Instant Answers! Windows 95

W9-CSN-080

To do this:	Click this:	or Press this:	
Activate menu bar	Menu bar	ALT or F10	
Activate selected object		ENTER	
Allow renaming of selected object		F2	
Bypass AutoPlay or AutoRun		SHIFT while inserting a CD	
Close active dialog box or menu without making a selection		ESC	Close from System menu
Close active window	X	ALT-F4	Close from System menu
Close current folder and all parent folders		SHIFT-click on Close button	
Collapse current selection in Explorer		Numeric keypad – or LEFT ARROW	
Copy a file while you drag it		CTRL	
Copy image of active window to the Clipboard		ALT-PRINT SCREEN	
Copy selected objects to the Clipboard		CTRL-C	Copy from Edit menu
Create a shortcut while you drag a file		CTRL-SHIFT	
Cut selected object and place it on the Clipboard		CTRL-X	Cut from Edit menu
Delete selected object without placing it in the Recycle Bin		SHIFT-DEL	
Discontinue the connection to a network drive			Disconnect Network Drive from Tools menu
Display a context menu, usually different from the context menu that appears with a right-click alone		CTRL-right-click	
Display properties of selected object		ALT-ENTER	Properties from File menu
Display the task switcher, where you can switch to another running application		ALT-TAB	
Establish a permanent connection with a network drive			Map Network Drive from Tools menu
Expand current selection in Explorer		Numeric keypad + or RIGHT ARROW	
Maximize current menu			Maximize from System menu
Minimize current Window			Minimize from System menu

Instant Answers! Windows 95

To do this:	Click this:	or Press this:	or Select this:
Minimize all windows when Taskbar is selected		ALT-M	Minimize All Windows from context menu
Move among the panes in Explorer or among areas in a dialog box or desktop		F6 or TAB	
Move selected objects into the Recycle Bin		DEL	Delete from File menu
Move selection in direction of arrow		Arrow keys	
Move selection to first object beginning with that letter		Letter keys	
Move selection to first object in a list or line		HOME	
Move selection to last object in a line or list		END	
Open context menu for selected item	Right-click on item	SHIFT-F10	
Open Find: All Files dialog box		F3	Find Files or Folders from Start menu
Open Go To command in Explorer	3½ Floppy (A:)	CTRL-G or F4	Go to from Tools menu
Open parent folder for active window		BACKSPACE	
Open Start menu and select Taskbar	Start	CTRL-ESC	
Open Start menu if no applications are running	Start	ALT-S	
Open Windows 95 Help		F1	Help from Start menu
Paste Clipboard contents into selected window		CTRL-V	Paste from Edit menu
Refresh current window		F5	Refresh from View menu
Return a maximized window to its previous size			Restore from System menu
Select all objects in current window		CTRL-A	Select All from Edit menu
Select second item on the context menu, usually Explore or Open		SHIFT-double-click	
Start a program	Double-click on its icon		Program from Start | Program menu
Switch among tasks on Taskbar	Taskbar	ALT-ESC	
Switch tabs in a dialog box	Tab	CTRL-TAB/ CTRL-SHIFT-TAB	
Undo last copy, move, delete, paste, rename		CTRL-Z	Undo from Edit menu

Windows 95

Answers!
Certified Tech Support,
Second Edition

About the Authors . . .

Marty Matthews and Carole Boggs Matthews are the best-selling authors of more than 45 computer books covering topics as diverse as Windows, FrontPage, Outlook, Excel, PageMaker, CorelDRAW!, Networking, and Paradox. They have been working with software for more than 25 years and are experts in Windows, Office, graphic design, and desktop publishing.

Windows 95

Answers!
Certified Tech Support,
Second Edition

Martin S. Matthews
Carole Boggs Matthews

Osborne **McGraw-Hill**

Berkeley • New York • St. Louis • San Francisco
Auckland • Bogotá • Hamburg • London
Madrid • Mexico City • Milan • Montreal
New Delhi • Panama City • Paris • São Paulo
Singapore • Sydney • Tokyo • Toronto

Osborne/**McGraw-Hill**
2600 Tenth Street
Berkeley, California 94710
U.S.A.

For information on translations or book distributors outside the U.S.A., or to arrange bulk purchase discounts for sales promotions, premiums, or fund-raisers, please contact Osborne/**McGraw-Hill** at the above address.

Windows 95 Answers: Certified Tech Support, Second Edition

4567890 AGM 998

ISBN 0-07-882399-4

Publisher	**Proofreader**
Brandon A. Nordin	Stefany Otis
Editor-in-Chief	**Indexer**
Scott Rogers	David Heiret
Acquisitions Editor	**Computer Designer**
Joanne Cuthbertson	Roberta Steele
Project Editor	**Illustrator**
Cynthia Douglas	Lance Ravella
Editorial Assistant	**Series Design**
Gordon Hurd	Peter Hancik
Technical Editor	**Cover Design**
John Cronan	Matt Nielsen
Copy Editor	
Jan Jue	

Contents @ a Glance

Contents

Acknowledgments

Stream International spent considerable time and effort collecting many of these questions and drafting their answers, thus providing the core of this book. For this we are very appreciative. Special thanks to Steven F. and Lala M. Thanks also to Dianne S., Todd B., Andrea G., Bob B., Allen M., Tony F., Lori F., Gretchen J., Kevin P., Michael W., Margaret M., Peter S., Scott H., Scott T., Joseph Y., Joseph K., Joseph H., George W., Dan G., Phil J., Chris L., Daniel W., John T.

John Cronan technically reviewed both editions of this book. John, who is an author in his own right, thoroughly tested everything the book says and gave us lots of feedback on the results. John made a significant contribution to this book and for that we are very grateful. **Thanks John!**

Patricia Shepard did much of the work turning the material in the first edition into the second edition. Pat, who is also an author in her own right, did this with much dedication and attention to detail, for which we are very appreciative. **Thanks Pat!**

The crew at Osborne was ably led by **Joanne Cuthbertson** in Acquisitions and **Janet Walden** in Editorial, with strong support from **Cynthia Douglas**, project editor, **Jan Jue**, copy editor, and **Gordon Hurd,** editorial assistant. As always, this team made the project as easy as possible and, in many instances, even fun. **Thanks Joanne, Janet, Cynthia, Jan, and Gordon!**

Carole and Marty Matthews

July, 1997

Introduction

Windows 95 represents a major change in the way you use your computer and includes many new facilities and features that were not available in the past. It is therefore natural that you'll have a great many questions about how to use what is available, as well as about how to handle the situation when things don't go quite right. With literally hours waiting on a toll phone line to get tech support from Microsoft, almost nonexistent documentation, and online help that never quite answers the question you are asking, there is a great disparity between the questions being asked and the answers that are available. The purpose of the book is to fill that void.

The more than 400 questions that are answered in this book have as their core the questions Stream International has been asked in its role of providing tech support to Windows 95 users. To these real-world questions the authors added their more than three years of using Chicago (the original code name for Windows 95) and Windows 95 itself in both beta and released versions. The authors have literally delved into every nook and cranny of the product and experienced a great many of the problems first-hand. As a result, they have located practically every source of answers and have referenced many of them here.

The book then brings together the "on the firing line" experience of a Windows 95 tech support company with the authors' experience in researching and using the product—about as much as two people can have and not be the programmers writing Windows 95 (and the Matthews have spent a lot of time talking to those people, too).

Windows 95 Answers is divided into 13 chapters, each of which focuses on a major subject. Within each chapter the questions and answers are further divided into topics, which group similar questions. To find a particular answer, use the table of contents to identify the chapter and section in which it's located. You can then look for the central topic of your question. Around your question, you'll find others that relate to it and that will add to the original answer. You can also go right to a chapter and then look at the Answer Topics! headings and alphabetical list of key terms at the beginning of the chapter. Finally, you can use the index to locate a topic that doesn't pop out at you from either the table of contents or the Answer Topics! at the beginning of each chapter.

Besides the questions and answers, there are many **Tips, Notes**, and **Sidebars** throughout the book that give you insight, which only considerable experience would otherwise bring, into how best to do something. In addition to the Tips, Notes and Sidebars, there are a number of **Cautions** that that point out areas that can cause considerable problems if they are not avoided. All chapters begin with a section called **@ a Glance**. These sections give you an introduction to the chapter's subject and how to address or accomplish the issues related to it. Reading all of the @ a Glance sections will give you a broad understanding of Windows 95 and answer many of your questions before you ask them.

Conventions Used in This Book

Windows 95 Answers uses several conventions designed to make the book easier for you to follow.

⇨ **Bold type** is used for text that you are to type from the keyboard. Bold type is also used for web addresses, as in "**http://www. osborne.com**"

⇨ *Italic type* is used to call attention to important terms or to words and phrases that deserve special emphasis.

⇨ Small capital letters are used for keys on the keyboard, such as ENTER and SHIFT.

⇨ When you are expected to enter a command, you are told to *press* the key(s). If you are to enter text or numbers, you are told to *type* them.

Versions of Windows 95

There are four versions of Windows 95 that you could possibly have:

⇨ The retail full or upgrade version that you as an individual or company bought and put on computers you already own. This is called the "original retail" version.

⇨ The OEM (original equipment manufacturers) version shipped in new computers prior to the spring of 1996. This is called the "original OEM" version. This differs from the original retail version in that in *most instances* it included Microsoft Plus! Companion for Windows 95.

⇨ The Service Pack 1 upgrade to Windows 95 that was published in December of 1995. It can be downloaded from Microsoft (**http://www.microsoft.com/windows95**) and applied to either of the original versions. It was also given to OEMs to install on new computers beginning in the spring of 1996 and was called OSR (OEM service release) 1. Service Pack 1 included several fixes and new system administration tools, as well as additional components and drivers, many related to Novell networking.

⇨ The latest OEM version of Windows 95, called OSR 2, shipped in new computers beginning in the fall of 1996. It includes a new 32-bit file system called FAT32 with all new disk support tools, the latest versions of Internet programs, support for many new hardware devices, enhanced power management, and support for additional networking directory services and protocols. There are also several drawbacks to using this version in that you can no longer dual-boot with Windows 3.1, DriveSpace does not work with FAT32, and older DOS programs that required the Share command will no longer run properly.

OSR 2 *Note   You can download most of the components of OSR 2 from* **http://www.microsoft.com/windows95/default.asp**. *Click on Free Software and then click on OSR 2 Downloadable Components.*

It is not easy to tell which version you have if you have an OEM version (it came on your computer) or you simply don't know the origin. One way is to right-click My Computer and select Properties. The second line under System is the versions number. If it says:

⇨ "4.00.950", it is one of the original versions

⇨ "4.00.950a", the Service Pack 1 has been installed or it is the OSR 1 OEM version

⇨ "4.00.950 B", it is the OSR 2 OEM version

You can tell if you have an OEM version in the same System Properties dialog box just described by the product ID number under the Registered To heading. If it has "OEM" in the number, for example 12345-OEM-1234567-12345, then you have an OEM version. Otherwise you have a retail version.

If you happened to run the Service Pack 1 or one of several third-party patches to the operating system on OSR 2, the version will change back to "4.00.950a" even though you still have OSR 2. So here are some other ways you can tell which version you have.

⇨ Right-click a hard drive. If it says "Local Disk (FAT32)," "Local Disk (FAT16)," or "Local Disk (FAT)", you are using OSR 2. The original versions and Service Pack 1 had no mentions of "FAT."

⇨ Open a DOS window (Start | Programs | MS-DOS Prompt) and type **ver**. If the response you get is "[Version 4.00.950]" you have one of the original versions with or without Service Pack 1. With the OSR 2 version the response is "[Version 4.00.1111]."

⇨ Right-click the desktop and choose Properties. Click the Settings tab. If you see an Advanced Properties button in the lower-left corner, as shown here, you have OSR 2. The original versions and Service Pack 1 did not have the Advanced Properties button.

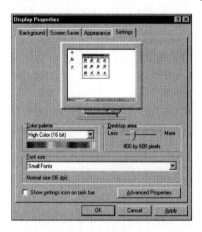

In this book we will talk about the first three versions of Windows 95 (original retail, original OEM, and Service Pack 1) without any differentiation because, to the user, the differences are almost transparent. We will refer to all of these as the "original version." When the OSR 2 version has some subtle difference not worthy of a note from what is being discussed, the OSR 2 icon will appear in the margin as shown on the left. When the OSR 2 discrepancy is significant, a special note to that effect will appear, as shown next.

OSR 2 *Note   With OSR 2 you can no longer dual-boot with Windows 3.1 or DOS.*

And now let's get to your questions...

Top Ten
FAQs

Top Ten FAQS @ a Glance

Whenever you install a new piece of software, questions arise simply because of its unfamiliarity. When the software is an operating system, those questions take on an even greater significance, because the operating system is so basic to everything that is done on your computer. Among the Windows 95 questions collected by Stream International, the following ten questions were those asked most often by callers. Here are the answers.

1. How do I find my files and programs?

To find any file, whether a program or a data file, you can take three independent paths through Windows 95 by using My Computer, Explorer, or Find.

To use My Computer, follow these instructions:

1. Double-click the My Computer icon on the desktop. The My Computer window will open, as shown in Figure 1-1.

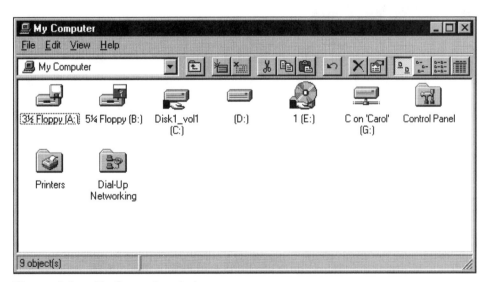

Figure 1-1. My Computer window

2. Double-click the drive that you want to search and then the directories or folders that you believe contain the files. Each folder that you double-click opens a new *folder window,* as shown in Figure 1-2.

3. When you find the file and the file is a program, you can load or start it by double-clicking it.

Tip   *If the file is a data file that is* associated *with a program (you can tell a file is associated with a program if it uses the program's icon), you can start that program and open the data file by double-clicking the data file.*

To use Explorer, follow these steps:

1. Click the Start button in the lower left of your screen. The Start menu will open.

2. Move the mouse pointer to Programs (you don't have to click), and then click Windows Explorer, as shown in Figure 1-3. Figure 1-4 shows the open Explorer window.

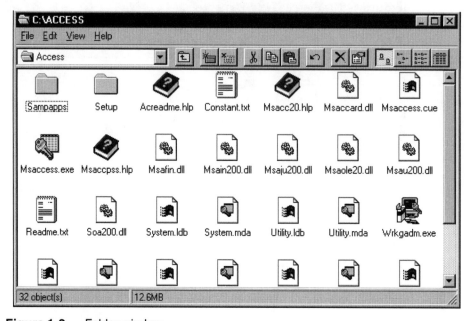

Figure 1-2.   Folder window

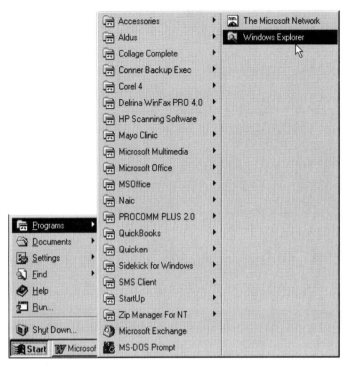

Figure 1-3.   Start and Programs menus

3. Click the drive and folder you want to open in the left pane, and then double-click the file you want to start or open in the right pane.

 Tip   *Right-clicking a file in the right pane of the Explorer window or in a folder window opens a pop-up menu, shown next, that allows you to copy, move, delete, or send a file to a floppy disk or to a fax.*

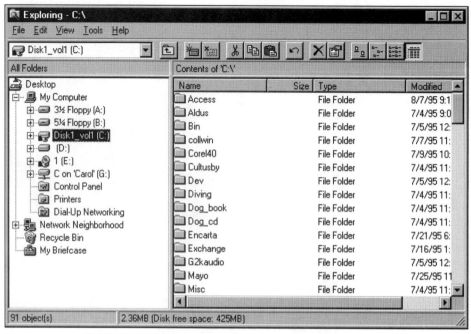

Figure 1-4.   Explorer window

The next set of steps shows you how to use Find:

1. Click the Start button, point on Find, and then click Files Or Folders. The Find dialog box opens as shown in Figure 1-5.

2. Select the drives (and folders, if desired) you want to search and click Find Now. When the search is complete, the files will be listed below the Find dialog box. You can do anything with those listings (open, start, copy, move, and delete them) that you can do in either Explorer or My Computer.

❓ 2. Do I have to reinstall my applications after installing Windows 95 on the system that had Windows before?

If you install Windows 95 over your existing Windows 3.x directory or folder, then you do not need to reinstall your applications. If you

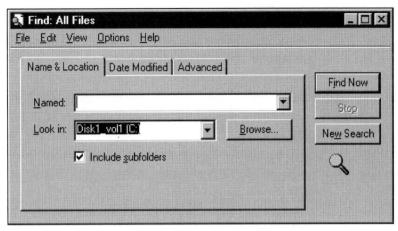

Figure 1-5.   Find dialog box

install Windows 95 into a new folder, then you will have to reinstall all your Windows applications. Copying files from your Windows 3.*x* folder to Windows 95 is not sufficient.

Tip   *There is almost no need to keep Windows 3.x on your computer (virtually all programs run as well or better under Windows 95), so Windows 95 should be installed over your existing Windows 3.x.*

? 3. What do I do if an application I am running stops responding?

You can use CTRL-ALT-DEL to end an application that is no longer responding to the system. When you press these three keys at the same time, the Close Program dialog box will come up, listing all active applications. Select your application and click the End Task button. Windows 95 will allow you to continue working in the other applications that are running without having to reboot the whole system.

Caution   *Do not press CTRL-ALT-DEL a second time, unless you want to reboot your computer and lose any information that has not been saved.*

❓ 4. How do I do a clean boot for Windows 95?

When troubleshooting Windows 95 or a specific application, you sometimes have to run the system in the simplest possible configuration to single out the source of the problem or a conflict. In the previous operating systems, you had to create a separate boot disk and boot off this floppy. Windows 95 gives you an easier way of creating a clean environment. Use these steps for that purpose:

1. Restart your computer.

2. When you see the message "Starting Windows 95," immediately press F8. You will see a menu of the following options:

   ⇨ **Normal**   **This starts regular Windows 95 without changes.**

   ⇨ **Logged**   This starts regular Windows 95, but creates a file called Bootlog.txt that lists all the steps during bootup. This is very useful in tracking down Windows 95 startup failure. You can read the Bootlog.txt file with Notepad.

   ⇨ **Safe Mode**   Windows 95 is started by use of the most generic default settings: VGA display driver, no network, Microsoft mouse driver, and the minimum device drivers necessary to start Windows. No CD-ROM drives, printers, or other peripheral devices are used. Config.sys and Autoexec.bat are ignored. You can also get this by pressing F5 at the "Starting Windows 95" message.

   ⇨ **Safe Mode With Network Support**   This starts Windows 95 in a minimum mode, as before, but adds networking for the situation where you must have access to network drives. You can also get this by pressing F6 at the "Starting Windows 95" message.

   ⇨ **Step-By-Step Confirmation**   This is also called *interactive start*. It starts Windows 95, but asks if you want to execute each line in your Config.sys and Autoexec.bat files (or the Windows 95 default if you don't have these files). Type **Y** if you want to process the line; type **N** if you don't. You will receive an error message if one of the command lines fails (an indicator of where the system fails). It will process the Registry and load all Windows drivers.

⇨ **Command Prompt Only**   This starts only the DOS part of Windows 95. All drivers are loaded and all command files processed, but the graphic user interface (GUI) is not started. You are left at the C:\ prompt. You can type **win** to load the GUI. You can also get the Windows 95 DOS command prompt by pressing ALT-F5 at the "Starting Windows 95" message.

⇨ **Safe Mode Command Prompt Only**   This is the same as the Safe Mode option, but stops at the C:\ prompt without loading the GUI. Type **win** to load the GUI. You can also get this by pressing SHIFT-F5 at the "Starting Windows 95" message.

⇨ **Previous Version Of MS-DOS**   (This is only available if you have dual-boot MS-DOS/Windows 95 set up on your system.) This starts your computer in the previous version of MS-DOS that was on your computer when you installed Windows 95. (See the next question.) You can also get this by pressing F4 at the "Starting Windows 95" message.

OSR 2 *Note*   *With OSR 2 you can no longer dual-boot with Windows 3.1/DOS. This applies to the following question as well.*

? **5. How can I go to my previous version of MS-DOS? I tried pressing F4 while booting when it says "Starting Windows 95," but nothing happens and I don't get the option "Previous version of MS-DOS" when I press F8.**

If pressing F4 does not work, dual booting is not enabled on your computer. You can enable this feature with these steps:

1. Open Notepad (Start menu | Programs | Accessories | Notepad), and open a file called Msdos.sys in your root directory or folder.

2. Locate the section entitled "Options," and change the line BootMulti=0 to **BootMulti=1**.

3. Save the changes and reboot. Pressing F4 during booting will load your previous version of MS-DOS, and pressing F8 will give you an option to start the previous MS-DOS version. If you boot into your previous version of MS-DOS, you must reboot your computer to return to Windows 95.

Tip   *If you have installed Windows 95 into a new directory without deleting Windows 3.x from your computer, you can start Windows 3.x by booting into the previous version of MS-DOS and then typing* ***win****.*

6. I have installed Windows 95 into a separate folder or directory. Now, when I am trying to run most of my programs, I get an error message that the specified path is invalid. But the path is correct, and the file is right there on the hard drive; I can see it. How do I run my applications and not get this message displayed?

Windows 95 gives an error message because it cannot locate different program components like *.DLLs that you probably have in your Windows 3.*x* \Windows\System folder. Since you did not install Windows 95 over your previous setup of Windows, Windows 95 is not aware of the location of these components. Under most circumstances, the only sure way around this is to reinstall your programs.

7. How do I recover from a power failure or unintentional rebooting during the Windows 95 installation process?

The Windows 95 installation program includes a Safe Recovery option. Depending on where the installation was interrupted, you may be able to turn your computer off and then on (don't just press CTRL-ALT-DEL), run Setup again, and choose the Safe Recovery option when you are prompted. If this doesn't work the first time, try running Setup a second time.

8. I have deleted a file by mistake. Can I get it back?

Yes. Any files that you delete in My Computer, Explorer, or any Windows 95 application are automatically moved to the Recycle Bin on your desktop. The deleted files can be recovered by opening the Recycle Bin, selecting the files, and choosing Restore from the File menu.

Caution   *You can permanently delete files in the Recycle Bin by right-clicking the Recycle Bin and choosing Empty Recycle Bin. Once this is done, though, the files cannot be recovered.*

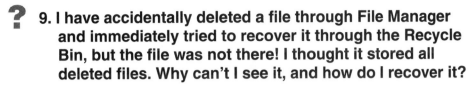

9. I have accidentally deleted a file through File Manager and immediately tried to recover it through the Recycle Bin, but the file was not there! I thought it stored all deleted files. Why can't I see it, and how do I recover it?

The Recycle Bin stores files deleted through 32-bit native Windows 95 utilities only. You can recover files deleted in My Computer, Explorer, or any Windows 95 application. File Manager is a 16-bit Windows 3.*x* application, and it does not support file recovery through the Recycle Bin. You can try to recover your file using disk utilities for Windows 95, such as Norton Utilities for Windows 95.

Tip   *Use only native Windows 95 file management utilities to have use of the Recycle Bin and long filenames.*

10. After I completed Setup, the system was trying to reboot but died. Now what do I do?

1. Turn the PC off and then back on (do not just press CTRL-ALT-DEL).

2. Press F8 when you see "Starting Windows 95," to open the Startup menu and choose Safe Mode.

If Windows 95 starts, change the video driver to the standard VGA driver by following these steps:

OSR 2   1. Right-click the desktop, choose Properties, click the Settings tab, and then click the Change Display Type button (or the Advanced Properties button in OSR 2).

OSR 2   2. Click the Change button in the Adapter Type section (or the Adapter tab in OSR 2) and click Show All Devices.

3. In the Manufacturers list, click Standard Display Types, and then click Standard Display Adapter (VGA). Click OK.

4. Click the Start button, choose Shut Down, and choose Restart The Computer.

If Windows 95 still does not work, reboot from a floppy disk with your previous DOS, rename your Config.sys and Autoexec.bat (at a DOS prompt, type **ren autoexec.bat autoexec.tmp** and **ren config.sys config.tmp**), and restart off your hard disk.

If the problem persists, use these steps:

1. Restart off your hard disk, press F8 at "Starting Windows 95," and choose Safe Mode.

2. Right-click My Computer, choose Properties, click the Performance tab, and click the File System button.

3. Click the Troubleshooting tab.

4. Check all of the available boxes, then click OK in all dialog boxes, and reboot.

chapter

2 Answers!

Installing
Windows 95

Answer Topics!

Installation @ a Glance

Given that Windows 95 replaces both DOS and Windows 3.1, you might expect that it would have a fairly complex and lengthy installation. In fact, just the opposite is the case. If you use the Typical installation and have a fairly standard system running Windows 3.1 or above, the Windows 95 installation is simplicity itself. You have to type **a:\setup** (or **d:\setup** if you're installing from a CD-ROM) in the Run command and answer fewer than half a dozen questions—that's it! It takes only a few minutes of your time, although it will take between 30 and 60 minutes of your computer's time.

Of course, there are always hitches, and that is what this book is for. The
questions and answers grouped under the following topics will help you
understand what to do before, during, and after installation:

⇨   The **Pre-Installation Questions** section presents several situations that you
     might encounter and, in general, discusses the decisions you must make
     before installation in order for it to go smoothly.

⇨   The **Equipment Considerations** section discusses equipment resources
     needed and specific equipment compatibility.

⇨   The **Operating Systems Considerations** section relates to operating
     system compatibility, addressing both installing from other operating
     systems, and installing other operating systems to run with Windows 95.

⇨   The **Problems During Installation** section presents several situations that
     could occur during installation and how to handle them.

⇨   The **Post-Installation Questions** section offers alternatives to decisions
     you made during a previous installation, solutions to new needs you have,
     and ways to use more of Windows 95 after it has been installed.

OSR 2 *Note*   *OSR 2 is installed at the factory and therefore much of this
discussion does not apply to it. If you reinstall it, you must do so on a
computer by itself, not with another operating system.*

PRE-INSTALLATION QUESTIONS

?   **I have just bought the Windows 95 upgrade. I have completely
erased all information from my hard disk and formatted it,
so that it is empty, clean, and ready for Windows 95 Setup.
Am I ready *to begin installing Windows 95*?**

Not just yet. Since you have an operating system upgrade, you have
to have an operating system already installed on the computer to start
Windows 95 Setup. Install your previous version of DOS, and then use
it to start Windows 95 Setup. Also, since this is a Windows upgrade,
you must have available an original installation disk (although the
program does not need to be installed) for Windows 3.0 or above,
Windows for Workgroups, or OS/2 version 2.0 or above. You'll be
asked to insert the prior version's first installation disk if Setup can't
find it on your hard disk.

❓ Must I make a lot of _decisions during the setup of Windows 95_?

The installation procedure is more automated and user friendly than in all previous operating systems. One of the advantages of the installation is that it can be done entirely from within Windows. If Windows has never been installed on the system, the setup procedure will install a small subset of Windows 3.*x* just to run the installation process. During the setup, the Setup Wizard walks you through making choices and selecting options, as you can see in Figure 2-1. At all times, extensive context-sensitive help is just a mouse click away, and you always have the option to return to the previous screen(s) if you decide that you made a wrong choice.

Windows 95 Setup autodetects the hardware components that are installed on your computer and automatically loads necessary drivers, configures them, and writes all the information into the *Registry*—the database that stores all configuration information for the system.

During setup, every operation is recorded in the setup log. If the setup fails at some point, Windows 95 will recover from just before the

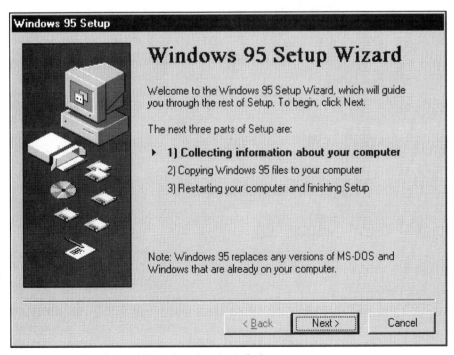

Figure 2-1.   The Setup Wizard makes installation easy

action that caused the setup to fail, and the user will be presented with an option to make necessary adjustments in the choices.

? What are the differences among *different types of setup*?

There are four options presented to you during setup, as shown in Figure 2-2: Typical, Portable, Compact, and Custom. The four choices allow you to choose the components that will be installed with Windows 95, depending on your disk space and whether you have a portable computer. The components that are installed by each option are listed in Appendix A. Briefly, the four choices are as follows:

⇨ **Typical setup** resembles the Express setup in Windows 3.*x*. This type of setup will run through most of the setup routine without requiring user input. The only choices that the user will have to make are the location of the Windows 95 folder and whether to create a startup disk.

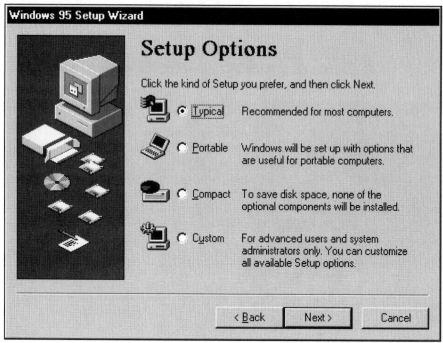

Figure 2-2.   Four options are presented to you during installation

⇨ **Portable setup** will install the files necessary to run Windows 95 on a laptop or notebook PC, including such components as power management; My Briefcase, a tool for file synchronization; and the system files necessary to establish a cable link between two computers for file exchange.

⇨ **Compact setup** will install the bare minimum files necessary to run Windows 95.

⇨ **Custom setup** resembles the Custom setup in Windows 3.*x*. This option will allow users to make their own choices on what components to install.

● ● ● ● ● ● ● ● ● ●

Pre-Installation Considerations

To prepare for the installation of Windows 95, run through the following steps. This will ensure that you and your computer are in the best possible shape for the installation.

⇨ **Compare your hardware** with the minimum and recommended hardware needed for Windows 95, as shown in Table 2-1, and consider upgrading your hardware before upgrading to Windows 95.

⇨ **Clean up your hard disk** by removing all unused files. Windows 95 requires a lot of disk space (40 to 80MB for file space and 10 to 20MB for temporary space). Use the installation of Windows 95 as an excuse to do the disk cleaning you always intended to do. Uninstall or remove the programs you aren't using, and delete the data and miscellaneous files that are no longer of value.

While it is a drastic step and you should consider it carefully, the very best way to clean up your hard disk is to back up all important files and to reformat it (which erases everything on your hard disk). After installing Windows 95, reinstall just the application and data files you need. You'll be amazed at how much more space you have.

Pre-Installation Considerations, continued

⇨ Back up important files on your hard disk. While the
    installation of Windows 95 will probably go without a hitch,
    there is nothing like the comfort of having a backup of *all*
    your important files in case the worst should happen. You
    need to back up all the data files you don't want to lose (these
    include word processing, spreadsheet, database, and drawing
    files). Back up your Config.sys and Autoexec.bat files from
    your root (\) directory or folder, and back up your .INI, .DAT,
    and .PWL files from your Windows folder. You may also have
    network and/or communications configuration and script
    files that need to be backed up. You don't need to back up
    your applications, since you already have them on their
    distribution disks.

⇨ **Create a bootable floppy** from your current version of DOS
    using the **format a:/s** command and a new disk, or one that
    can be written on in your drive A. This allows you to recover
    if something happens to your hard disk that prevents you
    from booting from it.

⇨ **Optimize your hard disk** by running ScanDisk (Thorough
    option), and defrag *before* you run Windows 95 Setup.
    ScanDisk checks your disk for both physical and software
    errors, and in many instances corrects them for you. Disk
    Defragmenter defragments your disk by putting related file
    segments together in the same area of the disk. Use the version of
    ScanDisk in the \Win95 folder on the Windows 95 CD or on
    the first Windows 95 floppy disk. You can't easily get to the
    Windows 95 version of Disk Defragmenter before installation,
    so use the DOS 6.*x* version if you have it, or use a recent
    version of Norton Speed Disk that is part of the Norton
    Utilities from Symantec.

⇨ Review the four primary decisions that you will have to make
    during installation:

    ⇨ **Install from Windows or from DOS?** If you are currently
        running Windows 3.1, 3.11, or Windows for Workgroups,
        it is recommended that you start Windows 95 Setup from
        Windows. In all other circumstances you need to start
        Setup from DOS.

Pre-Installation Considerations, continued

⇨ **Install into the current Windows directory?** When you install Windows 95 into your current Windows directory or folder, you'll replace your current version of Windows, and it will no longer be available. This is the reccommended approach. If you want to keep your current version of Windows available to you, you need to install Windows 95 into a new folder.

Remember that if you install Windows 95 into a new folder, you'll have to reinstall any Windows applications you want to use with Windows 95.

⇨ **Save your current DOS and Windows files?** If you choose to install Windows 95 in the same directory as your old Windows, you will then be given this choice. While it takes up to 10MB of your local hard disk (it can't be on a network drive or a floppy), it allows you to completely and cleanly uninstall Windows 95 and reinstall your previous DOS and Windows.

If, after Windows 95 is running for a while, you want to remove your old Windows and DOS files, you can do so by clicking Old Windows 3.*x*/MS-DOS System Files and then on Remove in the Install/Uninstall tab of theAdd/Remove Programs control panel reached from the Start menu | Settings | Control Panel option.

⇨ **Use Typical, Portable, Compact, or Custom installation?** If you have a portable (laptop or notebook) computer, or if you have a computer with very limited disk space, you should use either the Portable or Compact installation. If you know you want to install components not installed in a Typical installation, then use the Custom installation. In most circumstances, a Typical installation is the easiest and preferred type. See the discussion later in this chapter on the differences among the types of installation. Also see Appendix A for a list of components that are installed in the various types.

> ### *Pre-Installation Considerations, continued*
> By using the Add/Remove Programs Windows Setup tab in the Windows 95 Control Panel (opened from Start menu | Settings), you can easily add or remove Windows 95 components after installing Windows 95 and without rerunning Setup.

Table 2-1.   What You Need to Install Windows 95

Element	Minimum	Recommendation
Processor	386DX-20	Pentium 100
Memory	4MB	16MB
Free disk space	40MB	80MB
Display	VGA (640x480, 16 colors)	SVGA (800x600, 256 colors)
Mouse	None	Microsoft-compatible device
CD-ROM	None	8X CD-ROM
Modem	None	33.6 Kbps fax/modem
Sound board	None	16 bit

Can I *install Windows 95 without user input*?

Windows 95 allows system administrators to create batch setup scripts so that no input will be required from the users. The administrators can create an automated mandatory installation routine for the users on the network.

This new feature involves setting up Windows 95 on the file server by use of the file Netsetup.exe, which you can find on the Windows 95 CD in the Admin\Nettools\Netsetup folder. You then create custom batch scripts with the Batch.exe program in the same directory and store scripts in the Msbatch.inf file. Finally, you run the workstation setups, using the MS SMS (System Management Services) network login or any other network software management system to perform the mandatory setup. See the Batch.hlp file as well as the various text files in the \Admin\Nettools\Netsetup folder on the Windows 95 CD. Also, read the applicable parts of the Windows 95 Windows Resource Kit or its help file described later in this chapter.

OSR 2 *Note   The new OSR 2 version of Win 95 is only available when you purchase a new computer. You cannot buy it separately.*

My company is planning a migration to Windows 95. What are the *resources available to help me* with this migration?

Microsoft Press has published the Windows 95 Resource Kit, which has a wealth of technical information on how to implement Windows 95. It contains the following:

⇨ A guided tour

⇨ A planning guide

⇨ Technical information on installing, configuring, and networking

⇨ Software utilities

Tip   The complete Windows 95 Resource Kit is on every Windows 95 CD as a help file (Win95rk.hlp) in the \Admin\Reskit\Helpfile folder. As you can see in Figure 2-3, this folder also contains help files for Apple Macintosh users and system administrators.

Microsoft also offers the Windows 95 Migration Planning Kit, which contains the Resource Kit text in a help file format, a demo kit, a deployment guide, a Microsoft project deployment plan template, and a business analysis tool. Contact Microsoft at 800-426-9400.

You can order Microsoft Windows 95 TrainCast, which is a series of eight shows that explain and demonstrate how to plan, support, and implement the migration to Windows 95. For information on ordering tapes and local broadcast availability, check Microsoft's web site at **http://www.microsoft.com/mstv** or e-mail them at **mstv@microsoft.com**.

Third-party support is available through companies such as Stream International, which offers consulting services to help your company plan and implement enterprisewide migration to Windows 95.

 *Tip   For additional information on installing Windows 95, connect to the Microsoft Support web site (**http://www.microsoft.com/ WindowsSupport/**). They have an entire section on "Before You Install."*

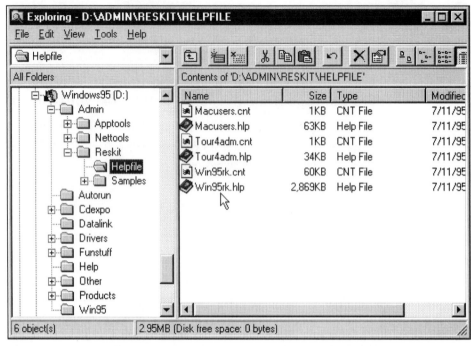

Figure 2-3.   The Windows 95 Resource Kit, available on the Windows 95 CD

EQUIPMENT CONSIDERATIONS

?   **Can I set up Windows 95 if I have _compressed my hard disk with Stacker_?**

Yes. Windows 95 Setup is compatible with Stacker version 2.0 or above. Before you start Setup, verify that there is at least 1.5MB of free hard disk space on the host drive, or 8MB if you use a permanent swap file. If there is not enough free space on the host drive, you must run the compression software to increase this amount.

**Note**   Windows 95 Setup may not find your boot drive if you have compressed it with SuperStor. If you get a message to that effect, you will need to decompress your hard drive, remove SuperStor, and then rerun Windows 95 Setup.

? **During installation, does Windows 95 _detect hardware devices and configure them_?**

Yes. During installation, if you choose (see Figure 2-4), Windows 95 analyzes your computer to identify the hardware resources that are available. To the extent possible, it configures the appropriate drivers and stores the hardware information in the Registry.

? **Can I install Windows 95 correctly on a _hard disk partitioned with OnTrack Disk Manager_?**

Yes. Windows 95 is compatible with all versions of Disk Manager. It also provides a protected-mode driver for Disk Manager version 6.03. If you use this version, Windows 95 automatically uses its protected-mode driver, which will give you faster 32-bit disk access.

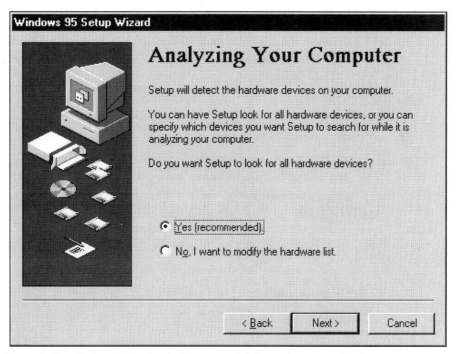

Figure 2-4.   Setup Wizard asks if you want it to analyze your hardware

❓ How much *hard disk space* do I need for Windows 95?

The installation requirement for hard disk space varies depending on the options you choose. For the basic components of the operating system in both a Typical and Compact installation, you will need the disk space as shown in Table 2-2. If you choose to install some of the features not included in a Typical install, you can as much as double the amount of disk space required. For example, if you install the Microsoft Exchange and the Microsoft Network, it will add 20MB to the basic components shown in Table 2-2, and Local Area Networking will add 5 to 10MB. Additionally, when you are done with the installation, you should have at least 10 to 20MB left for temporary files.

 Tip   *A good rule of thumb is that you need 50MB for minimum installation and 100MB for a full installation.*

❓ Can I *install Windows 95 on my PowerPC*?

No. Windows 95 is designed to run only on Intel-based computers. This means that you cannot install it on computers using PowerPC or DEC Alpha chips.

❓ How much *RAM do I need* to run Windows 95?

The absolute minimum is 4MB. Despite what you may have heard, Windows 95 will run fine with only 4MB. It is just that most people also want to run one or more applications. While that's possible with 4MB, it is recommended you have at least 8MB, and you will notice a major boost in performance with 16MB of RAM. The primary considerations are what applications you will be running and how many of them at one time. If you are running Microsoft Word or Excel

Table 2-2.   Disk Space Required for Basic Windows 95

Installation Option	Additional Disk	Space Required
	Compact	**Typical**
New installation	30MB	40MB
Windows 3.x upgrade	20MB	30MB
Windows for Workgroups 3.x upgrade	10MB	20MB

alone, 8MB is fine. You can even run them together in that space, although you can switch back and forth much faster with 16MB. If you are running CorelDRAW, you will be happier with 16MB.

❓ Will Windows 95 _run on my 286_?

No. Windows 95 is a 32-bit operating system and requires a 32-bit processor. You will need a 386-based or higher computer to run Windows 95.

OPERATING SYSTEMS CONSIDERATIONS

❓ Can I have _more than one operating system installed_ on my PC at one time?

OSR 2 Yes. You can install Windows 95 in its own folder and retain your old DOS and Windows. If you boot and do nothing, you will get Windows 95. If you boot and press F4, you'll get your old DOS, from which you can run your old Windows. Or you can partition your drive and use OS/2's Boot Manager to select the application operating system. Windows 95 must first be installed, and then you can partition your drive and make the new partition bootable. Then use OS/2 to install the Boot Manager menu system in the new partition. When you start, a menu will open asking which operating system you want to run this session. You have 30 seconds to choose, or by default it will go into the first partition that was made active—Windows 95.

 **Caution**   If you install Windows 95 into its own folder, you'll have to reinstall the applications you want to run under Windows 95.

❓ If Windows 95 is the operating system upgrade, what _operating systems can I upgrade over_?

You can install the Windows 95 upgrade over the following:

⇨ MS-DOS version 3.2 or above, or an equivalent version of DR DOS or PC DOS that supports partitions greater than 32MB

⇨ Windows 3.0 and above

⇨ Windows for Workgroups 3.1 and above

⇨ Dual-boot OS/2 with MS-DOS installed on the FAT partition

⇨   Dual-boot Windows NT with MS-DOS installed on the FAT
     partition

❓ Can I install Windows 95 on a computer that has *OS/2 and Windows and still dual-boot*?

OSR 2   Yes, you can. Be aware that Windows 95 cannot access the HPFS
partitions used in OS/2, so you have to have a FAT partition with
enough disk space to install Windows 95. Don't install Windows 95
on top of your existing Windows if you also want to keep it.

To install Windows 95, boot into DOS and start Windows 95 Setup.
Setup disables the OS/2 Boot Manager, because during the setup
process Windows 95 Setup has to have full control over the system.
You can reenable OS/2 Boot Manager after the setup is complete.
To do this:

1. Start Windows 95.

2. Click the Start button, choose Run, and type **fdisk**.

3. Choose Set Active Partition, as shown in Figure 2-5. Enter the
    number of the Boot Manager Partition. This partition is the 1MB
    Non-DOS partition.

4. Close Fdisk and restart the computer. You can now use the Boot
    Manager.

❓ If I am not ready to make the changeover, can I *set up Windows 95 and Windows 3.1 as a dual boot, and still have access to all of my files* on the hard disk using either version?

OSR 2   You can. When you install Windows 95, the Setup prompts you for the
folder to install to. The default is your existing Windows folder. Select
a different folder to install Windows 95 into, and you'll be able to
access your old Windows 3.*x* through dual boot.

Once installed, Windows 95 will not recognize your installed
applications. To correct that, start Windows 95 and reinstall your
applications into their existing folders. The result is that Windows 95
will register the applications, and you can still use them in your old
Windows without having to make two copies of each program, one
for each operating system. If you install new applications, make sure
to do two installs—one under Windows 3.*x*, one under Windows 95.

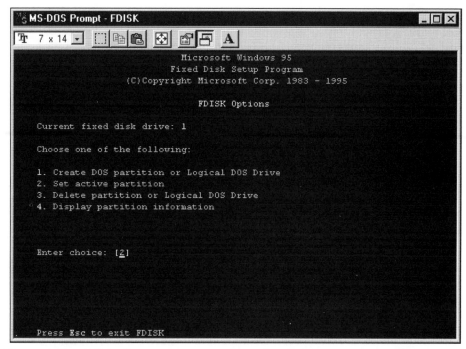

Figure 2-5.   Fdisk allows you to set partitions for dual operating systems

❓ Which is better _to start Setup from, Windows or MS-DOS_?

Starting Windows 95 Setup from Windows is the preferred option. However, you should start the setup from MS-DOS in the following cases:

⇨   You don't have Windows installed.

⇨   You have Windows 3.0 or an earlier version installed.

⇨   You have OS/2 installed either by itself or as dual boot.

⇨   You have Windows NT installed either by itself or as dual boot.

❓ What _versions of MS-DOS and Windows_ do I need to upgrade to Windows 95?

OSR 2 You need Windows version 3.0 and higher, Windows for Workgroups version 3.1 and higher, or MS-DOS or PC DOS version 3.2 or higher. You can also upgrade from OS/2 version 2.0 and higher.

Tip   *If you have Windows 3.0 or OS/2, you must run Setup from MS-DOS and then, in the case of Windows 3.0, choose to install Windows 95 in the same folder as Windows 3.0.*

? How do *Windows 95 and NT 3.5* operate on the same machine?

OSR 2   Windows 95 Setup will detect the presence of a Windows NT boot sector, and it will not overwrite it if you start Setup from MS-DOS or Windows 3.*x* and not NT. Setup will then load. However, Setup will make several changes to the folder structure and to the files in the System folder that will affect the operation of Windows NT.

Setup rewrites the Windows 3.*x* default .DLL files (such as Shell.dll) in the System folder. This is so that Windows 95 can run both 16- and 32-bit Windows applications. However, Windows NT's Windows on Windows (WOW) subsystem relies on the original Win16 DLLs (dynamic link libraries) to run Win16 applications. If Windows 95 is installed, certain Win16 applications, such as some of Microsoft's Setup programs and WinBUG, may not run under Windows NT.

Windows 95 moves all the screen fonts to a newly created Fonts folder. Since Windows NT uses the screen fonts normally present in the System folder, it will be forced to use a default Courier-type font rather than the normal system font. This default font is not proportioned correctly for Windows NT's dialog boxes, and some text may be unreadable.

? How can I install Windows 95 on my PC that has *Windows NT 3.5 installed*?

OSR 2   You can install Windows 95 on a Windows NT machine only if you have a dual boot between Windows NT and MS-DOS.

To install Windows 95:

1. Start the Windows NT computer in MS-DOS mode.

2. If Windows 3.1 or above is installed, start it, and then in the Program Manager's File | Run command, type *d*:**setup.exe**, where *d* is your Windows 95 CD-ROM or Setup disk.

3. If Windows 3.1 or above is not installed, type **d:\setup.exe** at the DOS prompt.

4. Follow the onscreen prompts of the Setup Wizard. Make sure to install Windows 95 into a separate folder rather than on top of existing Windows or Windows NT.

After you complete the setup, Windows 95 will become an option on your Startup menu, along with Windows NT and MS-DOS.

PROBLEMS DURING INSTALLATION

During setup I get the _error message "B1."_ What does that mean?

A "B1" error message indicates that Setup has detected an older 80386 processor that is not supported and instructs you to upgrade your processor. If your 80386 chip was made before April 1987 or has a label that reads "16-bit operations only," contact your hardware manufacturer for an upgrade.

I received the _error message "Cannot open file"_ while running Setup. What does this mean?

You may need to free up memory by disabling (typing **REM** in front of it) or removing the Smartdrv.exe statement in your Autoexec.bat, or by closing any applications that may be running in Windows. Windows 95 does not use SMARTDrive, so it is not necessary to have it in your Autoexec.bat.

When I am installing Windows 95, I get an _error message indicating that I don't have enough disk space available_. I know that I do have enough space. Is there anything I can do to get around this error message?

You can have Setup ignore the checking for available disk space by using the /id switch with the Setup.exe command (at the DOS prompt or in a Run command, type **setup /id**).

? **What does it mean when I get the *error message "Standard Mode: Fault in MS-DOS Extender"* when running Setup from DOS?**

There may be a conflict in the upper memory area. Upper memory blocks (UMBs) are the unused part of upper memory from 640K to 1MB. If an EMM386 statement appears in your Config.sys file (use Windows Notepad or DOS Edit to view it), it is enabling upper memory blocks. Disable this statement by typing **REM** in front of it, save your altered Config.sys, reboot, and then rerun Setup.

? **When running Setup, why do I get an *error message that my path is invalid*?**

The drive you are trying to install Windows 95 on has zero bytes available (such as a CD-ROM would have), or the drive is not ready or not mounted with a removable hard drive. Install Windows 95 to a different drive or make the removable hard disk drive ready.

If more than zero bytes of hard disk space are available, but not enough for Windows to be installed, you will receive an error message: "Insufficient disk space" or "Not enough disk space."

? **I am using a *Logitech mouse* on my computer. When I run Windows 95 Setup, the mouse does not work until I restart the computer to boot into Windows 95.**

If you have a Logitech mouse, you have to start the Setup program with the following command: **setup /il**. This will make your mouse available during the initial stages of setup.

? **I terminated the installation of Windows 95 after it requested the folder name to contain the Windows 95 files. On my second install, I was waiting for the prompt for the folder name but never got it. Windows 95 remembered my first try and automatically created the folder name originally entered. How do I *remove Windows 95 and start the installation over*?**

Windows 95 installation creates a file called Setuplog.txt to keep track of each step of Setup. If the setup fails at some point, Windows 95 Setup refers to this file to determine the last successful step. To restart

Setup from scratch, delete this file (it is in the root folder). You might also want to delete the Detlog.txt and Detcrash.log files if you have them.

❓ How do I *restart Setup after an earlier attempt has failed*?

Use the following steps to restart:

1. Turn off your computer (do *not* press CTRL-ALT-DEL), and wait ten seconds. Then turn it back on.

2. Start Setup again. Setup will prompt you to use Safe Recovery to recover the failed installation.

3. Choose the Safe Recovery option, and click Continue. Hardware detection will skip the part that caused the initial failure.

4. If the computer stops again during the detection process, restart Setup and repeat the process until the hardware detection process is finished.

5. After Setup is complete and Windows is running, you can use the information in Setuplog.txt and Detlog.txt to check for the devices that caused the problems.

❓ When I start Setup, I am advised by Setup to exit Windows and run *ScanDisk in MS-DOS*. I do that, but ScanDisk does not find any errors. I restart Setup and get the same error again. What should I do?

You can force Setup to run without running ScanDisk by adding the /is switch to the Setup.exe command line. (At a DOS prompt or in a Run command, type *d:***\setup /is**, where *d* is the drive with Setup on it.)

❓ *Setup fails to start*. What should I do?

You can do any of the following:

1. Check for sufficient conventional memory. Windows 95 requires 420K. If this is not available, remove any unnecessary drivers from your Config.sys file or terminate and stay resident (TSR) programs that are started in your Autoexec.bat file. As a general rule, to install Windows you need drivers only for your hard disk and maybe your CD-ROM, and you normally do not need any TSR programs. Use either Windows Notepad or DOS Edit to clean

out all unnecessary commands in your Config.sys and
Autoexec.bat files.

2. Check the RAM configuration in Config.sys.

⇨ Using MS-DOS 4.*x*, the commands should include

```
Device=Himem.sys
```

⇨ Using MS-DOS 5.*x* or later, the commands should include

```
Device=Himem.sys
Device=EMM386.exe NOEMS
DOS=High,UMB
```

⇨ Check for adequate extended or XMS memory; the
requirement is at least 3MB of XMS. If you are using MS-DOS
6.*x*, when you first see the MS-DOS message, press F8 and
choose Step-By-Step Confirmation to verify that Himem.sys is
loading. If it is not, verify that the file exists in your DOS or
Windows directory and that your Config.sys file has the
Device=Himem.sys statement.

⇨ At the DOS prompt or in a Run command, type **mem/c/p** to
check for free conventional and XMS memory.

❓ How can I *set up Windows 95 into a folder separate from my current Windows*?

During setup you are prompted to enter a directory or folder in which
to install Windows 95, and your current Windows folder is suggested
as a default, as shown in Figure 2-6.

To install Windows 95 into a new folder:

1. Click the Other Directory button.

2. Click Next and enter the new folder name. If the folder does not
exist, the setup routine will create it for you.

❓ I was running Setup and it *stopped during hardware detection*. What should I do?

Use the following steps:

1. Turn the computer off, wait ten seconds, and turn it back on. (Do
not press CTRL-ALT-DEL if Setup hangs!)

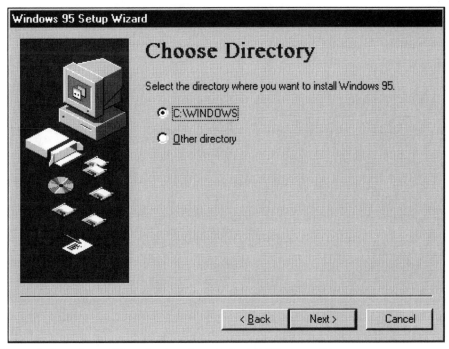

Figure 2-6.   Setup Wizard asks where to install Windows 95

2. When the PC is back online, restart Setup using Safe Recovery (you'll be prompted to do this). This will bypass the portion of hardware-testing detection that caused the problem. If your system stops again, it will be in a different detection module. Perform these steps as many times as necessary to allow your system to complete detection.

❔ What _switches can I use with Setup.exe_?

The Setup switches allow you to alter the Setup in a specific way. You type the switches at the time you enter a Setup command, as shown here:

```
C:\>d:\setup /?_
```

Following is a list of the command-line switches you may use with Setup when you start it in either the Run command or at the DOS prompt:

/?	This gives help on the possible switches of the Setup.exe.
/c	This prevents Windows 95 Setup from loading the SMARTDrive disk cache.
/d	This prevents Windows 95 Setup from using the existing version of Windows for the first stage of setup. Instead, it will load a brand-new small subset of Windows. This option is useful if the existing version of Windows is experiencing some problems.
/id	This prevents Windows 95 Setup from checking for the necessary disk space. This option can be used if the setup reports less space than you know you have.
/il	This tells Windows 95 to load the Logitech Series C mouse driver. This option is needed if you have a Logitech Series C mouse.
/im	This prevents Windows 95 Setup from checking for the necessary memory space.
/in	This prevents Windows 95 Setup from running the Network Setup module.
/iq	This prevents Windows 95 Setup from running ScanDisk at the beginning of setup from MS-DOS. This option is useful if you are using non-Microsoft disk-compression software.
/is	This prevents Windows 95 Setup from running ScanDisk at the beginning of setup from Windows. This option is useful if you are using non-Microsoft disk-compression software.
/T:_tmpdir_	This tells Windows 95 Setup to use the path and folder named _tmpdir_ to store all its temporary files.
/nostart	This copies the minimal Windows 3.x DLLs required by Windows 95 Setup and then exits without installing Windows 95.
batchfile	This tells Windows 95 Setup to use the file and path _batchfile_ to get the script containing the Setup options.

? I am installing Windows 95 from the CD-ROM. The _system went dead after the first reboot late in the process_. Why did this happen and what can I do about it?

You might have both real-mode and protected-mode drivers installed for the CD-ROM, and they are in conflict. Remove the CD-ROM real-mode drivers from your Config.sys and Autoexec.bat files (that is, all mention of your CD-ROM). If the problem persists, boot into Windows in Safe mode by pressing F8 when you see "Starting Windows 95" and choosing Safe mode from the Startup menu. If Windows will not start even in Safe mode, reinstall it. If you can get into Safe mode, reboot, press F8 again, and choose Logged to create a Bootlog.txt file to see where the system fails.

Look for the Detcrash.log file. If it is present, the problem is with hardware detection. Check Ios.ini in your Windows folder, and remark out the drivers that are loading in Config.sys (by putting **rem** and a space at the left of lines that load any drivers found on the unsafe list in the Ios.ini file) in case there is a problem with these protected-mode drivers. From the Start menu, select Settings | Control Panel and then double-click System. Then check the Device Manager for any conflicts. Change the display driver to standard VGA.

Try the Step-By-Step Confirmation boot after pressing F8 when you see "Starting Windows 95," and observe what is being loaded. Rename Autoexec.bat and Config.sys so they don't load on the next boot.

POST-INSTALLATION QUESTIONS

❓ I installed Windows 95 on a system with two CD-ROM drives. One *CD-ROM drive was not detected*. Why?

This happens if Windows 95 loads protected-mode drivers for the primary CD-ROM drive, but the secondary CD-ROM drive is running with real-mode drivers loaded by the Config.sys and Autoexec.bat files. Windows 95 assumes that both drivers reference the same device, so it assigns the same drive letter for both, making them appear as one drive.

Assign the CD-ROM drive that is running to a different drive letter with these steps:

1. Click the Start button, choose Settings, and click Control Panel.

2. Double-click the System icon, and then click the Device Manager tab.

3. Select the CD-ROM you want to change, click the Properties button, and click the Settings tab, shown in Figure 2-7.

4. In the Reserved Drive Letters section, set Start Drive Letter and End Drive Letter to the drive letter you want the CD-ROM to use. Click OK.

5. Click the Start button and click Shut Down.

6. Then click the Restart The Computer option.

? How do I know that Windows 95 Setup installed the *components that I want*?

Windows 95 Setup creates the following log files during the setup: Setuplog.txt, Detlog.txt, and Bootlog.txt. If the setup fails, another file is created called Detcrash.log. All of these files are in the root (\)

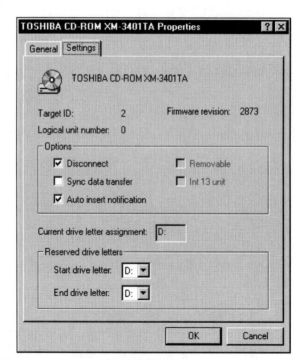

Figure 2-7.   You can change a CD-ROM's drive letter in the drive's Properties dialog box

directory or folder. You can view these files (but do not change them) by using Notepad, as shown in Figure 2-8.

⇨ **Setuplog.txt** is the file that keeps track of each step of setup. If the setup fails at the stage before hardware detection, Windows 95 Setup refers to this file to determine the last successful step. Setuplog.txt ensures that the setup does not fail twice due to the same cause. It will make the correction in the failed step and continue the setup.

⇨ **Detcrash.log** is created if the setup fails during hardware detection. This file stores information on what hardware component caused the failure and what resources the setup routine was accessing just before the crash. After such a crash, if you rerun Setup, it will automatically go into the Safe mode and will continue the recovery process, skipping the module that failed. If setup is successful, Detcrash.log is deleted upon completion of setup.

⇨ **Detlog.txt** contains a list of detected hardware components and the parameters for each detected device.

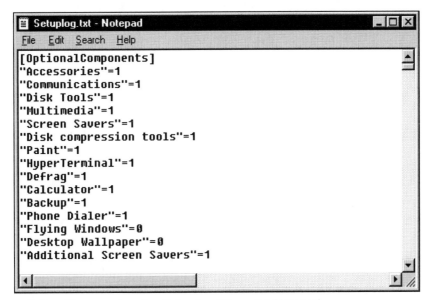

Figure 2-8. You can view the Setup log files using Notepad

⇨ **Bootlog.txt** is the file that describes what takes place during the system startup processes.

❓ How do I *install a feature of Windows 95 that I did not originally install*?

To add or remove a Windows 95 component outside of Setup, use the following steps:

1. Click the Start button, choose Settings, and click Control Panel.

2. Double-click the Add/Remove Programs icon.

3. Click the Windows Setup tab, as shown in Figure 2-9, and select/deselect the items you want to add or remove. Click OK when you are done.

   Tip   *You should have the Windows 95 disks or CD handy in case you need them.*

❓ When I look at the Windows 95 Installation disks in the Explorer, it only shows one *.CAB file on each disk. How can I get a *list of all the files that are on the installation disks*?

Follow these steps to list all files on the installation disks:

1. Insert the Windows 95 disk into drive A.

2. From the Start menu, choose Programs and MS-DOS Prompt. Then at the c:\ prompt, type the following command:

```
extract /d a:\win95_xx.cab > win95_xx.txt
```

where *xx* stands for the disk number. This action will generate a text file named after the .CAB file, and it will have the listing of the disk contents.

Alternatively, open an MS-DOS window, and for the Windows 95 CD, type the following to create a master list:

```
extract /a /d d:\win95\win95_02.cab > win95.txt
```

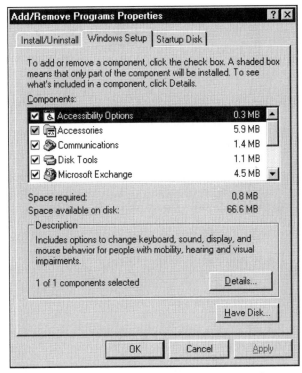

Figure 2-9.   Add/Remove Programs Properties dialog box allows you to install programs you did not install during Setup

where *d:\Win95_02.cab* is the filename of the first .CAB file. This will process all the .CAB files in sequence and generate a list of all files in the file Win95.txt.

Tip   *You can also download a .CAB file viewer from the Microsoft Power Toys utility package from the web site **http://www.microsoft.com/ windows/software/powertoy.htm**. The name of the utility is CabView. Be aware that the Power Toys are not a part of Windows and therefore are not supported by Microsoft.*

❓ How do I _remove Windows 95 from my computer_?

If during setup you chose the option of saving your system files so that you could uninstall Windows 95 (as described at the beginning of this chapter), and then after installation you want to remove Windows 95, you can use the following steps to completely restore your previous DOS and Windows:

1. Click the Start button and choose Settings | Control Panel.
2. Double-click Add/Remove Programs and, if necessary, on the Install/Uninstall tab.
3. Select Windows 95 and click Remove.

If you did not choose the option of saving your system files so you could uninstall Windows 95, use the following steps to remove Windows 95 and reinstall your previous system:

1. Reboot your computer using a DOS disk that contains the SYS.COM command.
2. At the DOS prompt, type **sys c:**. Remove the disk and reboot your computer.
3. Reinstall your previous version of DOS.
4. Delete the folders that contain Windows 95 files, and reinstall your previous version of Windows and all your Windows applications.

Note   *If you are having problems starting Windows 95 and want to remove it, boot into DOS by pressing* F8 *when you first see "Starting Windows 95," choose Command Prompt Only, and type* **uninstal** *at the DOS prompt.*

chapter

3 Answers!

What's New in Windows 95

Answer Topics!

What's New @ a Glance

One of the first impressions you'll have of Windows 95 is that it contains so many new features—and it does. Not only is the appearance of the product different, but so is the content. Windows 95 represents a major step forward in functionality on desktop and portable PC platforms by providing a system that is even easier, faster, and more powerful to use. In addition, it is designed to maintain compatibility with the existing Windows and MS-DOS applications and hardware in which you have invested.

This chapter covers the following:

⇨ **What About the Name?** gives an explanation of what the new Windows name means.

⇨ **New Features and Enhancements** includes information about plug-and-play, the Registry, multitasking, and the Recycle Bin.

⇨ **Accessibility Features** discusses features for people with vision and hearing problems, and with other disabilities.

> ⇨   **Enhancements to Previous Versions** covers changes in using the Clipboard, drag-and-drop between applications, handling games that require exclusive access to the system, improvements to system resources, handling memory, security features, and using Paintbrush.
>
> ⇨   **Help** includes a discussion of learning Windows 95 basics, using shortcut keys, and online help.
>
> ⇨   **Hardware Considerations** covers hardware requirements and capabilities.

WHAT ABOUT THE NAME?

? *__What does the name "Windows 95" really mean__*? **Does the numbering system mean that Microsoft will release a new version of Windows every year?**

"Windows 95" is a version number that gives users a sense for the "model year" of their software, in the same way that customers have a sense of the model year of their cars today. Microsoft won't release a new version each year.

? *__What is Windows 95__*? **And** *__what was Chicago__*?

OSR 2   "Windows 95" is the official product name of this new major version of Microsoft Windows. It replaces Windows 3.*x* and Windows for Workgroups 3.*x*. "Chicago" was the code name for the development project that produced the successor to these earlier products. Chicago was used as the name until the official product name, Windows 95, was announced. Since the first release of Windows 95 there have been several patches, upgrades, and fixes introduced, culminating in Windows 95 OSR 2, the FAT32 version that is only available when you buy a new computer (and cannot be used to upgrade an older release of Windows 95)—see the sidebar on OSR 2 in the Introduction.

NEW FEATURES AND ENHANCEMENTS

? *How is Windows 95 different from earlier Windows versions?*

Windows 95 is faster and is user friendlier than earlier versions. It also includes tools that make managing your files easier, as well as provide access to the Internet and to e-mail. See the sidebar "Some Important New Features of Windows 95" for a list of these features.

Some Important New Features of Windows 95

⇨ **32-bit architecture** takes advantage of the 32-bit data paths that have been available since the 386 processor. With this come faster response times and more sophisticated software.

⇨ **Backward compatibility** ensures that most of the programs and hardware with which you ran Windows 3.*x* and MS-DOS will run with Windows 95. There may be some glitches, but they are few.

⇨ **Taskbar** and **Start menu** are the focal points of a new graphic interface that provides an intuitive way to find the functions and programs you want. You simply click Start and a menu of your computer's contents makes it very easy for you to navigate the new operating system. This interface is called *discoverable*, because a user can discover how to use it with little or no training. Instead of searching for ways to perform a task, the user will easily discover the way to do it.

⇨ **Explorer, My Computer,** and **Network Neighborhood** provide the file management tools. With them, you can find out where files and devices are located—on your own disk or computer, or within your network—and open, copy, delete, rename, move, or perform other file and disk tasks.

Some Important New Features of Windows 95, continued

⇨ **Microsoft Exchange** acts as a centralized communications facility for sending and receiving e-mail, files, and faxes to and from LAN (local area network) and remote computers. It also provides a way of connecting with information services such as CompuServe or the Internet. It can be accessed by the Inbox icon, allowing you to quickly get your messages.

⇨ **Microsoft Network** is Microsoft's information service, which provides bulletin boards and chat rooms, as well as access to forums on a wide variety of subjects.

⇨ **Plug-and-play** allows you to "plug in your new hardware and play it." Windows 95 figures out what hardware you have or are installing, and handles the configuration setup and management for you (for the most part!).

⇨ **Recycle Bin** is where your deleted files are automatically placed. From there you can throw them away or restore them as you wish. The Recycle Bin is protection against inadvertently deleting a file you want to keep.

⇨ **Multimedia** accessories, including CD Player, Media Player, and Sound Recorder, are available to play and display your audio, video, and animated files. Also, Volume Control lets you control the volume for your special input and output devices, such as the CD player or microphone.

Some Important New Features of Windows 95, continued

⇨ **My Briefcase** allows you to keep the original and copies of a file synchronized. After you have edited a file (perhaps on another computer, or just in another directory or folder), you synchronize the original with the edited copy to keep all copies current with the latest changes.

⇨ **Multitasking** and **multithreading** allow you to easily and effectively run several programs at the same time. Multitasking was available in Windows 3.*x*, but multithreading is new to Windows 95.

⇨ **Drag-and-drop** allows you to use the mouse to drag a file or folder from one location to another. You can use this to open, copy, or move files, or even to print a document.

⇨ **Object linking** and **embedding** (OLE2) enables you to insert another application's files into a document by linking or embedding it. It facilitates how you update or modify the inserted file by calling in the creating application's toolbars and menus and then allowing you to continue with the current application. Although this is a facility that has been previously available, its handling of the interfaces with various applications has been enhanced.

⇨ **Accessories**, such as Calculator, Paint, Character Map, Notepad, and WordPad, as well as games (Solitaire, Hearts, Minesweeper, and FreeCell) enhance Windows 95's usability and your enjoyment.

⇨ **Security** of access can be controlled on several levels. For instance, you can restrict access according to an accepted password or to a list of persons allowed to log on to your computer.

⇨ **Sharing** of Windows 95 files and devices over a network is handled at several levels as well. You can share with others on your network everything on your computer, or just certain files or devices.

? **Are there special *keyboard shortcuts for the Microsoft Natural keyboard*?**

Yes. Here is a list of the shortcut keys for the Microsoft Natural keyboard:

WINDOWS-R	Display the Run dialog box
WINDOWS-M	Minimize all
WINDOWS-SHIFT-M	Undo minimize all
WINDOWS-F1	Open Help
WINDOWS-E	Open Windows Explorer
WINDOWS-F	Find files or folders
WINDOWS-CTRL-F	Find computer
WINDOWS-TAB	Cycle through Taskbar buttons
WINDOWS-BREAK	Display the System Properties dialog box

? **What are *multitasking and multithreading*, which I hear so much about?**

Multitasking enables you to run several programs at one time. *Multithreading* is a technique used to ensure that tasks run in the most efficient way possible without one program degrading the system by taking all the resources.

Windows 95 handles the scheduling of processes to allow multiple applications to run at the same time—multitasking. There are two types of multitasking: *cooperative* and *preemptive*. Under cooperative multitasking (implemented in Windows 3.*x*), the system required applications to check the system message queue and to give up control of the system to other running applications. Windows 95 supports cooperative multitasking for 16-bit Windows applications. For 32-bit applications, however, Windows 95 implements preemptive multitasking. In this environment, Windows 95 assigns system time to running applications, preventing a single resource-intensive application from monopolizing the system resources. With multithreading in Windows 95, the applications do not have to yield to other applications to share resources. Each 32-bit application can have multiple *threads*, distinct units of code that can receive a time slice from the system. A complex application can have several threads processed by the system at the same time through preemptive multitasking. This gives the application more stability and robustness.

? What is *plug-and-play*?

Plug-and-play makes it easier for you to add new hardware to your computer. It is a term for the PC architecture standard developed jointly by leading hardware and software vendors. Hardware labeled "plug-and-play" has been built according to these standards. When you add or remove plug-and-play hardware components and peripheral devices, such as modems, printers, video cards, and so on, the computer automatically recognizes the device (or its absence) and adapts to the new configuration. This eliminates some of the tedious procedures required to install hardware under previous versions of operating systems. Often you were required to manually change jumpers on the device to configure, for example, the IRQ (interrupt request), and then to spend hours troubleshooting hardware conflicts.

Full plug-and-play depends on having the following components:

⇨ A plug-and-play operating system, such as Windows 95

⇨ A plug-and-play BIOS (basic input/output system) on the computer's motherboard

⇨ Plug-and-play hardware devices (when you buy hardware, ask if it is plug-and-play compliant)

With Windows 95 you can still get some of the benefits of plug-and-play without the computer and other hardware being plug-and-play compliant, but as you buy new equipment, consider plug-and-play.

Windows 95 is the first PC operating system that supports plug-and-play. Information about the installed hardware devices is stored and maintained in the Registry database. When a new device is being added to the system, Windows 95 will check the Registry for available resources, such as IRQs, I/O (input/output) addresses, and DMA (direct memory access) channels, and dynamically assign it to the new device, avoiding the possibility of hardware conflicts.

? What is the *Recycle Bin*?

The *Recycle Bin* holds deleted files. Files are placed there automatically when you delete a file in My Computer or Explorer. Figure 3-1 shows the Recycle Bin window. You can also delete files in 32-bit applications like Microsoft Word 7 and CorelDRAW 6 by right-clicking a file in many dialog boxes, such as Open and Save As, and choosing Delete. Items in the Recycle Bin can be cut, copied, pasted, or dragged to

Name	Original Location	Date Deleted	Type	Size
0a03i19	C:\unzipped\097An...	6/7/97 1:36 PM	TIF Image Document	1KB
0a03i21	C:\unzipped\097An...	6/7/97 1:36 PM	TIF Image Document	72KB
0a03i22	C:\unzipped\097An...	6/7/97 1:36 PM	TIF Image Document	26KB
0a03i23	C:\unzipped\097An...	6/7/97 1:36 PM	TIF Image Document	123KB
0a03i24	C:\unzipped\097An...	6/7/97 1:36 PM	TIF Image Document	8KB
0a03i25	C:\unzipped\097An...	6/7/97 1:36 PM	TIF Image Document	18KB
0a03i26	C:\unzipped\097An...	6/7/97 1:36 PM	TIF Image Document	1KB
0a03i28	C:\unzipped\097An...	6/7/97 1:36 PM	TIF Image Document	2KB
0a03i29	C:\unzipped\097An...	6/7/97 1:36 PM	TIF Image Document	1KB
0a03i30	C:\unzipped\097An...	6/7/97 1:36 PM	TIF Image Document	40KB
0a03i31	C:\unzipped\097An...	6/7/97 1:36 PM	TIF Image Document	11KB
0a03i32	C:\unzipped\097An...	6/7/97 1:36 PM	TIF Image Document	14KB
0a03i33	C:\unzipped\097An...	6/7/97 1:36 PM	TIF Image Document	2KB
0a03i34	C:\unzipped\097An...	6/7/97 1:36 PM	TIF Image Document	1KB
0a03i35	C:\unzipped\097An...	6/7/97 1:36 PM	TIF Image Document	26KB
0a03i36	C:\unzipped\097An...	6/7/97 1:36 PM	TIF Image Document	1KB
0a03i37	C:\unzipped\097An...	6/7/97 1:36 PM	TIF Image Document	55KB
0a08f03	C:\My Documents	6/18/97 2:36 PM	TIF Image Document	468KB
W95ans10	C:\My Documents	6/13/97 2:33 PM	WinZip File	49KB

138 object(s)   12.4MB

Figure 3-1.   The Recycle Bin window allows you to recover deleted files and folders

another location. They can be restored to their original location by double-clicking the Recycle Bin icon, selecting files to restore, opening the Edit menu, and choosing Undo Delete. The Recycle Bin can easily be emptied when you are sure you want to get rid of its contents by right-clicking its icon and choosing Empty Recycle Bin.

Tip   To delete a file without placing it in the Recycle Bin (to save disk space), press SHIFT-DEL. But be aware that files deleted in this way cannot be restored.

Where is configuration data maintained? (What is the _Registry_?)

The _Registry_ is the database Windows 95 uses to store and retrieve information about user settings, hardware configurations, installed applications, application file types, and other system information. While there is no single file entitled "Registry," there are two files,

System.dat and User.dat, that contain the Registry information. You access much of the information in the Registry by clicking the Start button and selecting Settings | Control Panel. The Control Panel window, shown in Figure 3-2, is displayed. Each category of information contains its own access, such as Keyboard, Mouse, Passwords, Add New Hardware, Multimedia, or Network. Double-click the icon representing the data you want to change or add to. Because Registry information can be changed in several categories, there is no single Registry icon.

Windows 95 and Windows 95 applications use the Registry to store configuration and file association information. Whenever a new 32-bit application is installed, its information is stored in the Registry. Whenever a new hardware component is added or removed, or a user makes changes to the desktop, the information goes into the Registry.

 Tip   *In Windows 3.x, this information was stored in multiple .INI files (System.ini, Win.ini, and Progman.ini) plus the application-specific files (Winword.ini, Excel.ini, 123r4.ini, and so on), while the information for OLE was stored in the Reg.dat file. For compatibility purposes, Windows 95 will still maintain the .INI file settings for use by older applications.*

Figure 3-2.   Control Panel, which provides access to the Registry

The two Registry files, System.dat and User.dat, can be directly edited by use of the Regedit.exe program in the Windows folder. It is strongly recommended that this *not* be done, because there is nothing to tell you what you are doing, and you can cause major changes in the behavior of Windows 95.

Tip   *If you inadvertently make a change in the Registry files, System.dat and User.dat, you can recover with a backup set of files that Windows 95 maintains, System.da0 and User.da0. Revert to the backup files by renaming the .DAT files to .BAD and then the .DA0 files to .DAT.*

ACCESSIBILITY FEATURES

Where do you access the *features for disabled persons*?

Windows 95 contains a number of accessibility options to alter the way information is presented visually and aurally, and to alter the way the mouse and keyboard are used. You get to it by following these steps:

1. Click the Start button and select Settings | Control Panel, and then double-click the Accessibility Options. The Accessibility Properties dialog box is displayed, as shown in Figure 3-3.

2. Select the tab you want:

    ⇨ **Keyboard**, for changing the way the keyboard is used

    ⇨ **Sound**, for having sounds displayed on the screen

    ⇨ **Display**, for making the screen easier to see

    ⇨ **Mouse**, for implementing the mouse on the keyboard

    ⇨ **General**, for overall settings for when the Accessibility Options are used

What are the new *features for the hearing impaired*?

The Accessibility Properties dialog box's Sound and General tabs present features for the hearing impaired that allow you to

⇨ Set a global flag to let applications know you want visible feedback instead of or in addition to sound

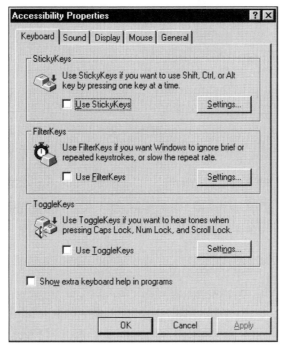

Figure 3-3. Accessibility Properties dialog box for persons with disabilities

⇨ Request a blinking title bar or screen flash instead of the system beep

⇨ Support alternative input devices such as headpointers or eyegaze systems

❓ What are new *features for people with tremors or limited hand motion*?

The Accessibility Properties dialog box's Keyboard and Mouse tabs have options for assisting those with limited hand motion or tremors that allow you to

⇨ Press a function key such as SHIFT, CTRL, or ALT in sequence with another key, so that you don't have to press two keys simultaneously. This is called *StickyKeys*.

⇨ Desensitize the keyboard so that tremors do not produce unwanted keystrokes by slowing the rate that a key may be pressed and ignoring repeated keystrokes. This is called *FilterKeys*.

⇨ Toggle the CAPS LOCK, SCROLL LOCK, and NUM LOCK keys to produce a sound when one of those keys is pressed. This is called *ToggleKeys*.

⇨ Use the numeric keypad on the right of your keyboard to move the mouse pointer on the screen and to press the mouse button without using the mouse itself. This is called *MouseKeys*.

? What are the new *features for people with vision problems*?

Using the Accessibility Options (Display and Mouse tabs) or the Mouse or Display control panels, users who have limited vision or eyestrain when working in windows can

⇨ Adjust the size of window titles, scroll bars, menu text, borders, and other standard screen elements.

⇨ Pick between two sizes for displaying the standard system font.

⇨ Choose one of three sizes for the mouse pointer: normal, large, or extra large. Also, the color can be adjusted or animation added to increase the pointer's visibility.

⇨ Select a high-contrast color scheme, making it easier to see screen objects. High-contrast mode has been added for users who require a high contrast between foreground and background objects to distinguish them.

ENHANCEMENTS TO PREVIOUS VERSIONS

? In Windows 3.*x*, I could only keep one piece of data on the Clipboard. This is a serious limitation when I need to manipulate multiple portions of documents. Do I still have the same limitation on *Clipboard contents in Windows 95*?

Yes and no. You still can retain only one item when you do Copy or Cut. However, Windows 95 provides a new mechanism for temporarily storing "document scraps" on the desktop. These are selected segments of a document that become a separate file when you drag it to the desktop.

To create a document scrap, open the original document and select the text or graphic that you want to copy, and then drag it to the desktop. This will create a *document scrap* on the desktop—a file with the copied piece of data. The item will have a title that includes the words "Document scrap..." and then the first several words of the copied piece, as seen here:

You can now drag this scrap to other documents or programs. You can create as many scraps as you want, and you can have not only text scraps, but pictures as well. You can only use this feature if the program used to create the document supports OLE2 drag-and-drop functions. For example, it will work with WordPad and Paint, but not Notepad.

I understand Windows 95 allows *drag-and-drop between applications*. Does this mean a new version of OLE is being used, and will "normal" Windows 3.1 applications lose their OLE functionality?

The 16-bit applications will not lose their existing OLE functionality, because Windows 95 still runs the 16-bit applications in the same manner that Windows 3.1 did. But 32-bit applications will have additional OLE2 functionality that 16-bit applications don't have, such as the ability to create scraps on the desktop.

Will Windows 95 be able to handle *games that require exclusive access to the system*?

Most MS-DOS applications can run concurrently with other MS-DOS, Windows 16-bit, and Win32-based applications. There are some MS-DOS applications (mostly games) that require exclusive access to the system. Such applications can be run in MS-DOS mode, which is still Windows 95. It is created by the Virtual Memory Manager as an exclusive operating environment. This mode does not allow multitasking and directs all resources to the MS-DOS application. To run in MS-DOS mode, choose Shut Down from the Start menu and select Restart The Computer In MS-DOS Mode.

? In previous versions of Windows, I was constantly running out of system resources. What improvements have been made to this _limitation of the system resources_?

While the system resources are still there, much of what was using them up is now handled in other ways. Specifically, much of the code has been moved from 16-bit into 32-bit code, which does not suffer from the 64K limitation. It is very unlikely that you will run out of system resources in Windows 95.

? Is there a _macro recorder_ like Windows 3._x_ used to have?

Not anymore. You are expected to use the scripting capabilities of the applications or a third-party batch programming language like that from Wilson WindowWare in Seattle at (206) 938-1740.

? How does Windows 95 handle _memory_?

Memory allocation is provided through the Memory Pager and is based on the _demand-paged virtual memory system._ Windows 95 is treating the memory as a flat, linear address space that can be accessed through 32-bit addressing. Each process is allocated a virtual address space of 4 gigabytes (Gb). This virtual memory space is divided into pages. A certain amount of information is stored in memory, and the rest is written back to the temporary storage space on the hard drive, called a _page file_ (_swap file_ in Windows 3._x_). When the application needs the information that is stored in this space, the information is paged back to memory. This process is called _demand paging._ Each process is only aware of its own memory, so it cannot accidentally overwrite information paged out by another process. This makes the whole system much more stable. Obviously, the more memory you have, the less disk activity you have for this purpose. Windows 95, therefore, can make good use of lots of memory.

? What *network security features* are implemented in Windows 95?

Windows 95 has several security features implemented directly in the system. These features are listed here:

⇨ *Logon security* can prevent a user from getting access to Windows 95 in two ways. In a stand-alone system or peer-to-peer network, you can set the Primary Network Logon by opening the Control Panel, double-clicking Network, and choosing the Configuration tab. In addition, in a client-server network, you can get server validation of the user logging on by opening Poledit.exe, the System Policy Editor (found on the Windows 95 CD under \Admin\Apptools\Poledit), and choosing Require Validation By Network For Windows Access. This is an improvement over Windows 3.*x*, where a user could still access Windows even if the server validation failed; he or she was only prevented from accessing the network resources.

⇨ In Windows 95, a user or administrator can enable *user-level security.* This security level can allow or prevent individual users or groups access to drives on that computer. A list of valid users and passwords is stored on a Windows NT or Novell NetWare server, and the access level for local resources is specified on the actual Windows 95 computer. This feature is accessed through Control Panel | Network | Access Control tab.

⇨ *Share-level security* allows or restricts access to specific resources, such as printers, disks, folders, and CD-ROMs on a computer. The password is assigned when sharing a resource through the Control Panel or Start menu (for printers), and My Computer or Explorer for disks and folders. This feature is available only in the peer-to-peer environment under Windows 95 or other Microsoft networks, but not under Novell NetWare. This feature is accessed through Control Panel | Network | Access Control tab.

⇨ In Windows 95, a system administrator can define user profiles through the System Policy Editor. In doing so, individual users can be prevented from accessing specific resources on the network or the workstation, and they can be restricted from modifying the system configuration or installing new hardware and software.

? What happened to _Paintbrush_?

Paintbrush was replaced by Paint, a new 32-bit application. Paint is an OLE server, which allows the creation of OLE object information that can be embedded or linked into other documents. It is also MAPI enabled, so it is easily integrated with Microsoft Exchange for sending images as e-mail or fax messages.

? I keep hearing rumors that Microsoft is working on a _portable version of Windows 95_ (one that works on multiple processors). Is this true?

No. Microsoft is not working on a portable version of Windows 95. Windows NT is a portable operating system, and it's already available for high-end Intel, MIPS, Alpha, and Clipper machines. It will be available on the PowerPC and other high-end platforms over time.

Windows 95 is optimized for Intel processors, and much of its internal code is Intel Assembler, which puts Windows 95 at the heart of today's mainstream line (but dedicates it to the Intel line).

? How are the _system resources_ handled by Windows 95?

In Windows 95, system resources are handled by Virtual Machine Manager, which replaced Win386.exe in Windows 3.1.

Virtual Machine Manager creates an environment in memory called the _virtual machine._ Each application sees this virtual machine as a separate computer that is running only this one application and dedicating all its resources to it. This allows each application to access all the resources it needs. Each Windows-based application, both 16-bit and 32-bit, runs in a single virtual machine called _System VM._ Each MS-DOS based application runs in its own _DOS VM._

? What _tools and utilities for my system_ are included with Windows 95?

Windows 95 has the following utilities for system maintenance:

⇨ **System Monitor**   This monitors system resources, threads, processor usage, and other system uses.

⇨ **DriveSpace**   This compresses hard and floppy disks, and configures disk drives that you have already compressed using DoubleSpace or DriveSpace.

⇨ **Backup/Restore**   This backs up or restores files to tape, floppy disk, and network drives.

⇨ **Disk Defragmenter**   This optimizes and speeds up your hard disk.

Net Watcher   This monitors network resource usage on your computer.

⇨ **ScanDisk**   This checks for and repairs logical and physical errors on your hard drives.

Tip   *Not all utilities might be installed during setup. You may have to add them through Add/Remove Programs. To do this, click the Start button, choose Settings | Control Panel, and double-click Add/Remove Programs.*

HELP

How can I learn the *basics of Windows 95*?

Use Windows 95 Help to learn the basics by clicking the Start button and choosing Help. You will find an online user's guide, as shown in Figure 3-4. Here you can take a ten-minute tour of Windows 95, get a quick introduction, or find many tips and tricks on its use.

How can I get more *information about Windows 95*?

For more information about Microsoft Windows 95, take a look on most major online services and networks.
The following list tells how to access this information:

⇨ On the Internet, use the World Wide Web (Microsoft Corporation at **http://www.microsoft.com**; Download.com at **http://www.download.com/PC/Win95**).

⇨ On the Microsoft Network, open Computers and choose Software | Software Companies | Microsoft, Windows 95.

⇨ On CompuServe, type **go winnews**.

⇨ On Prodigy, type **jump winnews**.

Figure 3-4.   Windows 95 Help window

⇨ On America Online, use the keyword **winnews**.

⇨ On GEnie, download files from the WinNews area under the Windows RTC.

❓ What *keyboard shortcuts* are used in Windows 95?

The command card inserted in this book contains the shortcut keys used in Windows 95.

❓ How do I use the *online help in Windows 95*?

In Windows 95, online help is not just context sensitive, it's also interactive. You can still press F1 and get the help that is appropriate for the situation you are in, but the Help in Windows 95 goes a step further. In many help windows, you will find a "Click here..." button that will walk you through the necessary steps to complete the task and take you to the necessary location.

You can resolve a lot of your problems and issues by going into Help, selecting the Index tab, and typing **troubleshooting**. This will take you to a menu with different troubleshooting scenarios. For example, if you are having problems printing, you can select "Troubleshooting, Printing…" and it will present you with an interactive printing troubleshooting guide (as you can see in Figure 3-5), which will step you through different troubleshooting steps. You will be able to quickly resolve the majority of common problems without having to call technical support or your friendly computer guru.

❓ Is there a way I can *view the online help in the old Windows 3.1 way*?

When you first launch Help, seeing the books and chapters of the Contents tab view with no search engine may be disconcerting. Click the Index tab and the search feature is there, looking very much like the default Help view of the Windows 3.1 online help.

HARDWARE CONSIDERATIONS

❓ What is the *cluster size on a disk under Windows 95*?

The cluster size for storing data on a disk is the same as for MS-DOS 6.x and Windows 3.x, which can be up to 32K, depending on the size of the logical partition. The sectors are 512 bytes.

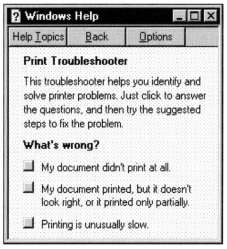

Figure 3-5.   Troubleshooting using Help can solve many of your problems

OSR 2 Note   In OSR 2 the cluster sizes are smaller for the same disk size than earlier versions of Windows 95, allowing better use of disk space.

▪ Will Windows 95 and Windows NT share the same *device drivers*?

Generally not, since Windows 95 and Windows NT have different device-driver models. However, since both products support a modular, layered device-driver architecture, there are areas of substantial synergy. For example, SCSI (small computer system interface) miniport adapters for Windows NT will be binary compatible with Windows 95, as will printer drivers and NDIS (Network Device Interface Specification) drivers for Windows NT.

▪ I have a lot of serial devices that I used to run with my DOS sessions. Are there any limits on the number of *ports supported by Windows 95*?

In Windows 95 there are actually more ports supported than in the previous versions of Windows. The actual number of ports with which Windows 95 can communicate is 128 serial and 128 parallel.

▪ Can I have a *RAM disk in Windows 95*? How do I use it?

Sure you can. Do the following:

⇨   Edit your Config.sys file to create a RAM drive by adding the line

```
Device=c:\Windows\Ramdrive.sys
```

This will create a 64K RAM drive and assign the next available drive letter to it. If you have enough memory available, you can specify a bigger size, for example:

```
Device=c:\Windows\Ramdrive.sys 256
```

This is still a very small area to serve as a temporary disk—2MB are needed in many instances to be effective.

 Tip   The purpose of a RAM drive is to give you a very fast disk by using RAM as temporary disk storage. However, this takes away from the memory you have available and can slow your programs, depending on the memory you have. So use it with caution.

⇨ To create a RAM drive in expanded memory, use the /E switch, as in

```
Device=c:\Windows\Ramdrive.sys /E
```

⇨ After rebooting your computer, you will see the new drive in My Computer or Windows Explorer.

? **After all the great things I've heard about Windows 95, I heard that these improvements will be available only if I am _running 32-bit applications_. Is this true?**

It is true that 32-bit protected-mode applications will utilize the robustness of Windows 95 to the full extent. However, Windows 95 has made important changes in the way that 16-bit applications are handled. Although 16-bit applications are still run very similarly to the way Windows 3.1 ran them (in the same memory space so they can see each other, or their OLE functionality would no longer exist), Windows 95 has improved cleaning up after the 16-bit applications. That is, while any 16-bit application is running, Windows 95 cannot track what resources are being used; once all 16-bit applications are closed, Windows 95 will go in, clean up the memory, and release any system resources the 16-bit applications may not have released. But during the execution of any 16-bit application, Windows 95 cannot clean up these resources, and the 16-bit applications will continue to use and not release the resources.

? **Can I _use Windows 95 with an IDE hard drive larger than 540MB_?**

Windows 95 will work on a hard drive over 540MB capacity in any of the following conditions:

⇨ Your PC's ROM BIOS supports logical block addressing (LBA).

⇨ Your hard disk controller supports LBA or geometry translation.

⇨ You only use the first 1,024 cylinders of the drive.

⇨ You have a vendor-provided real-mode driver for geometry translation.

If you are using any of the first three options just listed, you can take advantage of the Windows 95 protected-mode IDE (Integrated

Device Electronics) disk driver, ESDI_506.PDR, which allows the use
of 32-bit disk access. With the last option, 32-bit disk access is
available through ESDI_506.PDR only if you have OnTrack Disk
Manager's XBIOS drivers version 7.0 and above.

chapter

4 Answers!

Setting Up, Customizing, and Optimizing Windows 95

Answer Topics!

Setting Up, Customizing, and Optimizing @ a Glance

Different people like different things. That is as true with computers as with anything else. Windows 95 provides more accommodation for this facet of our nature than any previous operating system. Almost everything that you find in the Control Panel represents a way that you can set up, customize, or optimize Windows 95. These control panels enable you to set up your mail system, modem, network, and printer; to customize how your keyboard, mouse, and display behave; as well as to optimize how you use your file system and memory. In the Display control panel alone, you can change not only the color of the screen and the type of wallpaper displayed, but also the size, color, and font used in windows and their components like title bars, scroll bars, and message boxes. (See Table 4-1.)

Chapter 4 discusses the following ways to set up and change various Windows 95 features as well as to work more efficiently with Windows 95:

⇨ **Changing Your Display** discusses animated cursors, as well as how to change the way information on the desktop is displayed by customizing the colors, backgrounds, and screen savers. This section also covers changing icons, creating shortcuts that enable you to quickly start programs, and modifying the way various procedures are performed, such as changing wait times or changing the Logoff screens.

⇨ **Taskbar** shows you how you can work more efficiently by customizing the Taskbar. Options can be added to the Start menu, the location and size of the Taskbar can be changed, and the options in the Taskbar can be removed or added to.

⇨ **Customizing the Way You Use Windows 95** discusses how you can modify the Windows startup logo, how to use Full Screen Drag And Drop, and how to use some of the old Windows 3.1 features, such as displaying the file extensions. This section also covers how to use your Windows 3.1 Program Manager.

⇨ **Working with Programs** includes information about using Windows 95 more effectively, such as adding command-line switches to shortcuts, changing the sort order for folders, starting a program automatically, creating program groups, and assigning hot keys to start an application.

⇨ **Video Drivers** provides information about changing display and video drivers.

⇨ **Disk Drives** covers how to change the drive letter for the CD-ROM, changing the location of the swap file, and changing and modifying partitions on the hard drive.

⇨ **Mouse** gives information about changing mouse characteristics.

⇨ **Explorer** discusses ways you can change the display of drives and folders to meet your specific needs.

⇨ **Accessibility Options** shows how to activate and adjust the various accessibility features.

⇨ **Optimizing Windows** covers procedures for making Windows 95 functions more efficient.

For a quick view of some of Windows 95's more important features, see Table 4-1.

Table 4-1.   Some Important Features of Windows 95

Icon	Name	Function
Accessibility Options	Accessibility Options	Allows you to customize the keyboard, mouse, display, and use of sound to compensate for various disabilities
Add New Hardware	Add New Hardware	Leads you through the configuration of your system to accommodate adding and removing hardware
Add/Remove Programs	Add/Remove Programs	Provides the means to install or uninstall application programs, to add or remove Windows 95 components, and to create a Windows 95 Startup disk

Table 4-1.   Some Important Features of Windows 95 (*continued*)

Icon	Name	Function
Date/Time	Date/Time	Allows you to set the current date and time being maintained in your computer and to identify your time zone
Display	Display	Enables the selection of patterns and wallpaper to be used on your desktop; the screen saver you want to use; the appearance of your screen, including colors, sizes, and fonts; and the resolution and number of colors that are used in your display
Fonts	Fonts	Displays the fonts currently installed on your computer and provides the means to add and remove fonts
Keyboard	Keyboard	Allows the changing of the sensitivity, the language that is implemented, and the type of keyboard that Windows 95 thinks you are using
Mail and Fax	Mail and Fax	Provides the means to configure Microsoft Exchange and its Internet Mail, Microsoft Mail, Microsoft Fax, and Microsoft Network services
Microsoft Mail Postoffice	Microsoft Mail Postoffice	Enables the establishment and maintenance of a Microsoft Mail Postoffice for the immediate workgroup
Modems	Modems	Leads you through the configuration of your modem(s)
Mouse	Mouse	Provides the means to determine the use of the mouse buttons, the speed of double-clicking, the type of mouse pointers, the motion of the mouse pointer on the screen, and the type of mouse you are using
Multimedia	Multimedia	Allows the selection and configuration of audio, video, MIDI (Musical Instrument Digital Interface), CD, and other multimedia devices

Table 4-1.   Some Important Features of Windows 95 (*continued*)

Icon	Name	Function
Network	Network	Allows for the configuration of your network components, the identification of your workstation, and the type of access you want to allow to your files
Passwords	Passwords	Allows you to change your logon password and the passwords used in other services, to enable the remote administration of your computer, and to determine if everyone using your computer will use the same preferences
Printers	Printers	Leads you through setting up and sharing a new printer, as well as providing for the management of the work waiting to be printed
Regional Settings	Regional Settings	Provides for the setting of your preferences for number, currency, date, and time formatting
Sounds	Sounds	Enables the association of sounds with events such as the receipt of mail and exiting Windows
System	System	Allows you to manage and optimize your hardware resources

CHANGING YOUR DISPLAY

 I have seen *animated cursors* in NT. How can I get this for Windows 95?

Microsoft Plus! offers animated cursors. However, you need protected-mode disk drivers and a Windows 95-compatible version display driver running at 256 or more colors that uses the device-independent bitmap (DIB) engine. Animated cursors are not supported with the following display types: ATI Ultra (mach8), Diamond Viper, Standard display adapter (VGA), and Super VGA.

How can I _change the fonts_ used on my desktop?

Use the following steps to change the fonts used in Windows:

1. Right-click the desktop and choose Properties to open the Display Properties dialog box. Then click the Appearance tab, which is shown in Figure 4-1.

2. In the Item list, choose the desktop element that you want to change the font for (Icon, Title Bar, and so on); in the Font list, choose the font you want.

***

Tip   *You can also change the size, color, and style (whether it's bold or italic) of each font used on the desktop.*

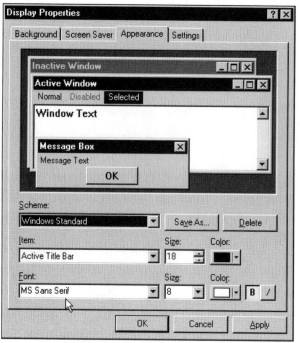

Figure 4-1.   Change your desktop fonts in the Display Properties dialog box

? How can I *change the icons for the folders* I have placed on my desktop?

If you drag the original folder or file to the desktop, you cannot change its icon. To work around this, create a shortcut for the folder or file, pick the icon you want for it, and place the shortcut on the desktop, rather than the original folder itself. To change an icon for a shortcut:

1. Right-click the icon and choose Properties.

2. Click the Shortcut tab and then click the Change Icon button, as you can see in Figure 4-2.

3. Enter or browse for the file in which you want to search for an icon, and then select an icon, as you see here:

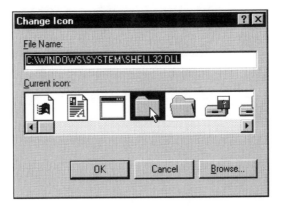

 Tip   *You can find Windows 95 default icons in \Windows\System\ Shell32.dll, in \Windows\System\Iconlib.dll, and in \Windows\Moricons.dll.*

? I want to *change the name of the My Computer icon*. How can I rename the icons on my desktop?

To rename desktop items, do the following:

1. Click the item you want to rename (for example, My Computer).

2. Press F2 and type a new name (for example, Bob's Computer).

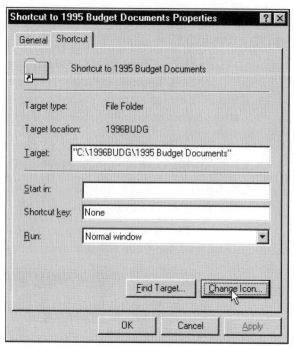

Figure 4-2.   Change the icon of a shortcut from the shortcut's Properties dialog box

---

Tip   *Using the preceding steps, you can rename My Computer, Network Neighborhood, Inbox, My Briefcase, and The Microsoft Network desktop icons. You cannot rename the Recycle Bin.*

How can I easily *change screen resolution* in Windows 95?

Screen resolution is the result of the number of pixels used to cover your screen and the number of colors that can be displayed. Standard VGA, the minimum for Windows 95, is 640×480 pixels and 16 or 256 colors (8-bit color). A higher resolution, sometimes called Super VGA, is 800x600 pixels and 16- or 24-bit color. You can change screen resolution in the Display properties dialog box with these steps:

1. Right-click the desktop for the pop-up menu, and choose Properties to open the Display Properties dialog box.

2. Click the Settings tab. Then change the pixel density (Desktop Area) and the number of colors (Color Palette) to get the resolution you want, as shown in Figure 4-3.

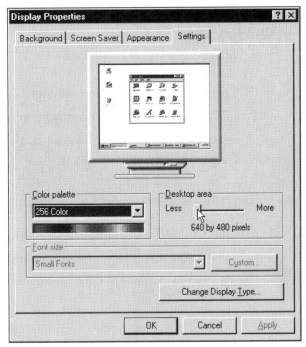

Figure 4-3.   You can change your display's resolution in the Display Properties dialog box

? How do I *change the wait time before my screen saver kicks in*?

To change the characteristics of your screen saver, do the following:

1. Right-click the desktop, select Properties, and click the Screen Saver tab.

2. In the Screen Saver list, choose the screen saver you want.

3. If the screen saver offers it, click the Settings button and complete the options for configuring that type of screen saver.

4. In the Wait spinner, pick the time you want the system to wait before the screen saver appears.

5. If you want to protect access to the computer by using a password to turn off the screen saver, make sure the Password Protected box is checked and click the Change button to specify the password.

6. Click the Preview button to test the screen saver and click OK when done.

How do I _change the way the date and time are displayed_ in Windows 95?

Use the following steps to do this:

1. Click the Start button, select Settings I Control Panel.

2. Double-click the Regional Settings control panel.

3. Select the Date tab or the Time tab to make the changes you want. Figure 4-4 shows an example of the Date tab.

 Tip   *You can also change Regional, Number, and Currency settings here.*

4. Click OK when done.

 Tip   *To actually change the date and time, right-click the time in the Taskbar and select Adjust Date/Time.*

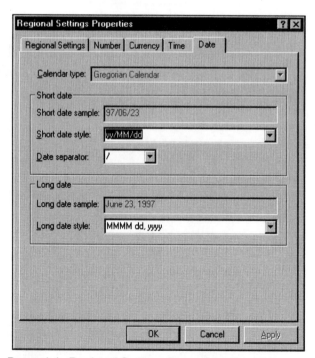

Figure 4-4.   Date tab in Regional Settings Properties dialog box

? How can I _create my own background_ (wallpaper)?

You can create your own Windows wallpaper with your company's logo or any graphics that you want by using the Paint program with the following instructions:

1. Click the Start button and choose Programs | Accessories.

2. Click Paint and create an image or Open an Existing Bitmap Image (files ending with .BMP, .PCX, and .TIF, among others) for the background that you want.

3. Open the File menu, choose Save As, and give a name to your new background.

4. Choose File, select either Set As Wallpaper (Centered) or Set As Wallpaper (Tiled), and it will replace your current background with your new one.

? What is an easy way for me to _customize my desktop—_ change colors, wallpaper, and screen savers?

All are easily changed. Right-click an empty spot on the desktop and choose Properties. This will open the Display Properties dialog box. In the Background tab you can set the pattern or wallpaper that you want to use. In the Appearance tab that you saw in Figure 4-1 earlier, you can change the color of your desktop, and in the Screen Saver tab you can choose which you want to use.

? How can I get _files and folders on my desktop_?

Very simply—drag them there from either My Computer or Explorer. Use these two steps:

1. Open My Computer or Explorer, and locate the file or folder you want to move.

2. Drag the file or folder to an empty spot on the desktop.

 Tip   When you drag a file or folder to the desktop, unless the file is a program, you will physically move the file or folder from its original folder to the desktop ("folder"). If what you really want is a copy on the desktop, then press and hold CTRL while dragging the object. You should also consider a third alternative, placing a shortcut on the desktop that points to a file or folder.

? I have chosen 800x600 small fonts, yet my _fonts and icons are not as small as I expect them_. What could be causing this, and how can I change it?

Most probably, one of the Accessibility options, High Contrast, has been enabled. To turn off this feature:

1. Click the Start button, choose Settings | Control Panel, and double-click Accessibility Options.

2. Select the Display tab, as shown in the following illustration, and clear the Use High Contrast check box.

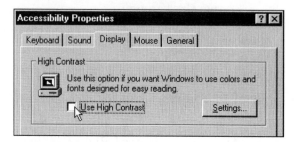

? Can I _modify the Windows 95 Logoff screens_?

There are two bitmap files in the \Windows folder that are used during logoff. Logow.sys is the "Wait while shutting down..." screen, and Logos.sys is the "You may now safely turn..." screen. Both are normal bitmaps. Back them up (right-click them, choose Copy, right-click white space in the Windows folder, and choose Paste), and modify them with Paint, opened from the Start menu under Programs | Accessories. Figure 4-5 shows Logos.sys being modified. Be sure to save the modified files under their original names. Windows will then use them when shutting down.

? How do I _remove the Network Neighborhood icon_ on a PC that is not networked?

It is not simple to get rid of the Network Neighborhood. You cannot just delete the icon from the desktop or drag it to your Recycle Bin. You can turn it off using the System Policy Editor, which you can find

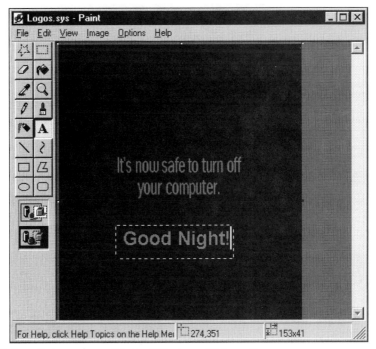

Figure 4-5.   Paint can modify the Windows 95 Logoff screens

on the Windows 95 CD in the \Admin\Apptools\Poledit\ folder as
Poledit.exe. Use the following steps:

1. Double-click \Admin\Apptools\Poledit\Poledit.exe on the
   Windows 95 CD, and open the default template, Admin.adm,
   when you are asked which template you want to use.

2. From the File menu, choose Open Registry, and then double-click
   Local User.

3. Click the plus sign opposite Shell to open it and then the plus sign
   opposite Restrictions.

4. Click Hide Network Neighborhood to enable it, as shown in
   Figure 4-6. Click OK and then close the System Policy Editor.
   You'll need to reboot for the icon to go away.

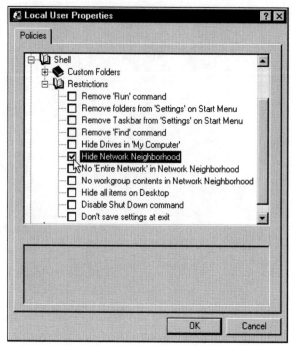

Figure 4-6.   The System Policy Editor can be used to customize some elements of your desktop

? What is a _shortcut_ and how do I use it to start programs from the desktop?

A *shortcut* is a very small file that represents or points to a usually much larger file or a folder in another location. A shortcut is useful because you can use it to remotely start a program, open a data file, or open a folder. For example, if you have an application that you use often, you can place a shortcut to that application on the desktop and start the application by double-clicking the shortcut, all the while leaving the application program file in its original folder.

To create a shortcut on the desktop, use one of the following techniques:

⇨   If you want a shortcut of a program file (one with an .EXE or .COM extension), all you have to do is drag the program file to the desktop or wherever you want the shortcut, and one will automatically be created for you. The original program file will remain where it was originally.

⇨ Press and hold *both* CTRL and SHIFT while dragging any file or folder to the desktop, and a shortcut will be created for you. Make sure you release CTRL-SHIFT before you release the mouse button.

⇨ Right-drag the file or folder to the desktop and select Create Shortcut(s) Here from the pop-up menu that appears.

⇨ Right-click the file or folder, select Create Shortcut from the pop-up menu, and drag the shortcut to the desktop.

I want my printer *shortcut on the right side of the screen*. I drag the icon there, but it snaps back to its position on the left. What can I do?

The icons are being automatically rearranged by Windows 95. Right-click the desktop, choose Arrange Icons from the pop-up menu, and then click AutoArrange to turn the check mark off. Without AutoArrange, the icons will remain wherever you drag them.

I am trying to *use the Pipes screen saver* from Windows NT. It says that I need the Opengl32.dll file. Where do I find this?

Support for OpenGL is not shipped with Microsoft Windows 95. OpenGL for Windows 95 will be available separately as a set of redistributable .DLL files. You can download them from Microsoft online forums (Internet: **http://www.microsoft.com; ftp:// ftp. microsoft.com** and CompuServe: **Go MSWIN95**, among others).

How can I make sure I am *using protected-mode disk drivers*?

You can determine if you are using protected-mode disk drivers with these steps:

1. From the Start menu choose Settings | Control Panel, and then double-click System.

2. Open the Performance tab, click File System, and choose the Troubleshooting tab.

3. If you have *not* checked Disable All 32 Bit Protect-Mode Disk Drivers, as you can see in Figure 4-7, you are using protected-mode drivers.

TASKBAR

❓ How can I *add options to my Start menu*?

The top part of the Start menu can contain options that you place there to start applications and/or open folders, as shown in Figure 4-8. You can place options on the Start menu in three ways:

⇨ Drag files and/or folders from My Computer or Explorer to the Start button on the Taskbar. This will automatically create a shortcut, place the shortcut in the \Windows\Start Menu folder, and place an option named after the shortcut on the Start menu.

⇨ Right-click a vacant area of the Taskbar, choose Properties, and open the Start Menu Programs tab. Click Add, browse for the program file of the program you want on the Start menu, click Next, click Start Menu, and click Next again. Type the name you want to use on the Start menu, and click Finish.

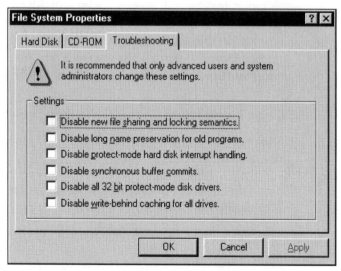

Figure 4-7.   You are using protected-mode disk drivers if Disable All 32 Bit Protect-Mode Disk Drivers is not checked

Figure 4-8.   The Start menu can contain options to start your applications

⇨ Open Explorer and locate the file or folder in the right window that you want to add to the Start menu. In the left window of Explorer, click the plus sign opposite the Windows folder. Then scroll the list of folders until you can see the Start Menu folder. If the option you want to add is a program, simply drag it to the Start Menu folder. A shortcut will be created in the Start Menu folder. For other types of files, press and hold CTRL-SHIFT while dragging the file to the Start menu folder. Then choose Create Shortcut(s) Here from the pop-up menu.

❓ How do I *change the location and size of the Taskbar*?

You can drag the Taskbar to any of the four sides of the screen, and you can drag an edge of the Taskbar to size it. Use these steps:

1. Point on a blank area of the Taskbar, hold down the left mouse button, and drag the Taskbar to another edge of the screen. For example, Figure 4-9 shows the Taskbar on the right edge of the screen.

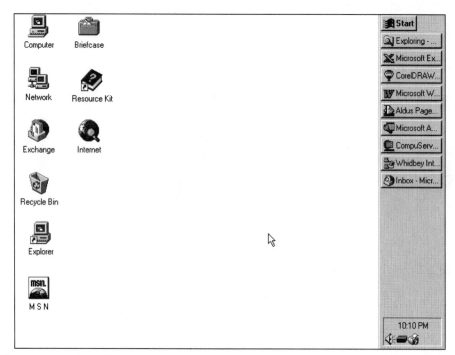

Figure 4-9.   The Taskbar can be dragged to any edge of the screen

2. Resize the Taskbar by moving the mouse pointer to the inside edge of the Taskbar. When the pointer becomes a double arrow, drag the mouse pointer in or out to size the Taskbar as you desire. You can see a three-task-high Taskbar in Figure 4-10.

❓ *What <u>customization can I do of the Taskbar</u>?*

You can customize the Taskbar by right-clicking an empty area of the Taskbar and choosing Properties. The Taskbar Properties dialog box will open as shown in Figure 4-11. Here you can control four attributes of the Taskbar, as follows:

⇨ **Always On Top** prevents the Taskbar from being covered by other windows. If this is turned off, then maximizing a window would cover the Taskbar.

⇨ **Auto Hide** will hide the Taskbar until you move the mouse pointer to the edge of the screen containing the Taskbar, and then the Taskbar will appear.

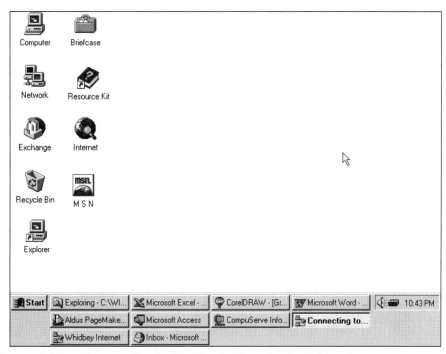

Figure 4-10.   You can size the Taskbar by dragging its inside edge

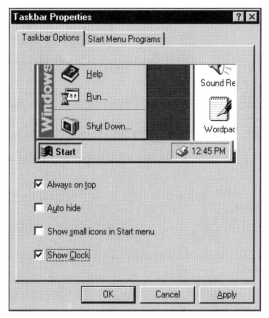

Figure 4-11.   The Taskbar can be customized in the Taskbar Properties dialog box

Tip   *Always On Top must be enabled for Auto Hide to work with maximized windows.*

⇨ **Show Small Icons In Start Menu** allows you to contain more options in the Start menu.

⇨ **Show Clock** turns the display of the clock in the Taskbar on and off.

In addition to customizing the Taskbar Properties dialog box, you can customize the position and size of the Taskbar, as you saw earlier in the question about changing the location and size of the Taskbar.

 ## How can I *turn off the clock on my Taskbar*?

The clock is controlled in the Taskbar Properties dialog box. Use these steps to turn it off:

1. Right-click an empty spot on the Taskbar and choose Properties.

2. Click the Taskbar Options tab, and clear the Show Clock check box to disable it. Choose OK.

 Tip   *You can set the clock (system time, date, and time zone) by double-clicking the clock in the Taskbar. If you hold the mouse pointer over the Taskbar clock, you can see the date, as shown here:*

CUSTOMIZING THE WAY YOU USE WINDOWS 95

 ## Can I *bypass the Windows 95 startup logo*?

Yes. You can turn off the logo by adding an entry to a file named Msdos.sys in your root folder. Msdos.sys, though, is a hidden, read-only file, so you must go through some extra steps. Do so with these instructions:

1. In Explorer, open the View menu and choose Options. In the View menu, choose Show All Files, as you see in Figure 4-12.

2. Also in Explorer, locate and right-click the file Msdos.sys (*not* Msdos.dos) in the root folder of your boot drive, and choose Properties to open the Msdos.sys Properties dialog box.

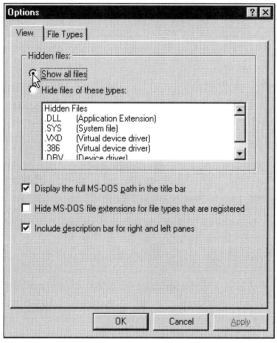

Figure 4-12.   To display all your files, use Explorer's View menu Options
dialog box

3. Click the Read-only and Hidden check boxes to turn them off, and
   then click OK.

4. Make a copy of Msdos.sys to serve as a backup by right-clicking
   Msdos.sys, choosing Copy, right-clicking an open area of the right
   pane of the Explorer window in the root folder, and choosing
   Paste. You can either leave the name "Copy of Msdos.sys" or
   change it to some other name like **Msdos0.sys**.

5. Right-click Msdos0.sys, choose Open With, scroll the list of programs,
   and double-click Notepad, with which you will edit the file.

6. Locate the section entitled "[Options]" and add the line **Logo=0**,
   like the one shown in Figure 4-13.

7. Choose Save As from Notepad's File menu, change the name to
   Msdos.sys (remove the "0"), and click Save. Close Notepad, reset
   the Read-only and Hidden attributes, and reboot your computer.
   You will no longer see the Windows 95 logo.

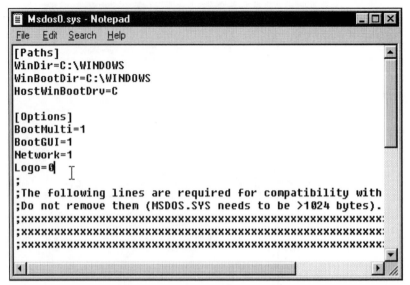

```
Msdos0.sys - Notepad                                    _ □ ✕
 File   Edit   Search   Help
[Paths]                                                        ▲
WinDir=C:\WINDOWS
WinBootDir=C:\WINDOWS
HostWinBootDrv=C

[Options]
BootMulti=1
BootGUI=1
Network=1
Logo=0    I
;
;The following lines are required for compatibility with
;Do not remove them (MSDOS.SYS needs to be >1024 bytes).
;XXXXXXXXXXXXXXXXXXXXXXXXXXXXXXXXXXXXXXXXXXXXXXXXXXXXXXXX
;XXXXXXXXXXXXXXXXXXXXXXXXXXXXXXXXXXXXXXXXXXXXXXXXXXXXXXXX
;XXXXXXXXXXXXXXXXXXXXXXXXXXXXXXXXXXXXXXXXXXXXXXXXXXXXXXXX
                                                               ▼
◄                                                          ►
```

Figure 4-13.   The file Msdos.sys provides some startup parameters to Windows 95

   Tip   *If you change your mind, changing the line to read* **Logo=1** *or removing it altogether will enable the logo again.*

❓ How can I *drag a screen and still see the contents of the screen*? I don't want just the outside of the window.

This is a feature called Full Screen Drag And Drop. It is available in Microsoft Plus! as part of its visual enhancements. Many vendors are shipping Microsoft Plus! along with Windows 95. You can also buy it as an add-on.

❓ I need to *exclude a certain area in upper memory*. How do I do this in Windows 95?

Upper memory is the area between 640K and 1MB. It is used for many purposes, including your ROM BIOS and video memory. Some of it can and should be used for the storage of Windows 95 itself, but you may want to prevent Windows 95 from loading into a certain area so you can use it for some other purpose. To do that, use the following steps:

1. Right-click My Computer and choose Properties. The System Properties dialog box will open. (This is the same dialog box you get when you open the System control panel.)

2. Click the Device Manager tab, and then double-click Computer. The Computer Properties dialog box will open, as shown in Figure 4-14.

3. Click the Reserve Resources tab and select Memory.

4. Click the Add button and type your exclude range. Click OK three times to close the various dialog boxes you opened.

? How can I get my _file extensions_ back? Just seeing the files and icons confuses me.

Use the following steps to show file extensions:

1. Open Explorer's or My Computer's View menu and choose Options.

2. In the View tab, uncheck the box Hide MS-DOS File Extensions For The File Types That Are Registered and select Show All Files.

3. Click OK.

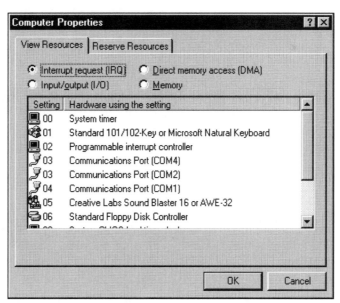

Figure 4-14.   The Computer Properties dialog box allows you to view and reserve computer resources

? How do I _remove the list of files under the Documents menu under Start_?

To clear the files in the Documents menu, do the following:

1. Right-click a blank area of the Taskbar and choose Properties.

2. Click the Start Menu Programs tab.

3. Click the Clear button in the Documents Menu section of the dialog box.

? How can I get my old _Windows 3.1 Program Manager_ to be easily available?

To get easy access to the Windows 3.1 Program Manager, do the following:

1. Click the Start button and choose Settings | Taskbar.

2. Click the Start Menu Programs tab and click Add.

3. Click the Browse button and double-click the \Windows folder.

4. In the \Windows folder, scroll down past the folders to the program files, select Progman.exe, click the Open button, and click Next.

5. Click Start Menu to select it as the folder where you want to place the Progman shortcut and then click Next.

6. Type the full name **program manager**, click Finish, and then click OK. Now when you click the Start button, the Program Manager option will be available.

Caution   *The Program Manager is a 16-bit application; by using it, you give up many of the features of Windows 95—most importantly, long filenames. You'll notice that the Rename option is gone from the File menu for this reason, and you can't click twice on a name in a Program Manager to change it. You also can't drag a file from the Program Manager to the desktop, My Computer, or Explorer.*

WORKING WITH PROGRAMS

? **How do I _add command-line switches to shortcuts for applications_ that are on my desktop?**

Use the following steps to add command-line switches to a shortcut:

1. Open the shortcut's Properties dialog box by right-clicking the shortcut and choosing Properties.

2. Click the Shortcut tab.

3. In the Target box, you should see the command line that is run when the icon is double-clicked. Add the switches to this line. For example, to run Microsoft Word 97 with the /n switch so that it doesn't automatically open up a new document, you would put the following entry in the "Target:" line: **C:\Program Files\ Microsoft Office\Office\Winword.exe /n**.

? **How do I _assign a hot key to quickly launch an application_?**

You can assign a hot key to any shortcut. Use the next set of steps to do this:

1. Right-click the Shortcut icon and choose Properties.

2. Click the Shortcut tab, click in the Shortcut Key box, and press a key combination you want to use for the shortcut key.

3. Click OK to complete the operation.

? **The program folders are listed alphabetically under Start | Programs. Is there any way I can _change the order of the program folders_?**

Yes. To reorder them, you can rename the folders with a number on the left of the name. With such a number, the folders will be sorted by number rather than alphabetically.

Use the following steps to rearrange the order of the folders:

1. Right-click the Start button and choose Open.

2. Double-click Programs. Every folder in this group appears under Start | Programs.

3. Click the folder you want to appear on the top of the list.

4. Press F2 to rename and type **1.** in front of the name.

5. Repeat this for the rest of the folders. For example, if you want the Microsoft Office folder to appear first, click it once, press F2, and type **1.** in front of the "Microsoft Office" label.

? I installed Windows 95 in a folder other than Windows 3.1. Can I *convert my Windows 3.1 program groups to the Windows 95 folders*?

Yes. Do the following:

1. Click the Start button and choose Run.

2. Type **grpconv /m**.

3. Select the group you want to convert.

4. Click Open and then click Yes in the Program Manager Group Converter dialog box. Close the Select A Group To Convert dialog box when you are done.

You can also convert the group by double-clicking the group name.

? How do I *create a file association* in Windows 95?

A file association relates a data file to a program that can open it, so that you can double-click the file in My Computer or Explorer and it will launch the application, which in turn will load the file. To create file association, use these steps:

1. Open My Computer, open the View menu, and choose Options.

2. Click the File Types tab and click New Type. The Add New File Type dialog box will open.

3. Enter the description and extension, and click New under Actions.

4. Type **open** for the Action, and then click Browse to find the application to associate with the file type. Click OK and then Close to complete the process.

? Can I *create a file disassociation* so that it will not open with its associated program?

Yes, to do this use the following steps:

1. Open My Computer or Windows Explorer.

2. Choose Options from the View menu.

3. Click the File Types tab. In the list of file types, select the one you want to change. The settings for that file type are shown in the File Type Details box as shown here.

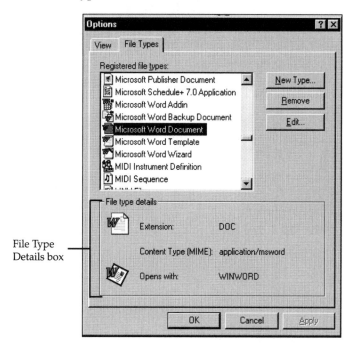

File Type Details box

4. Click Remove and then click Yes in the confirmation message box that displays. The selected file will no longer be associated with that program.

5. Click OK when done.

❓ How do I *create a program group* in Windows 95?

In Windows 95, a program group is nothing more than a folder in the \Windows\Start Menu\Programs folder. To create a new group, use the following steps:

1. Right-click the Start button and choose Open.

2. Double-click the Programs folder. Here are all your program groups.

3. Right-click inside the folder, choose New, and click Folder. This creates a new group, as shown in Figure 4-15. You can rename it to the name you want and drag to it the shortcuts you want there.

❓ I want to run a program minimized in the background at all times, but I don't want to have to manually minimize it every time it starts. How can I *load a program automatically and run it minimized when I start Windows 95*?

First you must place a program in the StartUp folder, as discussed in the next question about how to load a program automatically when

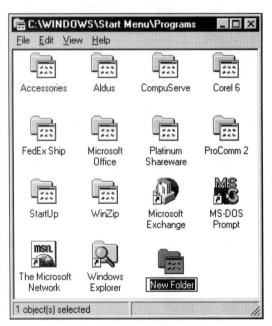

Figure 4-15.   A folder in the \Windows\Start Menu\Programs folder is a program group

Windows 95 boots. Then follow these instructions to have it minimized:

1. After placing a program in the StartUp folder, click the Start button and choose Settings | Taskbar.

2. Click the Start Menu Programs tab and click the Advanced button.

3. Double-click the Programs folder and open the StartUp folder.

4. Right-click the program you need and choose Properties.

5. Click the Shortcut tab and select Minimize in the Run drop-down list.

6. Click OK and exit. The program will now start up minimized.

? How can I *load a program automatically when I start Windows 95*?

Use the following steps to load a program when Windows 95 starts:

1. Click the Start button and choose Settings | Taskbar.

2. Click the Start Menu Programs tab, and then click the Add button.

3. If you don't know the exact filename of the application, click Browse, select the item you need, and click Open.

4. In the Create Shortcut window, click Next.

5. In the Select Program Folder window, select the \Start Menu\ Programs\StartUp folder. Then click Next.

6. In the Select A Title For The Program window, type a name for the shortcut, and click Finish.

7. Click OK to complete the task. The program will automatically start the next time you start Windows.

? How do I *load a program every time Windows starts without putting it in the StartUp folder*?

Add a run command within the Win.ini file. To do this:

1. Open the System Configuration Editor by typing **sysedit** in the Start menu Run dialog box, and then click the Win.ini tab.

2. Edit the Win.ini file by adding a Run command in the [windows] section—for example, **run=c:\progra~1\winzip\winzip32.exe**, as shown in Figure 4-16.

Tip   *You have to use 8.3 filename and extension format, because Win.ini is a rollover from 16-bit Win 3.x.*

3. Close System Configuration Editor and save the changes.

The next time you restart Windows 95 the program you entered in the Run command will open as well.

❓ How do I *remove an item from the Start menu on a local computer*?

To edit the Start menu, do the following:

1. Click the Start button and choose Settings | Taskbar.

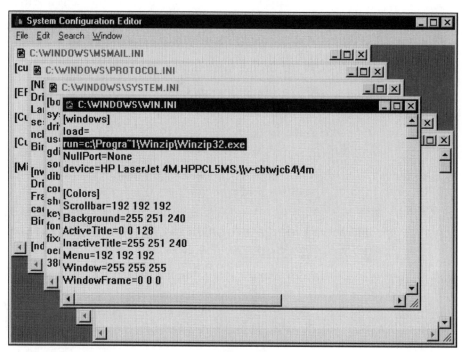

Figure 4-16.   A Run command in the Win.ini file

2. Click the Start Menu Programs tab and click the Remove button. A list of shortcuts and folders in the Start menu will be displayed, as you can see in Figure 4-17.

3. Select the shortcut or folder you want to remove and then click Remove.

❓ How can I *specify a working folder for a program*?

You cannot change the working folder for the original file in Windows 95—it must be done from within the program itself. However, you can create a shortcut to the original file and specify the working folder in the Properties. See the discussion earlier in this chapter on how to create a shortcut. Use the following steps to specify the working folder for a shortcut:

1. Right-click the shortcut and choose Properties from the pop-up menu.

2. Click the Shortcut tab.

3. Enter the working folder in the Start In text box.

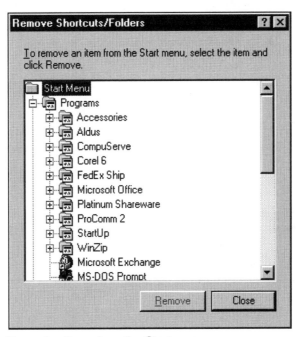

Figure 4-17.   Removing items from the Start menu

Tip   *Many applications, such as Microsoft Word 97, that have the capability within them to specify a working folder will override the specification in the shortcut.*

? What are the *techniques I can use to start my programs*?

You can use several techniques to start your programs, depending on how frequently you use them. Some of the most common options are to place shortcuts to your programs in the following locations (see the earlier discussion on creating shortcuts in the "Changing Your Display" section of this chapter):

⇨ **Directly on the desktop** by dragging the shortcut there. The shortcuts will remain where you drag them until you move or delete them.

⇨ **On the Start menu** by dragging the program files there. Up to 12 programs can be placed on the Start menu itself. (See the discussion on this earlier in this chapter.)

⇨ **In a folder on the desktop** by creating a new folder there and dragging shortcuts to it. If you leave the folder open, the shortcuts will be available at all times and you can ALT-TAB to the folder from any other program.

⇨ **In the Programs menu** by dragging shortcuts in Explorer to the \Windows\Start Menu\Programs folder, either directly or to a new or an existing subfolder to group the programs. When you group them, you get to them by clicking the Start button, selecting Programs, and then the group.

⇨ **In the StartUp folder** by dragging shortcuts in Explorer to the \Windows\Start Menu\Programs\StartUp folder. Programs in the StartUp folder are automatically started when Windows 95 is started.

Tip   *Objects on the desktop get covered by open windows, and you cannot use ALT-TAB to reach them. You can right-click the Taskbar and select Minimize All Windows to see your desktop, and then right-click the Taskbar again and select Undo Minimize All.*

❓ Can I *uninstall a program*?

If you installed an application with the "Developed for Windows 95" logo on it, you can uninstall it using the Add/Remove Programs control panel. This will remove the application and all its files. Try that with these steps:

1. Click the Start button and select Settings | Control Panel; then double-click the Add/Remove Programs icon.

2. Select the Install/Uninstall tab.

3. Select the program to be uninstalled, as shown in Figure 4-18 and click Add/Remove.

4. Click OK.

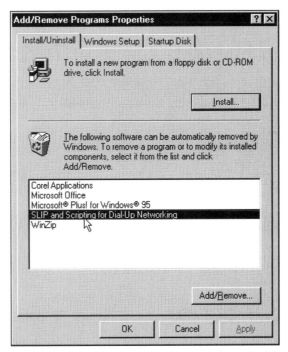

Figure 4-18.   Windows 95-compliant applications can be uninstalled in the Add/Remove Programs control panel

VIDEO DRIVERS

? **I thought that when I _changed my display driver in Windows 95_, I would no longer have to restart my computer to have the change take effect. Aren't these changes dynamic?**

They will only be dynamic if you don't change the color palette. If the color palette is changed, then a new driver file will have to be loaded, and hence the system needs to configure the color scheme based on what is available now with the newly installed driver.

 Tip   *You can download Power Toys from Microsoft's Free Download area: http://www.microsoft.com/windows95/info/powertoys.htm. One of its Toys is QuickRes, which allows you to change colors without rebooting.*

? **How can I _change my video driver_?**

To change your video driver, use the following steps:

1. Click the Start button and choose Settings | Control Panel.

2. Double-click the Display icon, and then click the Settings tab.

OSR 2 3. Click the Change Display Type button (or Advanced Properties button in OSR 2).

OSR 2 4. Click the Change button in the Adapter Type box (or in the Adapter tab in OSR 2), and then click the Have Disk button in the Select Device window.

5. Specify the path to the disk or folder containing the driver that you would like to use.

6. From the list select the driver to use and click OK to install.

DISK DRIVES

? **I have bought a second hard drive, and I want it to be drive D, but D is my CD-ROM. How can I _change the drive letter that is assigned to my CD-ROM_?**

Use the following steps to change a drive letter:

1. Click the Start button and choose Settings | Control Panel.

2. Double-click the System icon.

3. Click the Device Manager tab.

4. Click the plus sign next to CDROM and select your CD-ROM, click Properties, and click the Settings tab.

5. In the Reserved Drive Letters section, you can set Start Drive Letter and End Drive Letter to be the drive letter you want the CD-ROM to use, as you can see in Figure 4-19. Set it the way you want, and then click the OK button.

6. Reboot the computer. The CD-ROM will have the new letter. Remember, however, if you had some applications already installed from the CD-ROM using the old drive letter, you might have to reinstall them.

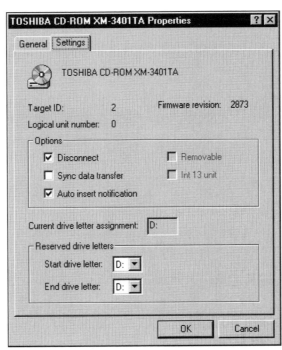

Figure 4-19.   Change a CD-ROM's drive letter in its Properties dialog box

I want to have my swap file on drive D. How do I _change the location of the swap file_?

To change the location, do the following:

1. Right-click My Computer and choose Properties.

2. Click the Performance tab and click the Virtual Memory button.

3. Select Let Me Specify My Own Virtual Memory Settings. Then, opposite Hard Disk, select the drive you want to use, as shown in Figure 4-20. Make sure to indicate that the Maximum size is the total amount of free space on the drive. Windows will then dynamically manage the swap file, and it will grow and shrink as needed.

**Caution**   Under most circumstances, Windows 95 can do a better job of real-time management of your swap file than you can. So you should not need to take over that function.

 How do I _change the partitions on the hard drive_?

The functionality for this did not change from DOS and Windows 3.*x*. Unlike Windows NT, in Windows 95 you cannot adjust the partitions

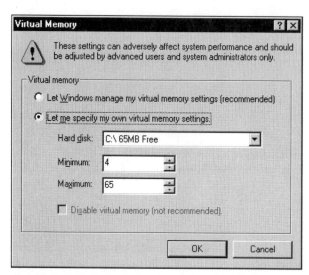

Figure 4-20.   The Virtual Memory dialog box lets you specify the drive and amount of space to be dedicated to a swap file or virtual memory

or create volume sets. You still have to use Fdisk to create partitions. See discussions in Chapter 2 on the use of Fdisk.

? My hard drive space is compressed with a third-party compression package. I wanted to partition using Fdisk to create an extra logical drive, but Fdisk shows only half of the disk space I can see using the DIR command. How can I _modify partitions_?

If you installed a disk compression program from Microsoft or another vendor, Fdisk displays only the uncompressed, not the compressed, size of the drives. In some instances Fdisk cannot delete partitions created by third-party applications. You will have to use that application to delete or modify that partition.

? How do I _use Windows 95 with SyQuest drives_?

To enable the support, you have to put **RemovableIDE=True** in the 386Enh section of the System.ini file. If this line is not there, then Windows 95's protected-mode IDE driver will not load. When the line mentioned here is added to the 386Enh section of System.ini, the Ios.log file will disappear, and the Windows 95 file system will provide 32-bit support for your SyQuest drive.

The other requirements for this support are that the SyQuest drive must have a formatted cartridge inserted when Windows 95 starts, and there must not be another 32-bit module loaded in System.ini, such as the one provided by DTC for their IDE boards.

There is another setting called Virtual Memory in Windows 95. This will be in "MS-DOS compatibility mode" if drive C is a removable drive, SCSI, or IDE.

MOUSE

? How do I _change my mouse behavior_?

You can adjust your mouse behavior with the following steps:

1. Click the Start button and choose Settings | Control Panel.

2. Double-click the Mouse icon to open the Mouse Properties dialog box that you see in Figure 4-21.

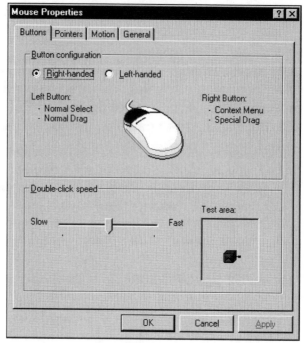

Figure 4-21.   Mouse behavior is controlled in the Mouse Properties dialog box

3. Click the tab for the behavior you want to change.

   ⇨ **Buttons** allows you to switch the left and right buttons and to change the speed of a double-click.

   ⇨ **Pointers** allows you to customize the pointers that appear in specific circumstances.

   ⇨ **Motion** allows you to specify whether you want to use pointer trails and the speed at which the pointer moves across the screen.

   ⇨ **General** allows you to specify the type of mouse you have and to change its driver.

4. After changing the settings, click OK.

❓ How do I _change my mouse driver_?

Use the following steps to change the mouse driver by use of the System Device Manager:

1. Click the Start button and choose Settings | Control Panel.

2. Double-click the System icon, and click the Device Manager tab.

3. Double-click the Mouse device, select your current pointing device, and click the Properties button.

OSR 2 4. Click the Driver tab and then click the Change Driver (or Update Driver in OSR 2) button. The Select Device dialog box will open (in OSR 2, the Update Device Driver Wizard opens and can search networks, the Internet, and so on for updated drivers automatically or manually by choosing the No Select Driver From List option).

5. Select the new driver to be used, or click Have Disk to use a non-Microsoft driver, and click OK.

Alternatively, you can change the mouse driver using the Mouse control panel in the next set of instructions:

1. Click the Start button and choose Settings | Control Panel.

2. Double-click the Mouse icon.

3. In the Mouse Properties dialog box, click the General tab.

4. Click the Change button. The Select Device dialog box will open.

5. Select the new driver to be used, or click Have Disk to use a non-Microsoft driver, and click OK.

? In my previous version of Windows I needed to have two mouse drivers—one for DOS and one for Windows. Do I still need two _mouse drivers_?

A single mouse driver is used in Windows 95, eliminating the need for two mouse drivers. This will even save you some system resources.

EXPLORER

? What are the _command-line switches that can be used with Explorer_ in shortcuts and batch files?

Explorer has several command-line switches that you can use in shortcuts and batch files to set it up in various ways, as you will see later in this section in the answer to the question about opening Explorer at the My Computer level. The switches are entered

following Explorer.exe and a space on a command line like the Start
menu Run command, a DOS command line, or the Target command
line in a shortcut.

⇨ **/e** specifies that the Explorer view will be used. Otherwise the
folder view is used.

⇨ **/n** specifies that a new window will be opened. Otherwise the
new view will use the existing Explorer window if one is open.

⇨ **,/root,***object* specifies that the root of the folders displayed will
be *object,* where *object* is a drive (network or local) or a folder.
Otherwise Desktop is the root. For example, the command line

```
Explorer.exe /e,/root,\\netdrive
```

opens an Explorer window with the network drive *Netdrive* as
the root drive. This would allow browsing *Netdrive,* but only
that drive.

⇨ **/select,***subobject* specifies that *subobject's* parent folder is opened
and *subobject* is selected. In the answer to the question about
opening Explorer at the My Computer level instead of at C:\

```
Explorer.exe /e,/select,c:\
```

opened an Explorer window with My Computer (the parent of
C:\) opened and C: selected.

⇨ **,***subobject* specifies that *subobject* is the initial selected object
unless it follows */select.* Otherwise nothing is initially selected.

Is there a *fast way to get from my desktop to the My Computer* view of my C:\ drive?

Yes there is. Just click the Start button, select Run, type a backslash (\),
as shown here, and press ENTER.

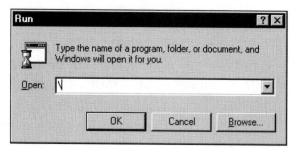

This is an easy way to bring up your C:\ drive.

❓ How can I _open Explorer at the My Computer level_ instead of at my C:\ level, so I can get to all my drives without using the scroll bar or Up One Level button?

To get Explorer to open at the My Computer level, you will need to add command-line switches in the Target command line of the shortcut used to open Explorer. Use the following set of instructions to do that:

1. Create a shortcut for Explorer on your desktop or in your Start menu that you will use to open Explorer.

2. Right-click the new shortcut, and choose Properties to open the Explorer Properties dialog box.

3. In the Shortcut tab, edit the Target command line so that it reads

    ```
    \Windows\Explorer.exe /e,/select,C:\
    ```

    (The C:\Windows\Explorer.exe may be different on your computer if you installed Windows 95 on a different drive and folder. Leave that part unchanged in your command line.) The command-line switches _/e,/select,_ are explained in answer to the question about command-line switches used with Explorer. The ending C:\ should be the first hard drive within My Computer.

4. Click OK and double-click your shortcut (or select it in the Start menu) to try it out. Your results should look like Figure 4-22.

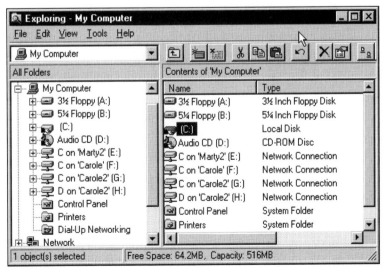

Figure 4-22.   You can open Explorer at different levels using command-line switches in the shortcut

? **When I use Find Files Or Folders, parts of the folder name or the long filename are cut off and I see something like "C:\windows\sys...." Is there a way I can _see the whole name_?**

Yes, you can increase the size of the box that shows the name by doing the following:

1. Point to the vertical line at the right of the box containing the field name you want to see. The pointer will become a vertical line with arrows pointing to the right and left as shown here:

Pointer becomes a two-way arrow

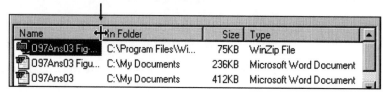

2. Double-click when you see the two-way arrow. The box will expand to fit the longest name on the list. Or when the two-way arrow is displayed, drag the side of the box to the size you want.

 **Tip**   You can also change the size of panes in Windows Explorer by dragging them.

? **Is there any way I can get a _separate window for each drive in Explorer_, like I could in File Manager?**

No. The only way to get two windows with different drives is to open two instances of Explorer. In Explorer, however, you can select one drive and have it displayed in the right pane, then scroll the left pane so you can see and open the second drive. You can then drag objects from a folder in the first drive to a folder in the second drive.

ACCESSIBILITY OPTIONS

 **Tip**   If you did not install the Accessibility Options during setup, you can still add them to your system. Click the Start button, select Settings | Control Panel, and double-click Add/Remove Programs. In the Windows Setup tab, place a check mark next to Accessibility Options. Insert your Windows 95 Install disk, click Have Disk, and follow the prompts.

❓ How can I *adjust the keyboard repeat rate*?

You can vary the time a key is held down before it begins repeating and the speed at which additional characters are produced in the Keyboard Properties dialog box. While these RepeatKey settings are not officially part of the Accessibility Options, they are important for people who can't lift their fingers off the keyboard quickly. Use the following steps to adjust the RepeatKey settings:

1. Click the Start button, choose Settings | Control Panel, and double-click Keyboard.

2. Click the Speed tab, shown in Figure 4-23, if it is not already displayed.

   ⇨ To adjust how long a key must be held down before it begins repeating, drag the Repeat Delay slider to the setting you want.

   ⇨ To adjust how quickly characters repeat when you hold down a key, drag the Repeat Rate slider to the appropriate setting.

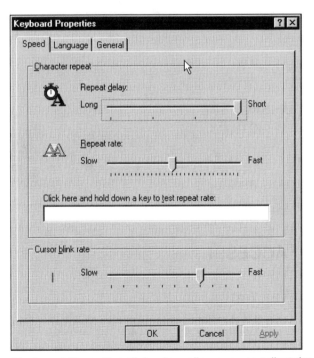

Figure 4-23.   Keyboard Properties dialog box allows you to adjust the repeat rate

3. Click in the test box and press a key to see if your settings work for you. If not, make the necessary adjustments and test them again.

4. When you are satisfied with the settings, click OK to finalize them.

? What is FilterKeys, and how do I implement it?

FilterKeys desensitizes the keyboard so that it is less likely that you will get unwanted keystrokes. Keystrokes that are not held down for a minimum period are ignored. This is useful for people who have tremors. FilterKeys is part of the Accessibility Options. Use the following steps to enable FilterKeys:

1. Click the Start button, select Settings | Control Panel, and then double-click Accessibility Options.

2. From the Keyboard tab, click Use FilterKeys to enable the feature.

3. Click Settings to open the Settings For FilterKeys dialog box, shown in Figure 4-24, to enable the shortcut (holding down RIGHT SHIFT for eight seconds); to ignore repeated keystrokes or quick

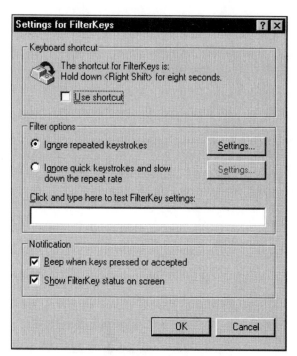

Figure 4-24.   FilterKeys removes unwanted keystrokes

keystrokes and slow down the repeat rate; to test the FilterKeys settings; and to determine the type of notification that FilterKeys is working—a beep or onscreen status display.

4. When you are finished, click OK twice to finalize the settings.

What is MouseKeys, and how do I implement it?

MouseKeys is part of the Accessibility Options that let users control the mouse pointer using the numeric keypad as follows:

⇨ Use the arrow keys on the numeric keypad to move the pointer horizontally or vertically.

⇨ Use HOME, END, PGUP, and PGDN to move the pointer diagonally.

⇨ Use 5 in the middle of the keypad as a single click and the + as a double click.

⇨ Use / at the top of the keypad to specify that the left mouse button will be clicked when 5 is pressed. Also at the top of the keypad, use - to specify the right button, and use * to specify both buttons.

⇨ Use 0 or INS at the bottom of the keypad to lock down the mouse button for dragging and/or DEL to release the mouse button.

⇨ Hold down SHIFT while you are using the mouse keys to move the pointer a single pixel at a time.

To implement MouseKeys, use the following steps:

1. Click the Start button, select Settings | Control Panel, and double-click Accessibility Options.

2. Click the Mouse tab, shown next, and select Use MouseKeys.

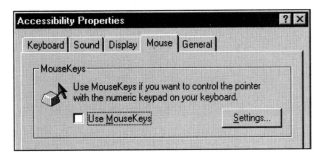

3. Click Settings to open the Settings For MouseKeys dialog box, shown in Figure 4-25, to vary the pointer speed and acceleration,

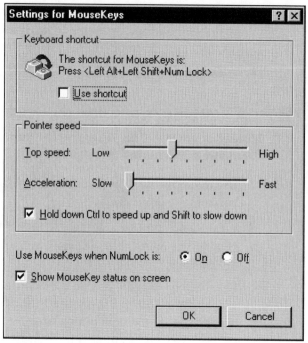

Figure 4-25.   Settings For MouseKeys lets you determine how fast the mouse
pointer will move

to use CTRL or SHIFT to speed up or slow down the speed, or to use
NUM LOCK as a toggle to switch MouseKeys on or off.

4. To turn MouseKeys on and off with a shortcut key, select Use
   Shortcut. This enables you to turn MouseKeys on or off by
   pressing LEFT ALT-LEFT SHIFT-NUM LOCK.

5. Click OK twice to finalize the settings.

❓ *What is StickyKeys,* and how do I implement it?

StickyKeys, part of Accessibility Options, allows users to press the
keys of a key combination one at a time and have Windows respond
as if the keys were pressed together. It is used with the CTRL, SHIFT, or
ALT keys. Use the following steps to implement StickyKeys:

1. Click the Start button, select Settings | Control Panel, and then
   double-click Accessibility Options.

2. From the Keyboard tab, click Use StickyKeys.

3. Click Settings to open the Settings For StickyKeys dialog box to enable the shortcut (pressing SHIFT five times); to press ALT, SHIFT, or CTRL twice to lock them in for repeated use; to turn off StickyKeys when two keys are pressed at the same time; and to determine notification by sound when CTRL, SHIFT, or ALT is pressed, or to show the status on the screen.

4. When you are finished, click OK twice to finalize the settings.

? *What is ToggleKeys*, and how do I implement it?

ToggleKeys, which is part of Accessibility Options, provides audio cues—high and low beeps—to tell users when CAPS LOCK, NUM LOCK, and SCROLL LOCK keys are pressed. A high tone will be sounded when one of the toggle keys is turned on, and a low tone when they are toggled off. Implement ToggleKeys with these steps:

1. Click the Start button and select Settings | Control Panel, and then double-click Accessibility Options.

2. From the Keyboard tab, click Use ToggleKeys.

3. Click Settings and select Use Shortcut to enable the shortcut (holding down NUM LOCK for five seconds).

4. When you are finished, click OK twice to finalize the settings.

OPTIMIZING WINDOWS

? I've got Windows 95 installed, but it's not performing as well as I had hoped. Is there anything I can do to *increase performance*?

Windows 95 is self-optimizing, so there isn't much you can do short of buying more memory. However, here are some things to try:

⇨ Click the Start button and choose Settings | Control Panel. Then double-click the System icon. Once the System control panel is opened, click the Performance tab and Windows 95 may give you some suggestions on what you can do to increase performance or tell you that your system is configured for optimal performance, as shown in Figure 4-26.

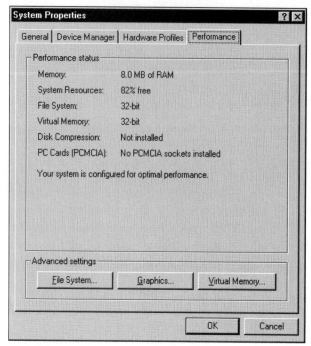

Figure 4-26.   The System Properties Performance tab will tell you if your system is optimally configured

⇨ Defragment your hard drive(s) using the Windows 95 Disk Defragmenter utility (from the Start menu, select Programs I Accessories I System Tools). This can greatly increase disk performance.

❓ In Windows 3.1, a _permanent swap file_ works better than a temporary one. Is it still true for Windows 95?

No. Windows 95 dynamically manages the swap file, which can grow and shrink as necessary. In this sense, its behavior is closer to a Windows 3.x temporary swap file. However, it is free of many limitations of Windows 3.x swap files as follows:

⇨ The Windows 95 swap file does not have to occupy contiguous disk space.

⇨ The Windows 95 swap file can be located on a compressed drive.

⇨ The Windows 95 swap file can be located anywhere the user wants, not just in the root of the boot drive.

It is recommended that you let Windows 95 manage the swap file for you.

How can I *speed up the Start menu*?

You can use Regedit to make changes to the Registry that speed up the menu display.

Caution   *Regedit is a very crude editing tool and gives you no help about what you are doing. It's like doing surgery blindfolded. Incorrect changes to the Registry can cause Windows not to boot. You therefore need to make very sure that you only change what you intend to change and that you understand exactly what to change.* **Always back up System.dat and User.dat before using Regedit.**

The Registry uses two files, System.dat and User.dat, and maintains a backup System.da0 and User.da0. All four of these files are in the \Windows folder. The .DA0 backups are frequently modified by Windows, so it is worthwhile creating your own verified backups before modifying the files with Regedit. Use the following instructions to make an additional backup and then use Regedit:

1. In Explorer, open the \Windows folder, right-click System.dat, and choose Copy from the pop-up menu that appears.

2. Right-click a blank area of the right Explorer pane within \Windows, and choose Paste to paste a copy of System.dat. It will be named "Copy of System.dat."

3. Repeat steps 1 and 2 for User.dat.

4. Click the Start button and choose Run.

5. Type **regedit** and click OK to open the Registry Editor.

6. In the left pane, click the plus signs opposite HKEY_CURRENT_USER and Control Panel to open them. (My Computer should already be open.)

7. Right-click Desktop and select New and String Value, as shown in Figure 4-27.

8. In the new entry that appears in the right pane, type **MenuShowDelay**, all one word, for the name and press ENTER.

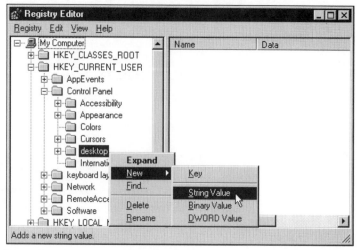

Figure 4-27.   Creating a new Registry entry

9. Double-click the new entry to open the Edit String dialog box. In the Value Data text box, type a value from 10 to 1, 1 being the fastest. Try **4** and click OK.

10. Exit the Registry Editor (the file is automatically saved) and restart Windows. Take a look at how fast you can access your Start menu items!

If you make a mistake and your system won't boot, boot into DOS, change to the \Windows folder, copy Copy of System.dat to System.dat and Copy of User.dat to User.dat, and then boot again.

❓ I tried to _use DriveSpace_, the disk compression program that comes with Windows 95, to increase the capacity of my new 850MB hard drive, but it is only compressing 512MB. Why?

The version of DriveSpace (version 2) in Windows 95 can only create a compressed drive of up to 512MB. Try Microsoft Plus! for Windows 95, which includes DriveSpace 3. This will give you a compressed drive up to 2Gb and a better compression algorithm than DriveSpace 2.

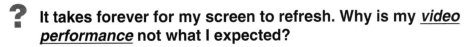

It takes forever for my screen to refresh. Why is my *video performance* not what I expected?

The controls that are available to change video performance vary, depending on your display adapter card. The controls you do have are reached by opening the Control Panel, double-clicking the System icon, selecting the Performance tab, and clicking Graphics. Depending on your controls, try dragging the Hardware Acceleration slider to Full. Try Fast ROM Emulation. Choosing this option will allow the system to emulate video ROM drivers in protected mode, letting the system write to the screen faster. Or try Dynamic Memory Allocation. If set, this switch will allow memory used by the application to be used for video display. This is very useful if you switch from text and graphics modes frequently.

I increased my *virtual memory swap file size* to 30MB, and now my system seems to run much more slowly. Why?

By default, Windows 95 will optimize your virtual memory settings for peak performance. When you force a given swap file size, it may adversely affect performance by causing Windows to manage (use) more of a swap file than it would otherwise be using in optimal circumstances.

Tip   *For your best performance, let Windows maintain your virtual memory settings.*

chapter

5 Answers!

Using
Windows 95

Answer Topics!

Using Windows 95 @ a Glance

When you're using Windows 95 and everything is working as expected, you're in fat city! Hopefully this occurs most of the time. This chapter, however, addresses unexpected situations. Some of the main questions revolve around these areas:

⇨   **Booting Situations** discusses problems that can occur while you are booting or loading Windows 95. Some of the questions involve other operating systems running with or instead of Windows 95.

⇨   **Shortcuts** describes how shortcuts are used and why they sometimes disappear.

⇨   **Drag-and-Drop** covers questions you may have while attempting to drag and drop objects and files.

⇨   **Windows Environment** describes several situations that cause your environment to look or act differently from what you expect. These questions often arise from differences between Windows 95 and 3.1, or from a lack of understanding of how Windows 95 now handles certain tasks.

⇨   **WordPad** is discussed for questions that commonly arise in this Windows 95 text editor.

⇨   **Equipment-Related Problems** discusses problems that can occur with equipment that is standard or nonstandard to Windows 95.

⇨   **Other Problems** covers a variety of questions arising while you are using Windows 95.

Starting Basics

Using Windows 95 begins with finding your way around the computer. You'll learn that it's easy and intuitive. First, you have a Start menu that calls to you, "Start here!" When you do, you'll find options that display programs neatly listed in a menu, documents and files that you frequently use, important settings that control your display and many other elements of your computer, a Find command for searching your files, system Help, and a Run option where you can enter DOS commands. In addition to these basic Start menu options, you can place up to 12 other options on the Start menu that let you quickly access the programs and folders you use most frequently.

On the Start menu and in Windows 95, there are a number of tools and convenient ways of getting around that make it easy and fun to use. For the first-time user of Windows 95, understanding four facilities of the system is of primary importance in effectively using it. These are the Start menu, the Taskbar, the right mouse button, and file management with Explorer, My Computer, and the Network Neighborhood. If you are just beginning, take a minute and look at what you can do with each of these.

⇨ The **Start menu** contains all the information, programs, and tools to get you started using your computer. You open the Start menu by clicking the Start button, and you can select one of the menu *options* by clicking it. The top four options open a submenu with additional options. You need only point to—you don't have to click—an option if its function is to open a submenu. The purpose of the seven initial Start menu options (before you add your own) is as follows:

⇨ **Programs** displays two or more *program groups* at the top of the submenu that, when you point on them, display another submenu listing programs and folders making up that group, as you can see in Figure 5-1. You'll find both Windows 95 groups, such as Accessories, with many valuable small applications or *applets*, and your own groups, perhaps with word processing, spreadsheet, or

• • • • • • • • • • •

Starting Basics, continued

database programs. At the bottom of the Programs submenu you will have two to four programs (depending on what Windows 95 options you installed) that you simply click to activate.

⇨ **Documents** lists the last 15 documents that you worked on and that were directly activated by double-clicking them or were opened from a shortcut. When you click a document or file that is *associated* with an application, that application will load and the selected file will be opened ready to use. You will find that this list rapidly fills up with documents, graphics, clip art, and other files that are handy to have at your fingertips.

⇨ **Settings** gives you fast access to the Control Panel, where you can change most of the hardware and user settings (Chapter 4 describes the most common control panels). Settings also gives you access to a Printers folder, where you can control all the printers, local and networked, including fax machines, that you have available. Finally, Settings gives you direct access to the Taskbar properties, which allows you to vary the Taskbar display, even hiding it if you want, and enables you to add programs to the Start menu, either on the top of it or contained within the Programs submenu.

⇨ **Find** allows you to search for files and folders on any disk drive to which you have access, to search for a computer on your network, or to search for an item on the Microsoft Network. Find is a powerful tool that allows you to search using criteria other than name, such as date, text content, file type.

⇨ **Help** brings up the Windows 95 Help system, which is comprehensive in its coverage of the features and how to use them. You can look at an overview of the Help system, learn some Tips and Tricks, or be led through a troubleshooting procedure. You can search for an item by subject, indexed alphabetically. Finally, you can search for all references to a subject in a database consisting of all words and phrases in the Help system.

Starting Basics, *continued*

⇨ **Run** provides a command line on which you can type a DOS command or directly initiate a program, or open a folder by typing in its path and name. This is the same as the Run Command line in Windows 3.*x*.

⇨ **Shut Down** allows you to gracefully shut down Windows 95 by first saving any open files or reminding you to do so, and then deleting any temporary files that have been in use and are no longer needed. The Shut Down option gives you the option to restart your computer, the equivalent of rebooting, either back into Windows or to DOS. You can protect yourself from losing unsaved information by always using Shut Down when leaving Windows 95 and, only when you are told it's safe, turning off your computer.

⇨ The **Taskbar**, which is normally at the bottom of the screen, enables you to switch among multiple programs that are running on your computer. It displays each program as a *task* on the Taskbar—a rectangle with the name and icon of the program (see Figure 5-2). After a program is started (see the discussion in Chapter 4 on starting programs), its task appears on the Taskbar. When you want to switch from one program to another, you simply click the task for the program you want to use. The program you are switching to opens on the screen. The program you left is still active in memory; it just may not be visible. With the Taskbar, you will always know what programs are active, and you'll be able to get to them immediately. In addition to the active program tasks, the Taskbar contains a *notification area* with special status icons that, for example, tell you that you have mail waiting, or that your printer or modem is active, or that allow you to control the volume of your sound system.

⇨ The **right mouse button**, which was largely ignored in previous versions of Windows, has taken on a significant role in Windows 95. Most importantly, when you *right-click* an object (a folder, a file, the desktop, or Taskbar), a *pop-up* menu appears that provides options related to the object you clicked on. These pop-up menus, some of which are shown in Figure

● ● ● ● ● ● ● ● ● ●

Starting Basics, continued

5-3, contain many different options. Most of them contain a Properties option that will open a Properties dialog box that gives you information about the object and lets you change its settings. Additionally, you can drag files and folders using the right mouse button and, when you are done dragging, get a pop-up menu that allows you to copy, move, or create a shortcut for the object you dragged.

⇨ **Explorer, My Computer, and Network Neighborhood** are the navigating and file management tools within Windows 95. You use them to find a file, a folder, or a networked computer. Chapter 6 discusses these tools more. Explorer is found on the Start | Programs menu. You'll want to place a shortcut to it on the Start menu, or even on the desktop. My Computer and Network Neighborhood are already on the desktop for your quick use.

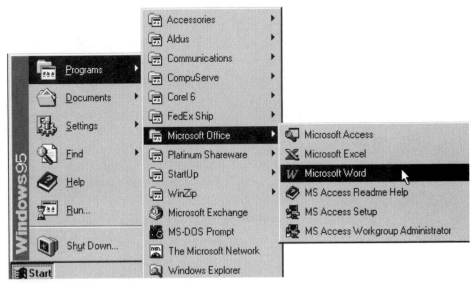

Figure 5-1.   From the Start menu you can open a program group and select a program

Figure 5-2.   The Taskbar lets you switch among programs that are running

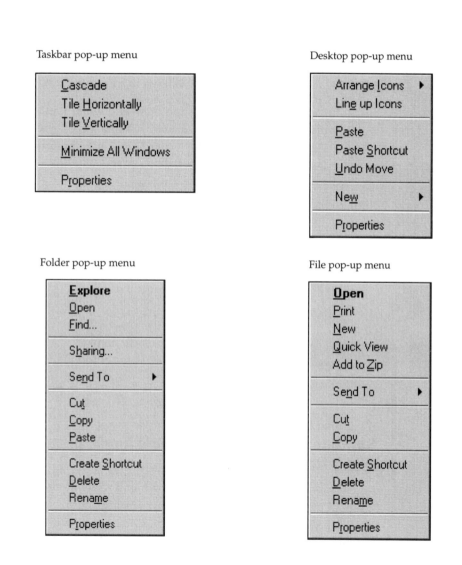

Figure 5-3.   The right mouse button opens pop-up menus such as these

BOOTING SITUATIONS

? **I installed Windows 95 to a clean folder instead of updating my current version of Windows 3.*x*. When I boot to my previous version of DOS and then launch Windows 3.*x*, I get a message that states my swap file is corrupt and that I can delete it and create a new one. How can I _boot both Windows 3.1 and 95 at different points_?**

OSR 2   You can do one of three things to rectify this problem:

⇨ Delete the swap file as prompted, and when Win3.*x* starts, go to the Control Panel and then to 386 Enhanced. Click the Virtual Memory button, and then click the Change button. Then create a temporary swap file instead of a permanent one.

⇨ You could install Windows 95 on a different drive than the previous version of Windows 3.*x*.

⇨ You could set up a permanent swap file in Win3.*x* and then add the following lines to the 386Enh section of the Windows 95 System.ini:

```
PagingFile=<Win31xPagingFile>

MinPagingFileSize=<SizeInk>
```

⇨ <Win31PagingFile> is the swap file (usually C:\386part.par), and <SizeInk> is the size of <Win31PagingFile> divided by 1024.

OSR 2 *Caution*   *OSR 2 does not support dual booting.*

? **How can I _boot directly into Safe mode, bypassing the Windows 95 Startup menu_?**

As the computer is booting, you can enter Safe mode by pressing F5 before Windows 95 begins loading. During booting, the computer first checks itself and then displays a list of the computer's components in a rectangle on the screen. After the check, it begins to load Windows 95 and displays a message, "Starting Windows 95." You must wait until the computer has checked itself, and then immediately press F5, either before the "Starting Windows" message is displayed or an instant after. You will boot directly into Safe mode.

Tip *If you press F8 at that time, you will get a menu of booting options. From the menu you can choose Safe Mode (or Safe Mode With Network Support). The Chapter 1 question, "How do I do a clean boot for Windows 95?" describes each of the booting menu options in detail.*

The Control Panel folder insists on loading every time I start my PC in Windows 95. How do I get the *Control Panel folder to stop loading on startup*?

There are three possible ways a folder will be automatically opened at startup. These are as follows:

⇨ The folder was open when Windows 95 was shut down. If so, close the Control Panel and then restart Windows 95. Normally that should take care of it.

⇨ A shortcut to the Control Panel was placed in the \Windows\ Start Menu\Programs\StartUp folder. If so, drag the Control Panel icon out of the folder.

⇨ The Win.ini file has a Run=Control Panel statement. Use Notepad to edit the Win.ini file, and change the statement to just Run=.

How do I *create a Windows 95 Startup disk* if I didn't do it during setup?

OSR 2 ***Tip*** *A startup floppy disk can be a lifeline if you can't boot from your hard disk. You should create, try out, and keep handy a startup disk now before you need it.*

You can easily create a *startup* or *boot disk* from within Windows 95. Follow these steps:

1. Click the Start button, choose Settings | Control Panel, and double-click Add/Remove Programs.

2. Click the Startup Disk tab, and click the Create Disk button, as shown in Figure 5-4. Follow the prompts. Make sure you are using a blank high-density disk, because all of the files on the disk will be deleted and replaced with the boot programs.

Figure 5-4.   Creating a new startup disk after installation

Tip   *If you originally installed from a CD-ROM, you'll be asked to insert your Windows 95 CD-ROM to create the startup disk.*

OSR 2 *Caution*   *Don't use a startup disk created in Windows 95 for OSR 2 or vice versa.*

? **When I start Windows 95, it comes up with an *error message asking me to change my video display settings*. How can I find the problem?**

OSR 2 To troubleshoot the problem:

1. Reboot your computer.

2. As soon as you see the "Starting Windows 95" message, press F8. Select Safe Mode. This starts with the most basic VGA display driver.

3. When Windows 95 is loaded, click the Start button and choose Settings | Control Panel.

4. Double-click the Display icon and click the Settings tab.

5. Now use Change Display Type to install and test successively more sophisticated display drivers. (In OSR 2, the Change Display Type button is called Advanced Properties.)

Note   *If you use a third-party display driver, you may have to get a new driver from the card manufacturer.*

6. Using Notepad, check System.ini to see what driver is installed by looking at the line display.drv=*some.drv*, where *some.drv* is the driver name you are looking for.

❓ When I reboot the system, I receive the following *error message: "Bad or missing Command Interpreter, enter name of Command Interpreter (c:\windows\command.com)."* What does this mean and what do I do about it?

OSR 2 This message can occur when the Windows 95 or the MS-DOS command interpreter (Command.com) is missing or has become corrupted.

To restore the operating system and make the disk bootable, do the following:

1. Boot the system using your Windows 95 Startup disk.

2. To move the Windows 95 basic programs to the hard disk from the floppy, type **sys c:** at the MS-DOS command prompt.

3. After the programs have transferred from the floppy disk to the hard disk, remove the disk and reboot the computer. You may need to reinstall Windows 95, but you will now be able to from your hard drive.

OSR 2 *Caution*   *Be sure to use the correct Startup disk for Win95 or OSR 2.*

❓ On one of my PCs I used to have the NT 3.5 Server with a dual-boot configuration. Since then I installed Windows 95 and deleted NT from my hard disk. When I boot, I still must choose between Windows 95 or NT. How do I safely *get rid of the dual boot for the deleted NT*?

To eliminate the NT dual boot, do the following:

OSR 2 1. Make sure you have recently backed up your critical files in case this gets messed up.

2. Use your Windows 95 Startup floppy disk (see earlier) to boot into MS-DOS.

3. Type **sys c:**, which overwrites the NT boot sector on the C drive with a DOS boot sector.

4. Reboot off your hard disk into Windows 95.

? **My system crashed, and the next time I started Windows, the screen came up with the words "_Safe Mode_" in each corner of the screen, the colors were different, and I could not access my CD-ROM. Why?**

If Windows 95 detects a problem during startup or detects that a previous startup did not successfully complete, it then starts in a special troubleshooting mode called Safe mode. This means that all your system files (Config.sys, Autoexec.bat, and all .INI files) are bypassed; no network, printer, or CD-ROM drivers are loaded; and only the standard VGA driver is loaded. This is done so that you can identify the reason for the system crash and make necessary changes.

To figure out what caused the problem, question yourself about what's been happening on your computer. For example: What was the last thing you did before the crash? Did you add a new driver? Retrace your steps and remove the driver. Did you install a printer? Remove it. If you were just working with an application, run ScanDisk (Start | Programs | Accessories | System Tools | ScanDisk). It will report any problems with your hard drive. Then click the Start button, Shut Down, and choose Restart The Computer. If everything is OK, you will get your regular Windows screen. If you are still getting the Safe Mode screen, you might have to continue troubleshooting.

? **What _switches are available to start Windows from the command prompt_ when I need to isolate an error?**

Using switches during booting enables you to diagnose problems. When you are having problems bringing up Windows 95, you can use the /d (for diagnostics) switch. This allows you to create an environment to troubleshoot your problem.

Follow these steps:

1. Boot to the MS-DOS environment either by selecting Restart The Computer In MS-DOS Mode from the Shut Down menu, or by pressing F8 and selecting MS-DOS mode during startup.

2. At the command prompt, type the following command:

   `win /d:switch`

   where _switch_ is one of the following switches:

   ⇨ **f** This disables 32-bit disk access. Use this if the computer seems to have disk problems or if Windows stalls. (This is the same as the statement "32bitdiskaccess=false" in the System.ini file.)

⇨ **m**   This starts Windows in Safe mode. Use this if you are having trouble booting. You can accomplish the same thing by pressing F5 when you first see "Starting Windows 95" while booting.

⇨ **n**   This starts Windows in Safe mode with networking. Use this if you need network access for your Windows 95 files. You can accomplish the same thing by pressing F6 when you first see "Starting Windows 95" while booting.

⇨ **s**   This prevents Windows from using the upper-memory ROM address space between F000 and FFFF for a break point. Use this if Windows stalls during startup. (This is the same as the "SystemRombreakpoint=false" statement in the System.ini file.)

⇨ **v**   This causes the system ROM to handle interrupts from the hard disk controller instead of Windows 95. Use this if you are having disk problems. (This is the same as the statement "VirtualHDIRQ=false" in the System.ini file.)

⇨ **x**   This prevents Windows from using any of the upper-memory area A000-FFFF. Use this if you suspect an upper-memory conflict. (This is the same as the statement "EMMexclude=A000-FFFF" in the System.ini file.)

❓ While Windows 95 is loading, an error occurs during _video adapter initialization_. My computer stalls and I have to press CTRL-ALT-DEL to restart it. How do I change my video driver back to VGA?

To change your video driver, do the following:

1. Restart your computer, and as soon as you see "Starting Windows 95," press F8 and choose Safe Mode.

2. When in Windows 95, click the Start button and choose Settings | Control Panel.

3. Double-click the Display icon and click the Settings tab.

OSR 2   4. Click the Change Display Type button, and then click the Change button in the Adapter Type section. (In OSR 2, click the Advanced

Properties button, and then click the Change button on the
Adapter tab.)

5. Click Show All Devices, click Standard Display Types under
   Manufacturers, click Standard Display Adapter (VGA) under
   Models (see Figure 5-5), and then click OK.

6. When asked to use the current driver or a new driver, select Current.

? Can I _warm-boot Windows 95 without rebooting the PC_?

Yes. Do the following:

1. Click the Start button and choose Shut Down.

2. Click Restart The Computer.

3. Hold down SHIFT and click Yes. This will only restart Windows 95,
   not the computer (warm boot). This is a lot faster than a normal
   (cold) reboot.

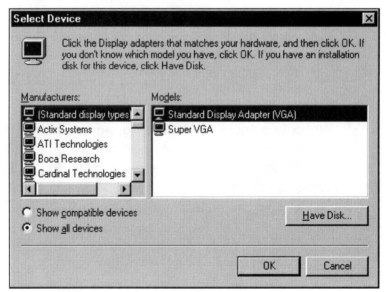

Figure 5-5.   Returning your display driver to standard VGA

SHORTCUTS

? **Sometimes I _create a shortcut and then it seems to disappear_. Where does it go?**

> As a rule of thumb, the shortcut is created in the same folder with the original. If the original is on the desktop, the shortcut will be added to the desktop. In My Computer or Explorer, the shortcut will be created in the same folder as the original. On the other hand, if you are in the Find window and create a shortcut, you may not see it unless you rerun the search. The shortcut to an object, such as a printer or a modem, will by default be placed on the desktop.

? **_How are shortcuts used?_**

> A _shortcut_ is a small (under 1K) file that references another file. A shortcut allows you to remotely load a program, open a folder, or access an object (like a printer or a dial-up network connection) by double-clicking the shortcut. You can place a shortcut in a convenient location, for example, on the Start menu (where you only have to single-click it) or on the desktop. That way, you don't have to search the computer or open a number of folders to find the original object, program, or folder.
>
> There are several ways to create a shortcut, as explained in Chapter 4. Probably the easiest is to right-drag the original file, folder, or object to where you want the shortcut and then select Create Shortcut(s) Here from the pop-up menu. If the file is a program file (a file with an .EXE, .COM, .BAT, or .PIF extension), you can drag it normally (using the left mouse button) to where you want the shortcut, and a shortcut will be created. You can tell that an icon represents a shortcut if the icon contains an arrow, like this:

DRAG-AND-DROP

? **How do I _drag an item from a Program Manager group to the Windows 95 desktop_?**

Program Manager, designed to ease the transition between Windows 95 and earlier versions, does not provide drag-and-drop from its groups to the Windows 95 desktop. Even though Program Manager ships with Windows 95, it is still a 16-bit application and only has drag-and-drop within its windows.

? **If I am dragging an .EXE file from the Explorer to the desktop, I get a shortcut. If I drag a document file, it is copied to the desktop! How do I know the _outcome of the drag-and-drop_?**

By design, Windows 95 treats program files differently from data files. If you drag an .EXE or .COM file to the desktop, you create a shortcut. If you drag holding down the CTRL key, the file is copied to the desktop. If you drag holding down the SHIFT key, the file is moved to the desktop.

If you drag a data file (a .DOC, .BMP, .XLS, or any type other than .EXE or .COM) to the desktop, the file is moved to the desktop. You get the same result of moving the file if you drag holding down the SHIFT key. If you drag holding down the CTRL key, the file is copied to the desktop, and if you hold down both CTRL and SHIFT, you will create a shortcut to the data file.

? **How can I _use drag-and-drop with the left mouse button and also with the right mouse button_? Is there a difference?**

Using the left mouse button and dragging a folder or file, you will have different results depending on the keys you hold down as you are dragging, as follows:

Keys Held	Effect
None	Moves folders and nonprogram files, makes a shortcut of program files (ones with an extension of .EXE or .COM)
CTRL	Copies all folders and files
SHIFT	Moves all folders and files
CTRL-SHIFT	Makes a shortcut for all folders and files

Right drag-and-drop gives you a pop-up menu when you drop the object, asking if you want to move, copy, or create a shortcut:

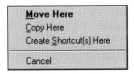

WINDOWS ENVIRONMENT

How can I _access the desktop if it is hidden_ behind open applications?

Right-click an empty area of the Taskbar, and choose Minimize All Windows from the pop-up menu shown next; or press ALT-M when the Taskbar is selected.

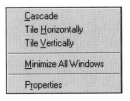

 Tip   *After using Minimize All Windows, you can again right-click the Taskbar, select Undo Minimize All, and restore the windows you closed to their original position.*

How can I _add a program that's on my Start menu to my desktop_?

You need to exercise a bit of caution when adding a program from the Start menu to the desktop. You can easily move it instead of copying it, as described in the Note that follows. Use these steps to add a program to the desktop:

1. Click the Start button and select Settings | Taskbar.

2. On the Taskbar Properties dialog box, select the Start Menu Programs tab.

3. Click the Advanced button.

4. Right-click the program to be added, and then drag it onto your desktop.

5. From the pop-up menu displayed when you release the pointer, choose Create Shortcut Here.

Note   *If you do a regular drag-and-drop here, you will move the program to the desktop, not copy it.*

In *Add/Remove Programs on the Control Panel (Windows Setup tab)*, the size in bytes in the Components list is different from the size specified for the Space Required displayed below it. Why?

The two sizes are calculated differently and give you different information. The size you see beside each component listed is the total of the files in that component. The size for the Space Required is calculated by use of the cluster size of the hard disk drive you are installing them on, which varies depending on the size of the hard disk and how it is formatted.

Other than using the Programs menu system, are there any *alternative ways that I can run an application*?

Yes, there are a number of alternatives. Here are some of them:

⇨ Double-click a shortcut icon created on the desktop by dragging the program's .EXE file there.

⇨ Click an option in the Start menu itself (not the Programs submenu), created by dragging the program's .EXE file to the Start button.

⇨ Double-click a shortcut icon created in a special folder left open on the desktop by dragging the program's .EXE file there.

Tip   *A special folder left open on the desktop containing shortcuts to your frequently used applications is superior to placing the shortcuts directly on the desktop, because you can use ALT-TAB to get to the folder but not to the desktop—you must minimize any open applications.*

Note   *Power Toys, available free as a download from Microsoft (**http://www.microsoft.com/windows95/info/powertoys.htm**), lets you choose the desktop icons from a menu similar to the Start menu.*

⇨   Click the Start button, choose the Run command, type the application's path and filename, and press ENTER.

❓ Why *can't I see my Taskbar even when Always On Top is checked* in the Taskbar Properties Options dialog box?

Sometimes the Taskbar is dragged too low on the screen and disappears from view. Place your pointer on the bottom of the screen until it turns into an arrow, as shown next. Then drag upward and release the mouse. The Taskbar will reappear on the screen.

Tip   *If you also have Auto Hide enabled, the Taskbar will not be visible until you move the pointer to the edge of the screen where the Taskbar is.*

❓ How can I *capture my screen* in Windows 95?

The PRINT SCREEN key on your keyboard will copy the image on your screen to the Clipboard. You can then paste that image into a document. You can use PRINT SCREEN in the following ways:

⇨   To copy an image of the entire screen, press PRINT SCREEN.

⇨ To copy an image of the window that is currently active, press ALT-PRINT SCREEN.

⇨ To paste the image into a document, open the Edit menu in the document window, and then click Paste.

❓ When using Explorer, I get an Edit option when I right-click the Autoexec.bat file, but not when I right-click Config.sys. How can I *edit Config.sys from the Windows Explorer window*?

Windows 95 has attached a special property to .BAT files that brings up the Edit option. You can edit your Config.sys file in Explorer in several ways:

⇨ Double-click it and then select Notepad as the application to open the file.

⇨ Right-click it, choose Open With, and select Notepad to open the file.

⇨ Run Sysedit by clicking the Start button, choosing Run, and typing **sysedit** on the command line. This opens the System Configuration Editor (see Figure 5-6), which opens many of the system files for editing.

Tip   *If you don't see the system files in Explorer, open the View menu and choose Options | Show All Files. By default Windows 95 will hide files with system and hidden attributes.*

❓ How do I *get rid of the Inbox icon on my desktop*? Why is it there when I told it not to install MSN?

The Inbox icon is there because you have chosen to install Microsoft Exchange and/or Microsoft Fax. You must remove them to get rid of the icon. You can do so with the following steps:

1. Click the Start button and choose Settings | Control Panel.

2. Double-click Add/Remove Programs, and then click the Windows Setup tab.

3. Scroll the list of components until you can see Microsoft Exchange and Microsoft Fax, as shown in Figure 5-7.

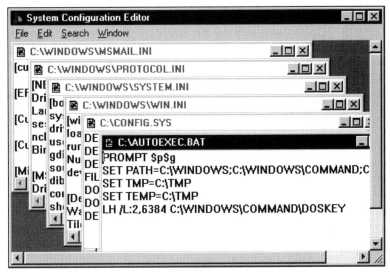

Figure 5-6.   The System Configuration Editor allows you to edit your system files

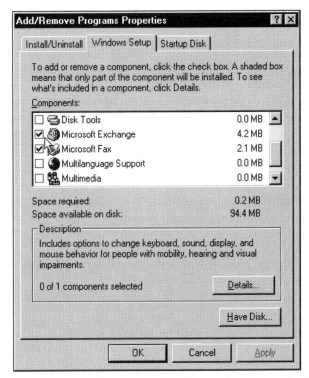

Figure 5-7.   Uninstalling MS Exchange and MS Fax will remove the Inbox

4. Uncheck the Microsoft Exchange and the Microsoft Fax check boxes, click OK, and click Yes to restart your system. When Windows comes back up, the Inbox icon will be gone.

? How can I *install a program in Windows 95 when there is no File / Run option*?

You may install a program in two ways: by directly loading the program's Install or Setup programs (see the following steps), or by using Windows 95's Add/Remove Programs utility. If you use Add/Remove Programs, you will be guided through placing the program on a menu, perhaps within a program group, and can assign an icon to it.

Follow these steps to directly run the program's own installation procedure:

1. Click the Start button and choose Run.

2. Type in the command (for example, **a:\setup**), or choose it from the drop-down list if you have recently run Setup from your A drive.

Follow these instructions to use Add/Remove Programs:

1. Click the Start button and choose Settings | Control Panel.

2. Double-click Add/Remove Programs, and the Add/Remove Programs Properties dialog box will open, as shown in Figure 5-8.

3. Click Install and follow along as the Installation Wizard leads you through the process.

Tip   *Only applications written specifically for Windows 95 can be completely removed by use of Add/Remove Programs.*

? How can I *minimize all open windows*?

There are two quick ways to minimize all open windows on the desktop:

⇨ Right-click an empty spot on the Taskbar, and then select Minimize All Windows from the pop-up menu.

⇨ Click normally on a vacant area of the Taskbar to deselect all objects on the desktop and then press ALT-M.

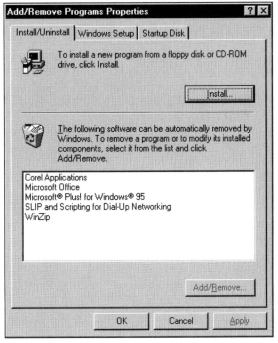

Figure 5-8. Add/Remove Programs leads you through the installation of your programs

❓ How can I *move an active window using the keyboard*?

To move an active window by use of the keyboard rather than the mouse, follow these steps:

1. Press ALT-SPACEBAR to display a command menu on the active window.

2. Press the DOWN ARROW key once to select Move and press ENTER. A four-way arrow will appear on the active window.

3. Press the arrow keys to move the window in whichever direction you want.

4. When you are finished, press ESC to end the move.

❓ How do I *open a file with a different application* than the one with which it is already associated?

An option of the right-click pop-up menu contains the Open With option in which you can select the application you want to open the

file. Follow these steps to get the Open With question on the right
mouse pop-up menu:

1. In My Computer or Explorer, *left*-click the file to select it.

2. Hold down the SHIFT key and right-click it. The Open With
    command will appear in the pop-up menu.

Tip   *You must first select the file before SHIFT right-click will cause Open
With to appear.*

? I see the terms *"real mode" and "protected mode"* used a lot in conjunction with Windows 95, but what's the difference between them, and is it really important?

Yes, it is important. *Real mode* was the original way that the 8086 and
8088 processors operated and the foundation on which DOS was built.
It was a single-tasking, 16-bit environment limited to slightly over
1MB of address space. The 80286 processor added *protected-mode*
instructions, and the 386 and 486 significantly improved on them.
These protected-mode instructions, which are 32-bit, provided for
multitasking, where two or more programs could be in memory at the
same time, and allowed addressing up to 4Gb in the later processors.
(The term "protected" comes from the memory protection routines
that are necessary when two programs run in memory at the same
time, whereas "real" addressing is what takes place if only one
program is running at a time.) DOS never made use of protected
mode, and all Intel processors (including the Pentium) have kept
the real-mode instructions for that reason. Since all processors have
real-mode instructions and it is the initial startup mode, most disk
drivers used real-mode instructions. This meant that every time you
went from Windows, which runs in protected mode, to the disk driver
in real mode, you had to switch the processor from protected to real
mode, taking time and going from a more efficient to a less efficient
environment. For these reasons, Windows 95 has made a considerable
effort to replace real-mode drivers with protected-mode drivers.

Tip *Wherever possible, use protected-mode drivers. The easiest way to do that is to use only the drivers that come with Windows 95 by removing any statements in your Config.sys and Autoexec.bat files that load drivers (under many circumstances you should be able to completely get rid of your entire Config.sys and possibly your Autoexec.bat files).*

How can I *rebuild Windows 95 default folders*?

You can run the Grpconv.exe program that rebuilds the Windows 95 folders (for example, all the folders within the \Windows folder). Follow these steps:

1. Click the Start button and choose Run.

2. In the Run dialog box, type **grpconv /s**. While the program is running, you will see the Start Menu Shortcuts message box appear.

Grpconv.exe is principally used to convert Windows 3.1 program groups to Windows 95 shortcuts in the \Windows\Start Menu\ Programs folder. When Grpconv.exe is used with the /S switch, it rebuilds the default Windows 95 folders.

As I open multiple applications, my Taskbar gets very crowded. How do I *see the applications that I am running in the list format*?

The easiest way is to drag the inside edge of your Taskbar in so you can easily see all of your tasks, like this:

You can also switch to each task individually using ALT-TAB. Or you can press CTRL-ALT-DEL (this is equivalent to pressing CTRL-ESC in Windows 3.x), and you will get a list of all running applications with the option to end tasks. Click Cancel to continue without ending a task.

? **How do I _select more than one icon on the desktop at a time_?**

You can select multiple icons on the desktop in two ways:

⇨ If the icons you want are grouped together, click a blank spot of the desktop and select the icons by dragging the mouse over them, surrounding them with the select rectangle.

⇨ If the icons are not contiguous, press CTRL and click the icons you want.

? **How can I _stop opening multiple windows each time I open a new folder in My Computer_?**

In your current window, select the View menu, choose Options, and on the Folder tab, choose Browse Folders By Using A Single Window That Changes As You Open Each Folder, as shown in Figure 5-9.

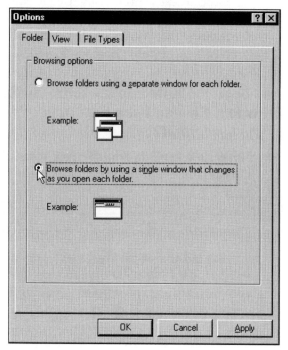

Figure 5-9.   The View menu Options dialog box contains a control for displaying a single window rather than cascading ones

❓ How do I find what *system resources are currently available to me*?

In My Computer, Explorer, or a number of other windows, open the Help menu and select About Windows 95. The About dialog box opens with both the free system resources and the free physical memory, as shown in Figure 5-10.

❓ When I am running an application, why does my *Taskbar sometimes disappear*?

The Auto Hide feature is enabled. Here are the steps to clear this:

1. Move your cursor to the edge of the screen where the Taskbar is located and the Taskbar will reappear.

2. Click the Start button and choose Settings | Taskbar.

3. Clear the Auto Hide box, as you can see in Figure 5-11, and click OK when you are done.

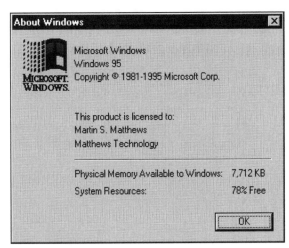

Figure 5-10. The About dialog box from most Help menus will give you the free system resources

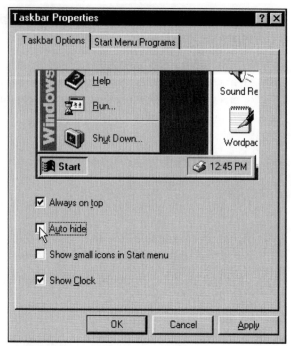

Figure 5-11.   If Auto Hide is checked, the Taskbar will only be visible when you move the mouse pointer to the edge of the screen, where it's located

? Why does Windows 95 change *the look of certain parts of my applications* and not other parts?

The programming code is often inconsistent throughout an application, probably because it was written by multiple programmers. In some instances an application may use Windows 95 tools to create some parts. For example, in Access 2.0, which uses Windows 95 to create its dialog boxes, the check boxes now come equipped with check marks, and there is a single-click "X" for closing the application in the upper-right corner. Some applications just show a slight appearance change, such as fonts and colors.

Note   Microsoft Office 95 and 97 have reduced this problem by making the Office applications more consistent.

? **How do I *tile or cascade windows in Windows 95*?**

> You can tile or cascade windows to get two or more windows on your screen at one time. Just right-click an empty spot on the Taskbar. You will see the options to Cascade, Tile Horizontally, or Tile Vertically on the pop-up menu.

? **How do I *use the question mark icon* on the right side of the title bars?**

> This is a Help aid found in dialog boxes. The question mark is known as the "What's this?" button. Click it and the pointer changes to a question mark, as shown here. Click any object in the dialog box, and a short description of the object is shown.

WORDPAD

? **I am in WordPad, and I am trying to save a file with the name C:\Test.txt, but I am getting an *error message: "This filename is not valid."* What is going on?**

> If all characters in the name are valid, the problem might be that all 512 root folder entries are used up. In MS-DOS and Win3.*x*, you could have 512 files and folders defined in the root (C:\) directory or folder. MS-DOS used one root folder entry for each file and folder. In Windows 95, the 512-entry maximum still applies, but you might get to use a lesser number of actual items because Windows 95 uses additional root folder entries to store long filenames and their associated 8.3 aliases, plus the normal files and folders. This means that you can run out of available root folder entries even if you have fewer than 512 files or folders in the root folder. To avoid this problem, save your files to a folder other than in the root. Folders other than the root do not have the root entries limitation—the only limitation is actual free disk space.

How do I set a *manual page break in WordPad*?

There is no provision for page breaks. They are handled automatically.

How do I *use WordPad*?

WordPad is a 32-bit editor that replaces the Write application that was in Windows 3.1. WordPad uses the same file format as Microsoft Word 6 (and Microsoft Word 95 and 97), but it also supports the reading and writing of text files (.TXT) and rich text files (.RTF) and the reading of Write files (.WRI).

Note   Word 97 uses a different file format than does Word 95, but can save to the true 6.0/95 format rather than the .RTF format with the new converter that's available from the Microsoft web site.

To start WordPad, open the Start menu and select Programs | Accessories | WordPad. Alternatively, you can open the Start menu, select Run, type **wordpad**, and press ENTER.

If you create a new document in WordPad, you are given a choice of the type of document you want to create, as shown next. You need to determine what you will do with the document and how much formatting it will have. Word 6 and rich text can handle a lot of formatting, but those formats cannot be used with system files like Autoexec.bat, Config.sys, and Win.ini.

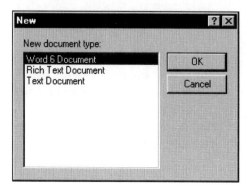

EQUIPMENT-RELATED PROBLEMS

? **How do I _add hardware to my computer_?**

Much of this question depends on what hardware you are adding. If you are adding plug-and-play hardware, Windows 95 will most likely handle the installation for you. If you are not using plug-and-play, you still have a good chance of Windows 95 handling the installation with no problems. However, if you do have problems, either with plug-and-play hardware or without, you can work with the system by finding out where the conflict is (most likely a conflict in how the IRQ, port, or DMA addresses are being assigned) and manually assign your new hardware to a different address.

Follow these steps to install new hardware:

1. From the Start menu, select Settings | Control Panel.

2. Double-click the Add New Hardware icon. The Add New Hardware Wizard will lead you through the installation. It will vary depending on the hardware being installed.

If the Wizard is unable to install your hardware, follow these steps to find out why and resolve it:

1. Click the Start button and select Settings | Control Panel.

2. Double-click the System icon.

3. Select the Device Manager tab, and select View Devices By Type, as shown in Figure 5-12.

4. Click the Print button for a list of all your devices and their assigned IRQs, ports, and DMA addresses. Any device conflicts will be flagged for you on the report that is printed.

5. Check with your hardware manuals or documentation, and determine what assignments are needed. You now know what is in conflict and what you need.

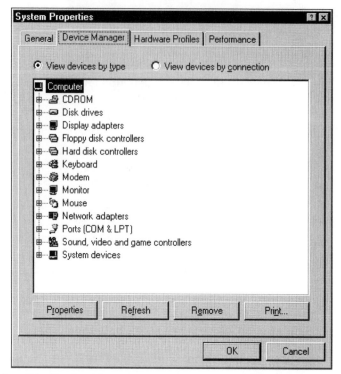

Figure 5-12.   The Device Manager provides several ways to see your device assignments

6. Manually assign your hardware to an available IRQ, port, or DMA.

7. Run Add New Hardware again with the new settings.

 Caution   *Sometimes with plug-and-play, Windows 95 will rearrange a device's resources to make room for new hardware. This is usually just fine. But sometimes software will be looking for a device at a particular IRQ or DMA. You must resolve the conflict by changing the software configuration to the new settings, or change the hardware assignments to something that will work with the software.*

? I'm having a problem with my _Conner external tape drive_. The Conner program is attempting to back up 800MB of data, but there is only 500MB of data. What is going on?

The Conner backup program is having problems with long filenames in Windows 95. To back up your data, use the Backup program that comes with Windows 95. You can access Backup by clicking the Start button and selecting Programs | Accessories | System Tools | Backup. Backup is a 32-bit application that is very easy to use and displays the standard tree and file list view you see in Explorer.

Tip   *If you can't find Backup, you may not have installed it, in which case you must rerun Setup—you cannot use the Add/Remove Programs Windows Setup tab to install Backup.*

Tip   *Only some types of backup tape drives are supported by Windows 95 Backup. QIC 40, 80, and 3010 drives connected to the primary floppy controller and made by Colorado, Conner, Iomega, and Wangtek are supported. All drives on a secondary floppy controller and QIC Wide tapes, QIC 3020, and SCSI tape drives as well as all drives made by Archive, Irwin, Mountain, Summit, and Travan are not supported. If your tape drive is not supported, contact your tape drive manufacturer for software that works with Windows 95.*

How can I *force Windows 95 to redetect my entire hardware configuration*?

To make Windows 95 redetect your hardware configuration, you must boot under Safe mode and then create additional hardware configurations. When you are asked to select one of the configurations during booting, you will not select one, to force Windows 95 to autodetect your hardware. Windows 95 will then create a new configuration based on your current hardware.

Follow these steps to do this:

1. Click the Start button and select Shut Down, and then select Restart The Computer and click Yes.

2. As the computer is rebooting, press F8 after the computer resources are listed and before Windows 95 begins to load.

3. Type **3** and press ENTER to bring up Safe mode. A message will be displayed telling you that the computer is running in Safe mode.

4. Click the Start button and select Settings | Control Panel. Double-click the System icon to open the System Properties dialog box.

5. Select the Hardware Profiles tab, and click Copy to make a copy of the Original Configuration. Name it **Original Configuration 1** and click OK.

6. Click the Original Configuration to select it and click the Rename button. Name it **Original Configuration 2** and click OK.

7. Click OK to close the System Properties dialog box.

8. Click the Start button and select Shut Down | Restart The Computer | Yes.

9. During the boot process you will be asked to select between Original Configuration 1, Original Configuration 2, and None Of The Above. Choose None Of The Above. This will force Windows 95 to go through the process of autodetecting the hardware installed.

10. Windows 95 will create a new profile for you called "Original Configuration." It may take a few minutes. You will need to click OK to allow the computer to be rebooted with the new configuration.

11. When the computer is rebooted, you will want to remove the other profiles (Original Configuration 1 and Original Configuration 2).

❓ Do I absolutely *have to have a mouse*?

It is strongly recommended that you use a mouse in Windows 95 because the whole environment is object-oriented and is strongly tied to pointing and clicking, now with both the left and right mouse buttons.

You can substitute the keyboard for many mouse actions by, among other things, using the shortcut keys listed on the command card inserted in this book. Also, the underlined letters in the menus and dialog boxes represent a shortcut—you can hold down the ALT key and press the underlined letter on the keyboard to activate the menu option or dialog box feature.

However, there are a few tasks, such as the following examples, that cannot be performed without a mouse:

⇨ In Explorer, you cannot move the vertical bar that divides the folder tree on the left and list of files on the right without a mouse.

⇨ In Explorer, when you are viewing files in Details view, there is no way without a mouse to change the size of the fields for the filename, type, total size, and free space listings.

⇨ Very long filenames may be truncated on dialog box properties tabs, and you can only see the whole name by holding a mouse pointer over it.

Tip   Even if you don't have a mouse, you can use the MouseKeys option to simulate the mouse pointer on the keyboard. You can access this option by choosing Start | Settings | Control Panel, and selecting the Accessibility Options icon. On the Mouse tab, enable the Use MouseKeys option. (You might have to install the Accessibility Options because they are not installed in every type of install.)

Do I need *Himem.sys or Emm386.exe* in Windows 95?

Yes, Windows 95 does need Himem.sys, but you do not need to include it in a Config.sys file. It is automatically loaded through the Io.sys file. If the Himem.sys file is missing or damaged, you will not be able to run Windows 95.

Emm386.exe is not required by Windows 95.

Where can I get an accurate view of my computer's *memory size*?

There are four places where you can see the physical memory you have on your computer:

⇨ As Windows 95 is booting, it displays the memory size.

⇨ In Explorer or My Computer, select Help | About Windows 95. The Physical Memory Available To Windows will be displayed as well as the percentage of System Resources currently available, as shown previously in Figure 5-10.

⇨ Right-click My Computer, and select Properties from the pop-up menu. In the System Properties dialog box, you can select either the General or the Performance tab for the RAM that is recognized by Windows. The Performance tab contains additional important system resource information, as shown here:

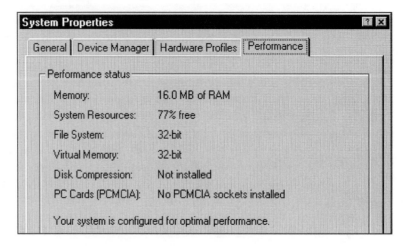

⇨   Click the Start button and select Settings | Control Panel |
     System. The System Properties dialog box will display the RAM
     on both the General and Performance tabs.

❓ My *SCSI controller* isn't working under Windows 95. What can I do?

This is probably due to a conflict between a real-mode driver in your
Config.sys file and Windows 95 trying to use a protected-mode driver.
(See discussion on real and protected modes in the "Windows
Environment" section earlier in this chapter.) Use either of the
following two methods to correct this problem.

⇨   First, try removing the SCSI driver (it probably has "ASPI" in its
     name) from your Config.sys file so that only the Windows 95
     protected-mode driver is loaded.

⇨   Alternatively, edit the Iso.ini file in your \Windows folder, and
     remove the reference to the real-mode driver.

❓ Can I use an *upper-memory manager such as QEMM with Windows 95*?

There is no need for such utilities. Windows 95 utilizes its internal
memory management system, which is superior to QEMM.

? **My _video display blinks_ (flickers). How do I avoid this?**

You probably selected the wrong display type, and your monitor is running at a different frequency than your video card. Use the steps in the earlier question (in the "Booting Situations" section of this chapter) related to changing video drivers to select the correct video device driver. If you don't know the display type, choose Standard Display Adapter (VGA).

? **I have been changing my _video display resolution_ back and forth, and now suddenly I cannot change it back to what I want. The option is no longer available. How do I restore the original defaults?**

OSR 2 Somehow you changed your display type and thereby your video device driver to one that does not have the resolution options of your original driver. You need to reselect your original display type, and the list will be set back to its original defaults. To do that, follow these steps:

1. Click the Start button, select Settings | Control Panel, and double-click Display.

2. Click the Settings tab, and click the Change Device Type button. Click Change for the Adapter Type. (For OSR 2, after the Settings tab, you must click the Advanced Properties button. Click Change on the Adapter tab.)

3. If you see your display adapter listed, select it and click OK three times to return to the Control Panel.

4. If you do not see your display adapter in the Models list, click Show All Devices; select your display adapter, as you can see being done in Figure 5-13; and click OK three times to return to the Control Panel.

5. If asked, restart your computer. When you are done, you should be able to select from among your original resolution settings ("Desktop Area" of the Display dialog box Settings tab).

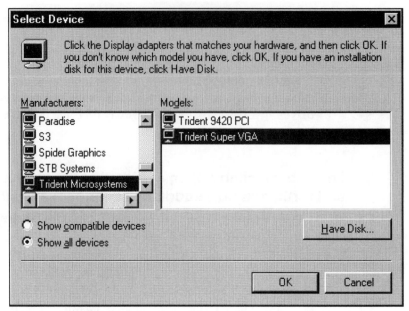

Figure 5-13.   Getting back to your original video driver will return your
resolution options

? **When I insert the Windows 95 CD so that I can add and
remove some of my components, a message is displayed
that says this is an older version CD and to obtain the
latest release of Windows 95. *What version of Windows 95
do I have and what can I do*?**

OSR 2 Microsoft has developed a newer version of Windows called OSR 2,
which was released at the end of 1996, for original equipment
manufacturer (OEM) computers. This message occurs if Windows
OSR 2 has been installed and then a Windows 95 CD is used to add or
remove applications. You must obtain the original OSR 2 disc to add
and remove applications.

To tell which version you have installed, double-click the System
icon on the Control Panel and look at the General tab. If "4.00.950" is
displayed, you have a Windows 95 original release.

If "4.00.950 B" is displayed, you have OSR 2, the newest release with FAT32. The introductory information on OSR 2 goes into detail on how to tell which version is which.

 Note   *You can also type **VER** at a DOS prompt to find out which version you have.*

OTHER PROBLEMS

I'm having problems trying to *access an open Properties dialog box*. Pressing ALT-TAB switches me to any open applications, but it does not switch me to the open Properties dialog box. How do I get back to it?

You can use ALT-ESC to switch to a Properties dialog box or to a wizard. ALT-TAB only works with applications.

Are *Autoexec.bat and Config.sys files required in Windows 95*?

No. Windows 95 does not require these files for operating. However, they are usually included and preserved for compatibility to earlier programs which have not been designed specifically for Windows 95.

How do I *close a failed application*?

If you cannot use any facilities within the application and you cannot close the DOS window it is running in (or if it isn't a DOS program), use the following steps to close it:

1. Press CTRL-ALT-DEL. Windows will display a list of all running applications so you can specify which one you want to end.

2. If Windows detects that any application is not responding to messages from the system, the text "not responding" appears after the related application in the list. In the Close Program dialog box, select the application you want to close and click End Task.

Tip   *After you use the Cancel or the End Task button to close the Close Program dialog box, the next time you press* CTRL-ALT-DEL, *the Close Program dialog box appears again and the computer is not restarted. If you want to press* CTRL-ALT-DEL *to restart the computer, you must press the keys again while the Close Program dialog box is displayed.*

 Caution   *If possible, use the Shut Down button in the Close Program dialog box or the Shut Down command on the Start menu to quit Windows. This ensures that all current information is saved in the Registry, and that each application is closed correctly before quitting Windows.*

I have deleted a large number of files over the last couple of days. When I wanted to recover some of them, I could not find the _deleted files in the Recycle Bin_! How can I avoid this?

You probably have exceeded the limit of the size of the Recycle Bin.

 Caution   *By default, the system allocates 10 percent of disk space to hold the deleted files in the Recycle Bin. When you exceed this limit, the system purges the oldest files to make space for the newly deleted files. You are not notified when this happens! You can avoid this problem in the future by increasing the disk space allocation.*

Use the following steps to increase the disk space allocated to the Recycle Bin:

1. Right-click the Recycle Bin and choose Properties.

2. Click the Global tab, as shown in Figure 5-14, and adjust the Maximum Size Of Recycle Bin setting. Click OK when you are done.

 Tip   *Remember also that you can have a separate Recycle Bin for every hard drive (or partition) that you have. To do this, click the individual drive tabs and adjust the disk space accordingly.*

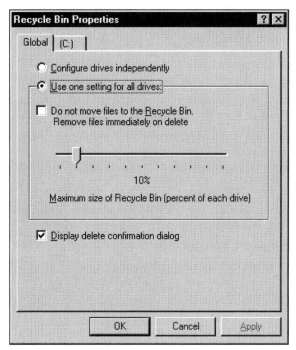

Figure 5-14.   You can change the size of memory allocated to the Recycle Bin in its Properties dialog box

? I think that a couple of the Windows 95 files are damaged. How do I _locate damaged files on the distribution disks_ so that I can manually verify them?

Unlike Windows 3.*x*, Windows 95 will spare you this effort. If you have Windows 95 installed on the system, you can run Setup to verify the integrity of files. When you run Setup, it will offer you a choice of reinstalling Windows 95 or just verifying the files. If you choose to verify the files, Setup will consult Setuplog.txt, the file that was placed into the root folder by the Windows 95 installation process, and verify the integrity of each of the installed components. If one or more files are missing or corrupt, Setup will reinstall them.

? **Can I use _Norton Utilities 8.0 or PC Tools for Windows with Windows 95_?**

OSR 2   You should never use Norton Utilities, PC Tools, or any other type of disk or file utility that was not specifically designed for Windows 95. The Windows 3.*x* versions of these utilities cannot handle long filenames in Windows 95 and might report the files as corrupt. An attempt to repair the "corruption" will lead to data loss and can seriously damage your whole system. Norton Utilities for Windows 95 is currently available as well as a Windows 95 version of PC Tools.

? **One of my 16-bit applications has crashed and has not returned the resources it used. How can I _refresh the resources without restarting_?**

Windows 95 will return all 16-bit resources once _all_ 16-bit applications have been closed. This includes screen savers such as MS Scenes, MS Office Manager (MOM), and other 16-bit Windows applications.

? **Why did Windows 95 put _"rem" in front of the SMARTDrive statement in my Autoexec.bat file_?**

Windows 95 made the SMARTDrive statement a remark so SMARTDrive will not be loaded during startup. Windows 95 replaces SMARTDrive with a protected-mode caching system that shrinks and grows as needed. The SMARTDrive was not totally deleted because you may need it if you boot into your previous DOS.

? **I ran a _virus utility_ on Windows 95 and it seemed to see the virus, but it will not remove it from my system. Is there a problem with my antivirus program or my system?**

Under Windows 95, most virus detection software will detect a virus, but it will not remove it from your system. This is because the virus utility uses low-level write commands to repair the damage to the disk. DOS-based virus utilities can only be run by use of the LOCK command. You need to get a Windows 95 antivirus program such as Norton AntiVirus for Windows 95.

File Management

Answer Topics!

File Management @ a Glance

File management, the handling of information written onto and read off of disks, was the primary focus of the first operating systems. Operating systems today do many other things, but file management remains critically important. It is a major area of enhancement in Windows 95 over the previous combination of Windows 3.x and DOS 6.x. Windows 95 provides a full 32-bit file system, many protected-mode drivers (see Chapter 5), long filenames, and Explorer, in addition to many smaller enhancements. The result of all these changes is a file system that is easier to use, more intuitive, and faster than its predecessors. Windows 95 almost transparently provides these basic services, without which computing would be useless.

DISK BACKUP AND COPY

? How do I make _backup copies of my original Windows 95 disk set_?

Windows 95 disks are shipped in Distribution Media Format (DMF), and the floppy disks are not compatible with the DOS Copy or DiskCopy commands. You cannot create backup copies of the Windows 95 disks. You must call Microsoft's sales center at 1-800-426-9400 if you need replacement disks.

? How do I _copy a disk_?

You can copy a disk in either My Computer or Explorer. Follow these steps:

1. Open My Computer by double-clicking the icon on the desktop. Alternatively, open Explorer by clicking the Start button and choosing Programs | Windows Explorer.

2. Right-click the floppy disk drive to be copied. This will open the pop-up menu shown here:

3. Click the Copy Disk command. The Copy Disk dialog box will be displayed, as shown here:

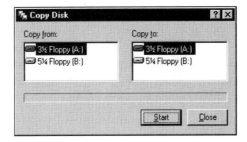

4. From the Copy From list, select the disk drive to be used as the source of the copy.

5. From the Copy To list, select the disk drive to be used as the destination of the copy.

6. Click the Start button and follow any prompts.

Can I *restore backups* made from previous versions of Microsoft Backup?

No. The Windows 95 Backup program only restores backup files that it has created.

File Management Tools

Here is a brief summary of some of the more important file management tools in Windows 95.

⇨ **Backup**, accessed through Start menu | Programs | Accessories | System Tools, will compress selected files and store them on multiple floppy disks or magnetic tape.

⇨ **Cut and Paste** can be used to move or copy a file, as well as text or graphics within a file. Use CTRL-X to delete or cut, CTRL-C to copy, and CTRL-V to paste. You can also click the Cut, Copy, and Paste icons in the folder window's toolbar, as shown here:

⇨ **Drag-and-Drop** allows you to move or copy files or *folders* (*directories* in DOS and Windows 3.*x*) by pointing on them with the mouse, pressing and holding a mouse button, and dragging them from one location to another. Using the right mouse button gives you a menu, shown next, when you release the mouse button ("drop" the object), whereas the left mouse button does different things depending on the type of file and the keyboard keys held down (see discussion in Chapter 5).

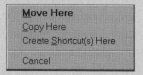

⇨ **Explorer**, **My Computer**, and **Network Neighborhood** are your primary access to files and folders within Windows 95. They allow you to locate files, folders, disks, and computers on a network; to look at files and folders in different views; to open, copy, move, delete, and rename files and folders; to create folders and shortcuts to files and folders; to format and copy disks; and to share disks and folders and to map disks on a network.

File Management Tools, *continued*

⇨ **Folder Window** is the standard window used by Explorer, My Computer, Network Neighborhood, and all folders that are opened. Figure 6-1 shows you its standard features.

⇨ **Long Names** are now allowed—up to 255 characters—and you can include spaces and all other characters *except* \ / : * " ? < > and |. You can give files descriptive names that are easily remembered, rather than the eight-character names with three-character extensions required in previous versions of Windows and DOS.

⇨ **My Briefcase** is used to synchronize files that are being modified or edited on another computer. This is a way to keep multiple copies of a file up to date.

⇨ **Recycle Bin** holds deleted files until it's emptied (or full, in which case the older files are deleted). You can cut, copy, paste, and restore files from this folder.

⇨ **Renaming Files** can be done by clicking the filename to select the file, clicking again to open the name for editing (or pressing F2), and then typing the new name. It is fast and efficient.

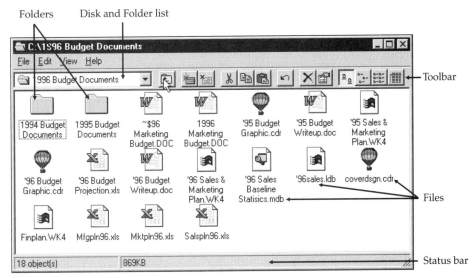

Figure 6-1. The Folder Window is used for all file management functions in Windows 95

OTHER DISK UTILITIES AND TASKS

? What is *Defrag* and how do I use it?

The Disk Defragmenter (which has the filename Defrag.exe) is a system utility that optimizes disk performance by reorganizing the files on a drive. When your disk begins to get full and you continue to save files, the files are broken up into segments, which are spread out over the disk in any unused space. Defrag's reorganization gathers up the segments and places them in one contiguous location. This considerably speeds up disk access. Unlike previous versions of Defrag, it can run from within Windows, and even while you are performing other tasks—although this is *not* recommended, since Defrag restarts every time you write something on the disk. You can defragment your local hard drives, compressed drives, and floppy drives. You cannot use Defrag on network drives or CD-ROM drives.

We recommend that you run Defrag regularly—at least monthly—if you use your PC fairly often.

Follow these steps to start the Disk Defragmenter:

1. Click the Start button and choose Programs I Accessories I System Tools I Disk Defragmenter.

2. Click the down arrow to open the Drive drop-down list, and select the disk drive to be defragmented. It will default to your hard drive. Click OK.

3. The Disk Defragmenter dialog box will examine your disk, display the percentage of fragmentation in your disk, and recommend whether you should defragment the drive. Click Select Drive to select a different drive. Click Advanced to set some options for how the defragmenting will be done. If you decide to proceed, click the Start button and a message box will open, giving you the status as shown here:

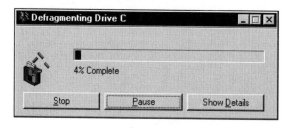

❓ Is there an easier way than going through the maze of menus if I want to run the _drive utilities such as ScanDisk and Defrag_?

There are two other ways to start the disk utilities: from the Start menu Run option and from the disk Properties dialog box.

Follow these steps to use the Run option:

1. Click the Start button and choose Run.

2. Type **scandskw** to start ScanDisk, or type **defrag** to start the Disk Defragmenter, and in either case, press ENTER or click OK.

Follow these steps to use the Properties dialog box:

1. Open My Computer or Explorer.

2. Right-click the drive you want to work on and choose Properties. The Properties dialog box will appear. Click the Tools tab as shown in Figure 6-2.

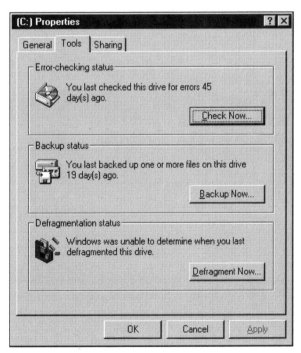

Figure 6-2.   The Tools tab of the disk's Properties dialog box provides access to some of the important disk utilities

3. Click Check Now to run ScanDisk, Backup Now to run Backup, and Defragment Now to run the Disk Defragmenter.

? How do I *format a disk* in Windows 95?

You can format a disk from either My Computer or Explorer using these steps:

1. Insert a disk into the floppy drive.

2. Double-click the My Computer icon, or open Explorer by selecting Start | Programs | Windows Explorer.

3. Right-click the disk drive that contains the disk and choose Format.

4. Choose the Capacity and Format type, or just accept the defaults that Windows 95 is offering if you are not sure (if the capacity is incorrect, you will have another chance to change it). Type in a Label if you want one on the disk. You can also select No Label, Display Summary When Finished, and Copy System Files (which will produce a bootable disk).

5. Click the Start button.

 Caution   *Formatting a used disk erases all data on it, and the lost data* cannot *be restored.*

? How can I *label a disk*?

You can label a disk while formatting it, as described in the previous question. You can also label a disk after it has been formatted by following these steps:

1. If you want to label a disk, place it in the disk drive.

2. Double-click the My Computer icon, or open Explorer by selecting Start | Programs | Windows Explorer.

3. Right-click the disk drive that contains the disk and choose Properties. Select the General tab if it is not already selected, as shown in Figure 6-3.

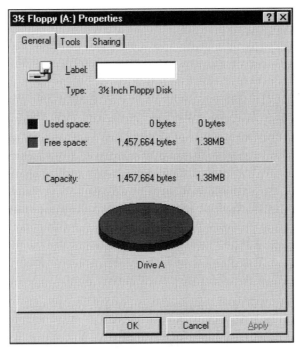

Figure 6-3.   The General tab of the disk's Properties dialog box allows you to label a disk

---

    Tip   If you click the Tools tab, you can find out the last time the disk was error checked, backed up, or defragmented. If it has not been recently, you can run the disk tools ScanDisk, Disk Defragmenter, and Backup from this dialog box.

4. Type the text for the label in the Label text box and then OK.

? After I ran a disk utility (an older version of Norton Utilities, for example), all my _long filenames disappeared_. Why?

You have to run a disk utility that supports long filenames, or the utility will look at the information in the Virtual File Allocation Table (VFAT) that stores the long filename, consider it corruption or garbage, and clean it up. Be sure to use Windows 95 utilities, such as the Norton Utilities for Windows 95 or the new version of ScanDisk that is long filename-aware.

? Windows 95 seems to have two versions of *ScanDisk*. What is the difference in the two versions?

One version of ScanDisk on the Windows 95 startup disk is a DOS program that checks your hard drive for errors before allowing setup. The other is a Windows-based version that can be run through Explorer or from the Start menu. Both versions check the File Allocation Table (FAT), long filenames, system structure, folder structure, surface damage (bad sectors and lost allocation units), and any DriveSpace or DoubleSpace volume and compression.

After Windows 95 has been installed, you can use ScanDisk from your Accessories menu with these instructions:

1. Click the Start button and select Programs | Accessories | Systems Tools | ScanDisk. The ScanDisk dialog box will be displayed, as shown in Figure 6-4.

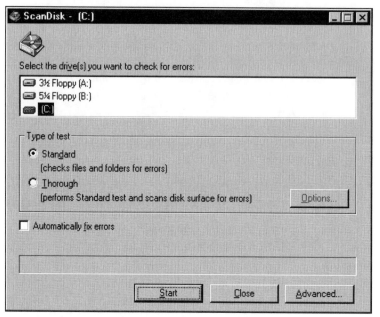

Figure 6-4.   ScanDisk searches your disk drives for errors

2. Select the disk drive to be checked.

3. Click the Type Of Test: Standard or Thorough. If you choose Thorough, you can click Options to select the area of the disk to be scanned. Also under Options you can choose whether to perform write testing and to repair bad sectors in hidden or system files.

4. If you want the errors automatically fixed without alerting you, click Automatically Fix Errors.

5. Click the Start button to begin the error checking.

FOLDER AND FILENAMES

I renamed a folder in Explorer. Can I get *back to my original name*?

Yes. After you perform a move, copy, or rename operation on a file or folder in Windows 95, you can undo it. Just press CTRL-Z. In Explorer or My Computer, open the Edit menu and choose Undo. If you are undoing a rename operation, the option will be Undo Rename; if you are undoing a move, it will be Undo Move.

Tip   *You can undo the last* ten *copy, move, or rename operations that you performed.*

FILENAMES

After I restored a tape backup, I *lost my long filenames*. Why?

Not all tape backup programs support long filenames. Windows 95 includes a backup utility that supports long filenames. You access it by clicking the Start button and selecting Programs | Accessories | System Tools | Backup.

What are the *valid filenames I can use* in Windows 95?

Filenames in Windows 95 can be up to 255 characters in length and can use all of the valid DOS filename characters, plus additional characters now valid in Windows 95. Windows 95 filenames are not case sensitive, but the case is preserved. Also in Windows 95 you can have any number of characters after a period and multiple periods, so long as the total number of characters does not exceed 255. In addition to the normal letters and numbers on your keyboard, the special characters shown in Tables 6-1 and 6-2 can be used.

To see the DOS 8.3 name corresponding to a long filename, right-click the file and then click Properties. You will see the long filename at the top of the dialog box and the MS-DOS name in the middle, as you can see in Figure 6-5.

Table 6-1.   Valid Special Characters in DOS and Windows 95

Symbol	Valid in DOS and Windows 95
$	Dollar sign
%	Percent sign
’	Apostrophe or closing single quotation mark
‘	Opening single quotation mark
-	Hyphen
@	At sign
{	Left brace
}	Right brace
~	Tilde
!	Exclamation point
#	Number sign
(	Opening parenthesis
)	Closing parenthesis
&	Ampersand
_	Underscore
^	Caret

Table 6-2.   Valid Special Characters in Windows 95 Only

Symbol	Valid Only in Windows 95
	Space
+	Plus sign
,	Comma
.	Period
;	Semicolon
=	Equal sign
[	Opening bracket
]	Closing bracket

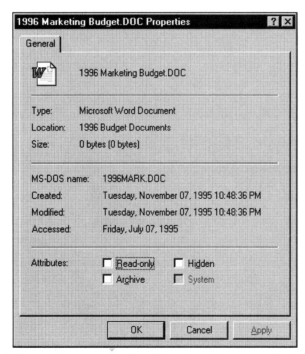

Figure 6-5.   A file or folder's Properties dialog box shows both the long and short filenames

FILE AND FOLDER OPERATIONS

? **Can I _add new options to the Send To menu_ that I get when I right-click a file?**

Initially, the Send To menu shows the floppy drives and other destinations that you have installed, as shown in Figure 6-6. However, you can specify any other disk and/or folder as a destination by adding shortcuts to the \Windows\SendTo folder. For example, adding a shortcut to the Recycle Bin saves time and avoids the prompt "Are you sure you want to send _filename_ to the Recycle Bin?" Alternatively, any other folder such as a temporary folder can also be used.

To add a disk and/or folder to the Send To folder, follow these steps:

1. In the right pane of the Explorer window, locate the drive and folder or device (such as a printer) to place in the Send To folder.

2. In the left pane, locate \Windows\SendTo, but do not select it. Simply display it on the left of the Explorer window.

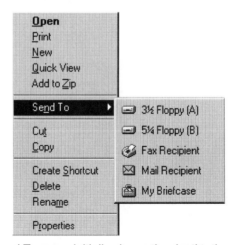

Figure 6-6.   The Send To menu initially shows the destinations you have installed

3. Drag the drive and/or folder from the right pane to the \Windows\SendTo folder in the left pane.

Now when you right-click a file and select Send To, the new destination will appear.

Tip   *Here is a bonus. If you have different but related places to send a file, you can create another level of submenu. You place an additional folder (not a shortcut) in the SendTo folder—for example, a Customers folder. Then, within that folder, place shortcuts to all your customers' individual folders, naming each shortcut appropriately. As a result, when you right-click a file icon, your Send To quick menu will show the new Customers option. When you move to it, you will see a submenu listing all your customers' shortcuts. (You may want to remove the "shortcut to" text from the icons in the SendTo folder.)*

? How do I *check my free and used disk space* in Windows 95?

Follow these steps:

1. Double-click the My Computer icon on the desktop.
2. Right-click the disk drive you want to check.
3. Choose Properties from the pop-up menu.
4. Choose the General tab. The disk space, free and used, will be displayed.

? How do I *copy files and folders in Explorer or My Computer to a different name in the same folder*? For example, I want to make a copy of Win.ini to Win.old. How do I do this?

You can make such a copy with the following instructions:

1. In Explorer or My Computer, right-click the file you want to copy.
2. Choose Copy from the pop-up menu, as shown here:

3. Right-click an empty area inside the same folder you copied from, and choose Paste. This will create a copy of your file at the end of the folder. If the original was called Win.ini, the copy will be called "Copy of Win.ini."

4. Type the name you want in place of the default name.

? Can I _create a copy of a file on my A:\ drive without using a second disk or copying the file to my hard drive_?

Yes, so long as there is enough room on your floppy to hold the copy. You can use the technique discussed in answer to the earlier question on "how to check free and used disk space," or you can do the following:

1. Open My Computer, double-click A:\ disk drive, and select the file or files you want to copy.

2. Open the Edit menu and choose Copy.

3. Open the Edit menu again and choose Paste. A copy of the selected file or files will be created with the words "Copy of" in front of the filename.

4. Select the name and type the name you want over the default name.

When I delete a shortcut from my desktop, it is placed in the Recycle Bin. How can I just _delete a file and not have it go into the Recycle Bin_?

First select the file and then hold down the SHIFT key and press the DEL key. You can also right-click the file and then hold down the SHIFT key before selecting Delete from the menu.

Caution   _Of course, if you delete a file without sending it to the Recycle Bin, it cannot be restored._

How do I _drag one file to another folder_ using just Explorer?

To drag a file from one folder to another using only one instance of Explorer, use the following steps:

1. Locate the file or folder you want to move in the right pane of the Explorer window.

2. Drag the file or folder into the left pane near but not on top of the top or bottom border of the pane. This will cause the pane to scroll, either up or down, depending on whether you moved to the top or bottom (this is called _nudging_). When you see the destination folder, drag the file or folder you are moving to it.

I am getting an _error message: "This folder already contains a file ..."_ What does that mean?

An example of this message is shown in Figure 6-7. It's telling you that you are trying to place two copies of the same file in the same folder, and asking if you want to replace the original file with the one you are trying to copy or move there. You cannot have more than one file with exactly the same name in the same folder. You can replace the existing file with the new one by clicking Yes. Alternatively, you can click No and copy or move the file to a different location or modify its filename.

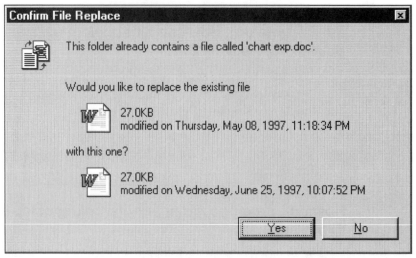

Figure 6-7. A message like this appears when you try to place two files with the same name in the same folder

? Where do I *find the Recycle Bin files*?

There is a hidden system folder, \Recycled, in the root folder of every drive. This folder stores the deleted files.

The following are procedures that you can use when working with the Recycle Bin:

1. If you delete or rename this folder in Explorer, Windows 95 will recreate a new one when you restart Windows 95. Of course, the new Recycled folder will not contain your previously deleted files.

2. If you rename the old Recycled folder back to its original name, all the previously deleted files will be displayed in the Recycle Bin again.

? What are some tips and tricks for quickly *moving and copying files*?

If you drag an object, varying the use of SHIFT and CTRL while you drag, you'll get the results described next.

⇨ If you drag a file or folder *without* using SHIFT or CTRL, you will have these effects:

⇨ Dragging within the same drive will move the object.

⇨   Dragging to a different drive will copy the object.

⇨   The exceptions to this are if you drag a file without using SHIFT or CTRL and it is a program file (one with an .EXE or .COM extension). Then

   ⇨   Dragging within the same drive will create a shortcut.

   ⇨   Dragging to a different drive that is not removable will create a shortcut.

   ⇨   Dragging to a different removable drive will create a copy.

   ⇨   Using SHIFT only always moves the object.

   ⇨   Using CTRL only always copies the object.

   ⇨   Using SHIFT and CTRL together while dragging always creates a shortcut.

 Tip   *Certain folders do not allow objects to be dragged to them, such as the Control Panel and Printers folders. Dragging to other folders always creates a move regardless of SHIFT and/or CTRL status, such as dragging to the Recycle Bin.*

? What is *My Briefcase*?

My Briefcase is a tool that you can use to synchronize files on different computers. You can change a file and then make sure that a copy on another computer is also changed. To install the Briefcase on your desktop, choose the Portable option when you set up Windows 95. If you do not do this, you can install it later using the Windows Setup tab on the Add/Remove Programs control panel.

To use My Briefcase, follow these procedures:

1. Using Explorer or My Computer, drag the files you want to maintain or keep synchronized from folders on your computer to the My Briefcase icon in Explorer or on your desktop. That places a copy of the files in the folder named My Briefcase.

2. Drag the My Briefcase icon to a floppy that you will use to transport the files to another computer.

3. Update your files in My Briefcase on the other computer, making sure that updates are saved to the My Briefcase folder.

4. When finished working on the files on the other computer, insert the updated floppy onto your main computer.

5. Double-click the My Briefcase icon, and the My Briefcase window will be displayed, as shown in Figure 6-8.

6. From the Briefcase menu, select Update All to update your files on the main computer. Select Update Selection if you only want to update some of the files. The files on the main computer are automatically revised.

Tip   *When you edit a file in My Briefcase, you are changing the file in the Windows\Desktop\My Briefcase\ folder, not the original file in another folder. However, that original file is linked with the My Briefcase file, and when you choose Update All or Update Selection, you will update the original file.*

❓ What is the *Recycle Bin*?

The Recycle Bin holds deleted files. These are automatically placed there when you delete a file by pressing DEL or by selecting Delete from the Edit menu or a pop-up menu. Items in the Recycle Bin can be cut, copied, pasted, or dragged to another location; or they can be restored to their original location by double-clicking the Recycle Bin icon, opening the Edit menu, and choosing Undo Delete. Items remain in the Recycle Bin until it is emptied by right-clicking it and choosing Empty Recycle Bin.

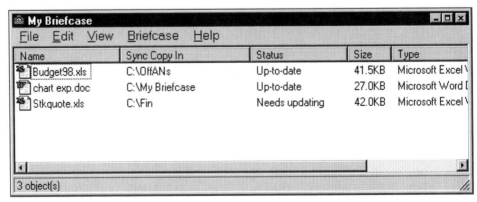

Figure 6-8.   My Briefcase tells you when two copies of a file are not in synch

Tip   *In Windows 95-compliant applications, such as Microsoft Word 97, if you right-click a file in the Open dialog box and choose Delete, the file will be placed in the Recycle Bin.*

How can I *select multiple folders or files*?

The method used depends on whether the files are contiguous. For contiguous files use one of these methods:

⇨ Click just above or to the right of the first item (not on an item), hold down the left mouse button, and drag the resulting outline box to include all items you want included.

⇨ Click the first file in a group, press SHIFT, and then click the last file in the group. All files in the group will be selected.

For noncontiguous files, click each file while holding CTRL.

How can I *select noncontiguous files from a list one at a time*?

Hold the CTRL key and click the files.

Why is a *shortcut not created when I drag a file from File Manager to the desktop*?

File Manager is a Windows 3.1 application. It does not support the functionality of creating shortcuts. Nor does it support dragging and dropping in any form outside of its windows. Use My Computer or Explorer to create shortcuts.

VIEWING FILES AND FOLDERS

I have *changed the property of a file to hidden*, but it still shows up in Explorer. What's wrong?

You have Explorer set to display hidden files. To change that, do the following:

1. Open Explorer's View menu and choose Options.

2. Choose Hide Files Of These Types.

3. Click OK.

❓ How do I *clear out the files from the Documents menu*?

To remove files from the Documents menu, do the following:

1. Click the Start button and choose Settings | Taskbar.

2. Click the Start Menu Programs tab, and click the Clear button in the Documents Menu section, as shown in Figure 6-9.

❓ How do I know which *.DLL files are being called by a given program*?

Right-click the program file (a file with an .EXE or .COM extension) in the right pane of the Explorer window and choose Quick View. The Import Table will show you the list of .DLLs being called by the program, as shown in Figure 6-10.

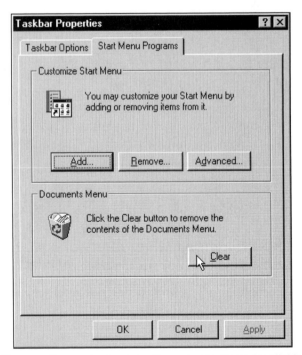

Figure 6-9.   Remove the contents of the Documents menu by clicking the Clear button

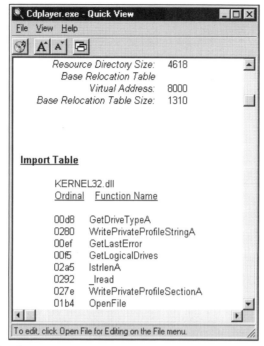

Figure 6-10.   The Quick View Import Table of a program file will tell you the .DLL
files loaded by the program

? When I save a file in Word 6.0, it does not appear under _Documents in the Start menu_. If I save the same file in WordPad, the file shows up on the list! Why?

The documents will only show under Documents in the Start menu if
they were saved by a Windows 95 application. Word 6 is a 16-bit Win3.x
application and does not support the Windows 95 environment in this
way. If you use Word 97 you will see your documents on the list.

? What _file formats can I see in Quick View_?

The following are among the file formats Quick View can open:

.ASC	ASCII text
.BMP	Windows bitmap
.CDR	CorelDRAW!
.DOC	Microsoft Word for DOS 5-6
	Microsoft Word for Windows 2-8
	WordPerfect 4.2-6.1

.DRW	Micrografx Designer
.INF	Setup information
.INI	Windows initialization
.MOD	MultiPlan 3-4.1
.RTF	Rich text format
.SAM and .AMI	AmiPro
.TXT	Text
.WB1	QuattroPro
.WKS, .WK1-.WK4	Lotus 1-2-3, 3-4
.WPD	WordPerfect demo
.WPS	Works word processing
.WQ1	QuattroPro 5 for DOS
.WRI	Write
.XLC and .XLS	Excel 4-8

Other viewers might be available from the manufacturer of a specific application.

? How do I *find a file when I have forgotten its name*?

The Find command for a file will first try to find a file by its filename, so if you have forgotten its name, you must use another search criterion. You can search for files created on a certain date, or search for text contained within the file.

Follow these steps:

1. From the Explorer Tools menu, select Find | Files Or Folders.

2. To search by date, click the Date Modified tab. Type the date, or the date range that the file was last created or modified.

3. To search by text string, click the Advanced tab. Type in the type of the file (such as **.doc**), the text string to be searched for, and the size of the file if you know it.

4. Click Find Now to begin the search.

Note   *You can combine searches by filling in all the known parameters on the three tabs, for instance, date and text string.*

❓ I often use *Find to search for the same files*. How can I save and reuse my criteria?

You can save your search criteria with these steps:

1. Click the Start button, select Find | Files Or Folders.

2. Fill in the details of the search, such as the filename to search for and the disk and/or folders to search in.

3. After all of the search parameters have been entered, click Find Now to perform the search and confirm that the criteria produced the desired results.

4. When the search is complete, open the File menu and select Save Search. Your search will be saved on the desktop with a filename that contains the search criteria and the file extension of .FND.

 Tip *You can also save the* results *of a search, not just the criteria, by selecting Options and then Save Results.*

To use a saved search, simply double-click the Find file (one with an extension .FND) on the desktop.

❓ What is a *folder*?

A folder is a directory as that term was used in earlier versions of Windows and DOS. It is a subdivision of a disk in which you can store files or other folders.

❓ How do I *make a new folder*?

Making a new folder is easy. Use the following steps:

1. Open Explorer or My Computer and open the folder to contain the new folder (the contents of the folder should either appear in the folder's own window or in the right pane of the Explorer window).

2. Right-click an empty area in either the folder window or the right pane of Explorer.

3. Choose New | Folder, as shown next. The new folder is created and placed in the parent folder.

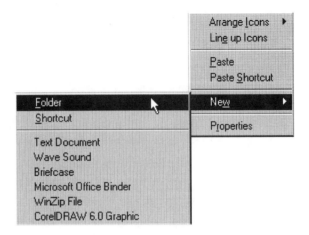

4. Type the name over the New Folder default name and you're done.

❓ I thought I *moved some files around in My Computer*, but they still show up in the old place. Why does this happen?

You probably haven't done anything to cause the screen to be refreshed. Press F5 and the display will be refreshed.

❓ I really *prefer File Manager from Windows 3.x to Explorer*. Is there any way to get it back?

Sure. Do the following to restore the File Manager:

1. Right-click the desktop.

2. Choose New | Shortcut.

3. Type in the filename **winfile.exe** and choose Next.

4. Type in the name of the shortcut **File Manager**, and then click Finish. A shortcut to the old Windows File Manager will appear on your desktop, as shown here.

❓ The *Quick View feature* is supposed to allow users to preview a file without having to open the application that created the file. How do I access this feature?

To use Quick View to see a file, follow these instructions:

1. Right-click the file in Explorer or My Computer.

2. Select Quick View, as shown here:

If the file extension cannot be opened by Quick View, this pop-up menu option will not be available. If you don't get the Quick View option at all (try it on a .DOC or .TXT file), Quick View may not be installed. To do this, use these steps:

1. Click the Start button and choose Settings | Control Panel.

2. Double-click Add/Remove Programs, and click the Windows Setup tab.

3. Select Accessories and then click the Details button. If Quick View doesn't have a check mark next to it, as shown in Figure 6-11, it means that it was not installed during the initial setup. In this case, just click this item to select it, choose OK, and follow the prompts for the disks.

How do I *search for a document that contains a specific word*?

Using Find, you can conduct a search using specific text for the criteria. Use these instructions:

1. Click the Start button and choose Find | Files Or Folders. (Alternatively, you can start by selecting Find from the Tools menu in Explorer.)

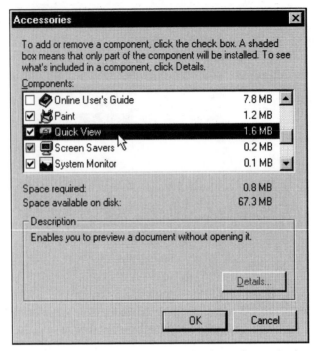

Figure 6-11.   Select Quick View by placing a check mark next to the name

2. In the Name & Location tab in Look In, type the disk drive or the path to be searched. Click Include Subfolders if you want the search to be extended to these. If you do not know the name of a folder or disk drive you want to search, click Browse and find it that way.

3. Click the Advanced tab and type the keyword or phrase for which you want to search in the Containing Text box, as shown in Figure 6-12.

4. Click Find Now to activate the search.

 Tip   *You can quickly open Find by pressing F3. The currently active drive and folder will be the basis for the search, so if you select the drive and folder first and then press F3, you will get exactly the Find dialog box you want.*

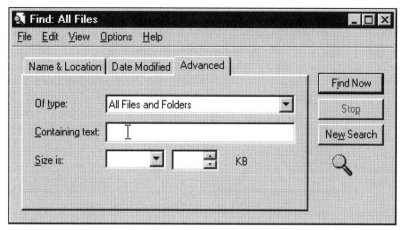

Figure 6-12.   Find allows you to search for a document containing specific text

? **When I save a _search that contains a wildcard_, the filename of the search contains different characters in place of the wildcard. Why does this happen?**

This is because wildcards (asterisks and question marks) are not valid characters to use in filenames. Windows 95 replaces asterisks with the @ symbol and question marks with !, the exclamation point, but only in the filename. When you use the saved search, the original criteria with the wildcards reappear as you can see in Figure 6-13.

? **In My Computer, how do I _select the details that appear in a folder_?**

To select a file or folder in My Computer or Explorer, you must click the filename or the icon itself. You cannot click the details that appear to the right of the icon and filename in Details view. My Computer and Explorer are designed this way so you can select multiple files and/or folders by pointing to the upper right of the objects, pressing and holding down the mouse button, and dragging a rectangle to the lower left of the objects.

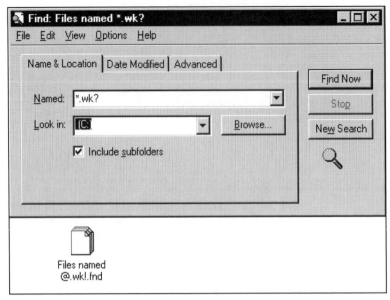

Figure 6-13.   Although wildcards are replaced in the filename of a saved search, the actual search criteria remain unchanged

❓ In Windows 95, since there really is not a File Manager, is there any way I can still _view files by type_?

Yes, there are two ways you can see all files of a certain type together: by sorting the files by type and by excluding the files you don't want to see.

To sort the files by file type in My Computer or the Explorer, use these instructions:

1. Open the View menu and choose Arrange Icons.

2. Click By Type, as shown in Figure 6-14.

Tip   _In Details view you can sort by clicking the heading buttons in the upper part of the window._

You can exclude certain system file types from being viewed and therefore see only the files that were not excluded. The following steps show how:

1. In either Explorer or My Computer, open the View menu and select Options, and the Options dialog box View tab will open.

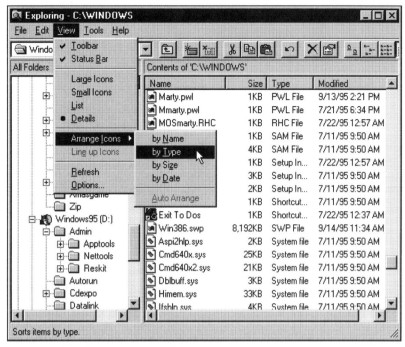

Figure 6-14.   Any Explorer or My Computer view can be sorted with Arrange Icons

2. Click Hide Files Of These Types. This will hide all of the system and hidden files, leaving only the files that you might normally use.

3. Click OK. You'll only see the file types that were excluded from the "hide files" list.

How do I *view only one type of file* (for example, only .DLL files) in Explorer?

You can look at all your .DLL files in two ways, either using Explorer directly or using the Find option in either the Explorer Tools menu or the Start menu.

Follow these steps to sort Explorer so all the .DLL files in a given folder are together:

1. Open Explorer and select the folder in which you want to see the .DLL files.

2. Open the View menu and select Details to see the file types.

3. In the right-hand pane, click the Type button in the heading above the files. This will sort the files in ascending order on the file type or file extension as shown in Figure 6-15.

 Tip *If you click the Name button once, you will sort the files in ascending order; if you click twice, you will sort in descending order.*

Follow these steps to use Find to gather together the .DLL files in all folders:

1. In the Explorer, open the Tools menu, choose Find, and click Files Or Folders.

2. In the Name & Location tab, type ***.dll** in the Named box. Choose the disk or folder to be searched in Look In. Use Browse if you are not sure.

3. Then click the Find Now button. Your results will look like those shown in Figure 6-16.

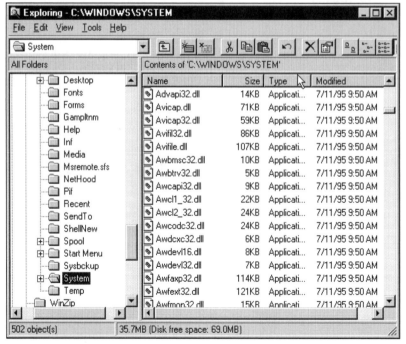

Figure 6-15.   Clicking the column buttons in the heading of the Details view sorts the files by that column

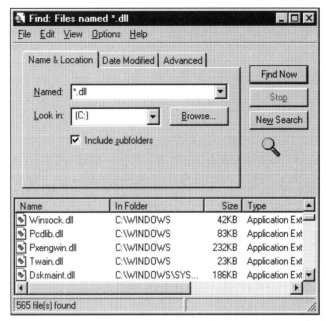

Figure 6-16.   The Find option can gather similar files across many folders

FILE ALLOCATION TABLE (FAT)

I am getting *errors trying to save from a Windows 95 application to another folder* on my PC. I have a configuration that allows dual booting between Windows 95 and Windows NT. I know it is not a matter of insufficient disk space, because the FAT partition that I created under NT is 4Gb. Why am I getting these errors?

Windows 95 only supports a 2Gb primary partition. Windows NT can create FAT partitions of up to 4Gb. The reason is that for Windows 95 (like MS-DOS), the maximum cluster size is 32K, while for Windows NT it is 64K. (The maximum number of clusters in both cases is 64K.) This means that Windows 95 can create a maximum drive of 32K × 64K = 2048MB (or 2Gb). For Windows NT, the numbers are 64K × 64K = 4096MB (4Gb).

Tip   *Fdisk in MS-DOS or Windows 95 can create extended partitions of more than 2Gb and then create several logical partitions of under 2Gb. But it cannot create primary partitions over 2Gb.*

OSR 2 *Tip   OSR 2 theoretically can support up to 2Tb (terebytes). Practically speaking, however, unless your BIOS supports interrupt 13 extensions, only 7.9Gb can be fully addressed. To determine whether your BIOS supports the interrupt 13 extensions, you must consult the documentation for the motherboard and drive.*

? I have both FAT and High Performance File System (HPFS) for OS/2 partitions on my computer. Windows 95 *Explorer does not seem to recognize the HPFS partition*. Why?

Windows 95 can only read an HPFS-formatted file from a remote server or with the use of a third-party application that will convert it to VFAT. Windows 95 does not have the capacity to recognize the HPFS partition directly.

? Does Windows 95 utilize a *File Allocation Table (FAT) file system*?

It does; however, it is a protected-mode implementation of the FAT system known as VFAT (Virtual File Allocation Table). FAT limits a file or folder's name to the 8.3 design; for example, Filename.ext, which provides eight characters for the name and a three-character extension. VFAT allows for both short and long conventions. The 32-bit VFAT driver provides a protected-mode code path for managing the file system stored on a disk that provides smoother multitasking performance.

OSR 2 *Tip   With OSR 2 using FAT32, you have real 32-bit addressing that replaces the VFAT virtual addressing. This accomplishes two things: you have additional address space and file access is faster.*

chapter

7 Answers!

Printing

Answer Topics!

Printing @ a Glance

After entering information into your computer and saving it, the next most important job is printing it. Sometimes this is the most troublesome and often the most time-consuming of the tasks. You have the problems associated with the mechanical device, with connecting it to your computer, with using the correct software drivers, and with scheduling and handling the print queue. If you are printing over a network, all of these problems increase exponentially. If that weren't enough, with today's printers you also have to worry about fonts—loading, using, managing, and removing them. Refer to the sidebar, "Printing Enhancements in Windows 95," for more specific information about new features that deal with common printer problems.

This chapter covers the following:

⇨ **Installing a Printer** discusses printer installation and point-and-print.

⇨ **Using a Printer** gives information about printing from Explorer, using drag-and-drop to print, using the Print Manager, printing offline, changing the print order, and printing from various applications.

⇨ **Fonts** covers how to view fonts, the number of fonts that can be installed, and how to install additional fonts.

Printing Enhancements in Windows 95

Windows 95 addresses all of the major printing concerns and goes a long way toward making printing truly easy. Among the many enhancements in Windows 95 are the following:

⇨ **Easier printer installation** and setup by use of plug-and-play, the Add Printer Wizard, and point-and-print. With a plug-and-play-compliant printer, all you need to do is plug it in and start Windows 95; the rest is done for you. With the Add Printer Wizard, you are quickly led through the setup process step by step. Using point-and-print, you use the Network Neighborhood to locate a shared printer on the network and then double-click it. This starts the Add Printer Wizard to complete the process.

⇨ **Faster printing** is a reality as a result of a 32-bit printing system, bidirectional communications, enhanced metafile (EMF) spooling, and support for the extended capabilities parallel port (ECP). Windows 95 replaces the Windows 3.x Print Manager with a faster 32-bit protected-mode print spooler using 32-bit virtual device drivers for the popular printers. With the printers that can support it, these device drivers will more closely interact with the printers through bidirectional communications and the extended capabilities parallel port. Using the enhanced metafile encoding scheme, Windows 95 can quickly spool a print job to the disk and then, with very little overhead, feed the job to the printer. This gets the user back to his or her work sooner and provides true background printing.

⇨ **More printing support** with Image Color Matching (ICM), deferred printing, improved font handling and flexibility, and the sharing of printers through a NetWare server. Using Image Color Matching, you can better match the colors on the screen with those produced with a color printer. If you are using a portable computer or are for some other reason disconnected from your printer, you can use deferred printing to hold the print job until you are next connected to a printer, at which time the job will automatically be printed. Windows 95

> *Printing Enhancements in Windows 95, continued*
> provides for font substitutions, enhanced and more accurate
> font generation, and the ability to store and print many more
> fonts. Windows 95 also allows its printers to be shared
> through a NetWare server.

INSTALLING A PRINTER

? **How do I *install a new printer* on my computer in Windows 95?**

You can install a new printer using the Add Printer Wizard from your Printer's dialog box. The wizard will prompt you in the installation of your printer. Use these steps:

1. Click the Start button and choose Settings | Printers.

2. Double-click Add Printer. The Add Printer Wizard window will be displayed.

3. Click Next. Choose Local Printer.

4. Click Next. The lists of Manufacturers and Printers will appear, as you can see in Figure 7-1.

5. In the Manufacturers list, select the manufacturer's name and in the Printers list, double-click the model you want to install, or select the model and click Next.

6. If you are installing a local printer, select the port it will use. The LPT1 parallel port is the most common choice.

7. Click Next. The wizard will prompt you for a friendly name (type a name that easily identifies the particular printer).

8. Decide if this printer will be your default printer and click Next.

9. Decide if you want to print a test page and then click Finish. Windows begins to copy the necessary files. If the files are already installed, you can use them or choose to install new files. You can install new files from Windows source files or from a disk from the manufacturer.

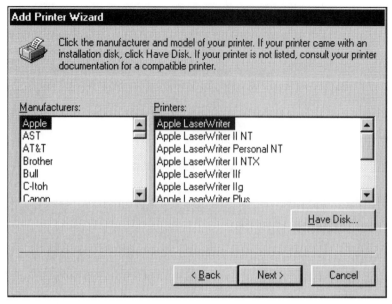

Figure 7-1.   Windows 95 gives you a wide choice of printer manufacturers and models to choose from

❓ I keep hearing about *point-and-print*. How does it work?

Point-and-print allows you to easily install a printer driver on your computer so you can use a shared network printer. Here's how:

1. Double-click the Network Neighborhood to open it.

2. Browse through your network by opening (double-clicking) various computers until you find the printer you want to use.

3. Double-click the printer and click Yes to install it on your computer.

4. Answer the various questions from the Add Printer Wizard, clicking Next and finally on Finish. The print queue for the network printer will open. Click Close.

The network printer is now set up on your computer and can be used by any of your Windows (and DOS, if you selected that option) programs. You can see the new printer on your computer by double-clicking Printers in My Computer or by clicking the Start button and selecting Settings | Printers. In both cases, the Printers folder will open and display a new networked printer, one with a cable beneath it, as shown in the lower right of Figure 7-2.

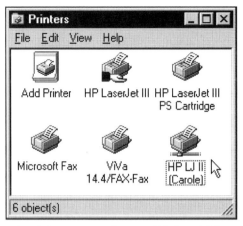

Figure 7-2.   A network printer appears in your Printers folder with a cable beneath it

USING A PRINTER

? **I have sent a number of files to the printer. One of them is urgent. How can I _change the order in which the files will be printed_?**

To change the print order, do the following:

1. Double-click the printer icon in the notification area on the right of the Taskbar. Your printer's print queue window will open, as you can see in Figure 7-3.

Document Name	Status	Owner	Progress	Started At
Microsoft Word - W95ans04.doc	Printing	marty	2 of 34 pages	10:18:46 AM 9/16/95
Benz.cdr:CorelDRAW		marty	1 page(s)	10:21:55 AM 9/16/95
C:\MPUB\KENRTNEV.PM5		marty	2 page(s)	10:25:57 AM 9/16/95
Microsoft Word - W95ans03.doc		marty	18 page(s)	10:28:34 AM 9/16/95

HP LaserJet III

Printer   Document   View   Help

4 jobs in queue

Figure 7-3.   The print queue window shows you what is waiting to be printed and in what order

2. Select the file you want to print sooner, hold down the left mouse button, drag it up to the top of the queue, and then let go of the mouse button.

? **In Windows 3.*x*, printing was closely connected to the video driver and I could resolve a lot of strange printing problems by replacing the video driver. Is this troubleshooting option of *changing the video driver still available*?**

In Windows 95, printing and video display are completely independent. The Windows 95 video driver and the Windows 95 printer drivers get graphical display information from separate sources and not from a common graphical device interface (GDI), as was the case in previous versions of Windows.

This is true only for the native 32-bit Windows 95 printer drivers. If you are using Windows 3.*x* printer drivers, the printer drivers would still access the common GDI for printing information. In this case, changing the video driver might directly affect printing.

? **In Windows 3.1, the colors on the printout did not match the colors on the screen. Does Windows 95 improve *color printing*?**

This has been addressed by a new Windows 95 feature called Image Color Matching (ICM), which provides the user with real color WYSIWYG (what you see is what you get). Applications that directly support ICM will match the formatting of the printed output to colors onscreen based on the specifications of the printer and display. Even older applications that are not ICM-aware (Windows 3.*x* applications) would benefit from this, because the ICM can be enabled directly through the printer driver. The printer driver has to be a native 32-bit Windows 95 driver that supports color printing.

? **How do I set the *default printer* for Windows 95?**

1. Click the Start button and select Settings | Printers.

2. Right-click the appropriate printer, and click Set As Default in the pop-up menu.

Tip   *In most applications you can set a printer to be the default printer for all Windows applications by choosing the printer in the application's Print dialog box and selecting Set As Default.*

I have been told that *drag-and-drop printing* is the quickest way to print. Is this so? How do I do it?

Yes, it is the fastest way to print. If you create a shortcut to your printer on your desktop, you can drag a file from My Computer or Explorer and drop it on the printer shortcut. This will send the document to the printer without you having to open the application that created the file. To create a shortcut to a printer, follow these instructions:

1. From My Computer, Explorer, or the Control Panel, double-click Printers. The Printers folder will open.

2. Drag the printer for which you want a shortcut to the desktop.

3. Answer Yes, indicating that you want to create a shortcut.

4. Rename the shortcut if you wish.

 Tip   *Drag-and-drop printing only works for documents that have a registered association with an application and have a printing option defined.*

To see if drag-and-drop printing has been defined for a type of file, use these steps:

1. From Explorer or My Computer, open the View menu and choose Options.

2. Click the File Types tab, and select the file type you want to check in the Registered File Types list box.

3. Click Edit. The Edit File Type dialog box will open, as you can see in Figure 7-4.

4. Check to see if the list of Actions includes Print. If so, drag-and-drop printing will work with that file type.

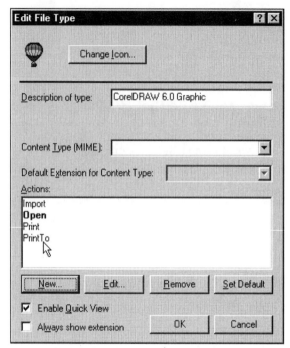

Figure 7-4.   The drag-and-drop actions available for a file type are listed in the Edit
File Type dialog box

5. If Print is not shown in the list of Actions in the Edit File Type
dialog box, you can add it to the list by clicking New, typing **Print**
in the Actions text box, and clicking Browse to select the application
you want to use to print the job.

What is *EMF*?

EMF is an enhanced metafile. It is a nondevice-specific picture of what
is being sent to the printer. A print job can be quickly captured
as an EMF on disk and then sent to the printer in the background.
Spooling with an EMF allows you to get back to work faster after
printing a file and to do more while the EMF is being sent to the
printer.

? **Since Windows 95 does not use a "Print Manager" but sends the pages to be printed in a queue as metafiles, will my printer be required to have enough _memory to print a full page of my graphics in metafile format_?**

No, your printer will not need additional memory. The Windows 95 EMF format (see the earlier question about EMF format for additional information) increases the actual printing speed, but does not require the printer to hold or process more information.

? **Sometimes I _print a document, but nothing comes out_. How do I avoid this problem?**

If you are trying to use a network printer or one that is sometimes not connected to your computer, check to make sure the printer has not been set to work offline. Use these steps to do that:

1. Click the Start button and choose Settings | Printers, or open My Computer and double-click the Printer icon.

2. Right-click the printer you are trying to use. The printer's pop-up menu, shown here, will open.

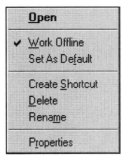

3. If Work Offline is selected and you can in fact connect to the printer, deselect the Work Offline option.

If you are using a local printer and having the problem, check all the obvious things like the cable being connected to the port you think you are using, the printer being turned on and online, and the driver

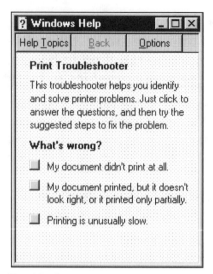

Figure 7-5.   The Print Troubleshooter will help you solve your printing problems

you are using being the correct one for your printer. Windows 95 has an excellent printer troubleshooting section in online help. The next set of steps will open it for you:

1. Click the Help menu in the Explorer, My Computer, or Printers window and select Help Topics. The Windows Help dialog box will open.

2. In the Contents tab, double-click Troubleshooting and then double-click again on it if you have trouble printing. The Print Troubleshooter will open, as shown in Figure 7-5.

3. Click the button that best describes your problem, and follow along as additional questions are asked until your problem is fixed. See the sidebar for other things you might do.

Other Things You Might Do

⇨ Empty the Recycle Bin. See Chapter 6 for several questions on using the Recycle Bin.

⇨ Delete .TMP files in your Temp folder, usually c:\windows\temp. This is a common problem for printing.

> *Other Things You Might Do, continued*
>
> ⇨ Reboot your computer.
>
> ⇨ If your printer is a network printer, the print queue may be hung on the server end. Wait for the print jobs to be processed, and if that doesn't work, contact the system administrator in charge of the server.
>
> ⇨ Check the printer path. Check the Details tab in the printer Properties dialog box (Start menu | Settings | Printers) of the printer you are trying to print to.
>
> ⇨ Make sure the correct printer is selected in the application you are printing from. Check the Print dialog box (or Print Settings dialog box in some applications) to see which printer is selected.

❓ How can I *print a file from Explorer*?

If printing has been defined as an option in a file type's registration, then there are three ways to print that file type from Explorer:

⇨ Drag the file from Explorer, and drop it on a shortcut to a printer that you have created on your desktop. (See the earlier question about drag-and-drop for how to do this.)

⇨ Right-click a file and select Print from the pop-up menu that opens.

⇨ Right-click a file and select Send To | Printer if you have added a shortcut to your printer in your \Windows\SendTo folder.

To add an item to the Send To list, use the following steps:

1. Create a shortcut to a printer on your printer as described earlier in the drag-and-drop question.

2. Open Explorer and then the \Windows\SendTo folder.

3. Right-click the right pane of the Explorer window, which should be the \Windows\SendTo folder.

4. Choose New Shortcut from the pop-up menu that appears.

5. Click Browse in the Create Shortcut Wizard that appears.

6. Select Desktop in the Look In drop-down list and All Files in the Files Of Type list. Your printer shortcut should appear in the list of objects on the desktop.

7. Double-click the printer shortcut and click Next.

8. Type the name you want to use and click Finish. Your printer will now appear in your Send To list.

When I *print from my DOS application*, I get an error message and I can't print. Why does this happen?

This happens because you only configured the printer to print from Windows applications. You will need to reconfigure the printer to print from DOS applications by deleting the current driver and using the Add Printer Wizard to install a new one with support for DOS. Use these steps to do that:

1. Click the Start button and choose Settings | Printers.

2. Select the printer you want to reconfigure, press DEL, and answer Yes you are sure you want to delete the printer.

3. Double-click Add Printer and click Next.

4. Select Network Printer and click Next.

5. Type in or browse for the path to the printer; select Yes you print from MS-DOS-based programs, as you can see in Figure 7-6; and click Next.

6. Click Capture Printer Port; select the device, such as LPT3; click OK; and click Next.

7. Type in a name for the printer, decide if you want to make it your default printer, and click Next.

8. Print a test page if you wish and click Finish.

Tip   *DOS programs cannot print directly to a network printer. You must map the network printer to a port address on your computer (such as LPT3, as was done in step 6) that DOS can print to.*

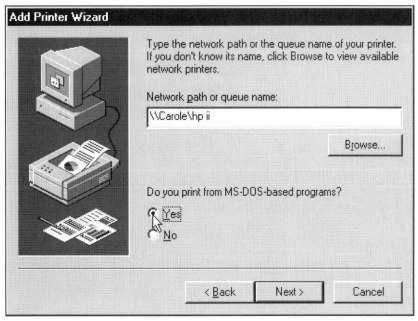

Figure 7-6.   You must establish the capability to print from DOS applications while you are setting up the printer

How do I *print from Lotus Notes* under Windows 95?

When you install a network printer on your computer, the default port is the path to the printer in the form *server\printername.* This works fine with many products. Notes, like DOS applications, is looking for a port address such as LPT3, as opposed to just *server\printername.* You can fix this problem by capturing the network printer to a port address on your computer. Use these instructions to do that:

1. Click the Start button and choose Settings | Printers.

2. Right-click the icon for the printer you want to use and choose Properties.

3. Click the Details tab and then select Capture Printer Port.

4. In the Device list, select the port address that you want to use.

5. Select or type the network path for the printer, select Reconnect At Logon, as shown next, and then click OK.

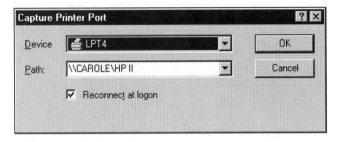

6. In the Print To The Following Port box, select the port you mapped, and click OK.

If I *print offline*, will I lose my print job if I turn off my laptop?

No, the whole idea behind deferred printing is that you can process the print job while not being actually connected to the printer. The job is spooled to the disk, and an EMF (enhanced metafile) print output is created. It will stay on your hard disk until you connect to a printer. Then when you connect to the printer and turn Work Offline off, your print job will be completed and the temporary spool file deleted.

I used to be able to *print offline on my laptop computer*, but then I changed something in my settings and this option is gone. What did I do?

If you have turned off spooling in your printer properties, you cannot print offline. Follow the next set of steps to turn this back on:

1. Click the Start button and select Settings | Printers to open the Printers folder.

2. Right-click the printer and select Properties from the pop-up menu.

3. Click the Details tab and the Spool Settings button. The Spool Settings dialog box will open, as shown in Figure 7-7.

Tip   *The Spool Settings dialog box allows you to begin printing after one page has spooled (which increases printing speed) or after all pages have spooled (which gets you back to your application faster).*

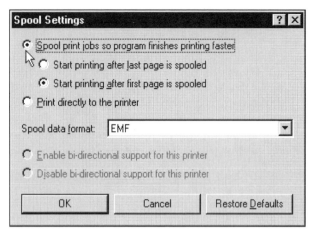

Figure 7-7.   The Spool Settings dialog box allows you to turn print spooling
on and off

   Tip   *If you have shared your printer on a network, you will not be able to
turn spooling off.*

4. Click the Spool Print Jobs option and click OK twice.

How do I *print out information about my computer configuration*?

To print your computer configuration information, use the
following steps:

1. Right-click My Computer.

2. Choose Properties and click the Device Manager tab.

3. Select Computer and then click Print.

4. Make sure the System Summary option is selected in the Print
dialog box and click OK.

How can I *print to a file*, and can I do it from Explorer?

You can send your output to a file and print later from a different PC.
You must either create a new printer, or change the configuration of

one of your existing printers so that you have a printer defined that prints to a file. Then you can use one of the techniques in the question about printing from the Explorer to do the printing. Here's how you change the configuration of an existing printer to have it print to a file (if you want a new printer to serve that purpose, use the Add Printer Wizard, as described in the question about installing a new printer):

1. Right-click the printer you want to reconfigure, and select Properties. The printer's dialog box will open.

2. Click the Details tab, and open the Print To The Following Port drop-down list box.

3. Select FILE, as shown in Figure 7-8. Click OK.

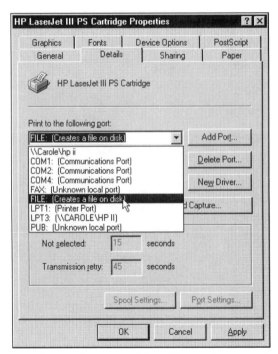

Figure 7-8.   You can direct printer output to a file or a fax as well as to an actual printer by changing the port you are printing to

When you issue the Print command, the print will be sent to a file and you will be prompted for a filename, as you can see here:

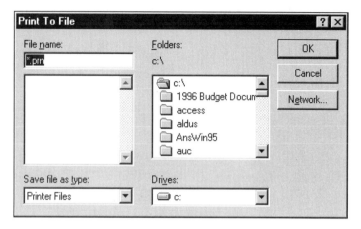

To print the file later, use these steps:

1. Click the Start button and choose Programs | MS-DOS Prompt to open a DOS window.

2. At the DOS prompt, type **copy c:\\<*path*>*filename lpt1*,** where <*path*>*filename* is the full path and name of your file, and *lpt1* is your printer port. Make sure you are printing using the same type of printer you selected when you printed to a file.

? I was trying to *print to a file (for example, Device Manager information) but it isn't readable*. What happened?

When Windows 95 prints information to a file, it uses printer language output rather than straight text format. To print to a file and have it in a readable format, you have to print to the Generic Text Only printer. To install the Generic Text Only printer, do the following:

1. Click the Start button and choose Settings | Printers.

2. Double-click the Add Printer icon, and click the Next button.

3. When you are prompted, click the Local Printer button, and then click the Next button.

4. In the Manufacturers box, select Generic; in the Printers box, select Generic/Text Only.

5. Click Next and in the Available Ports box, select FILE, and click Next.

6. Enter the name you want for the printer, and answer No to "Do you want your Windows-based programs to use this printer as the default printer?"

7. Click Next. Answer No to testing the printer and click Finish.

❓ I thought I should be able to *print to a printer connected to a UNIX machine* because I am running TCP/IP and can see the UNIX box. Why am I not able to do this?

In Windows 95, you cannot print directly to a printer on a machine running UNIX only. You can print to a printer on a Windows NT 3.5 server or on a NetWare server that is also running UNIX. For example, you can connect to a UNIX printer through a Windows NT machine and then share it to Windows 95 clients.

❓ Can I change the *spooling options* for my printer?

Yes, do the following:

1. Click the Start button and select Settings | Printers.

2. Right-click the appropriate printer, and choose Properties from the pop-up menu.

3. Click the Details tab and then click Spool Settings to go to the Spool Settings dialog box.

4. You can choose whether to spool print jobs or print directly to a printer, when to start printing after spooling, the spool data format, and whether to use bidirectional printer support. Make any changes and click OK when done.

Refer to the question earlier in this chapter about printing offline on your laptop computer for additional information.

FONTS

? How do I *add new fonts*?

Use the following steps to install new fonts.

1. Click the Start button and select Settings | Control Panel.

2. Double-click the Fonts control panel, and choose Install New Font from the File menu.

3. In the Add Fonts dialog box, browse to the location of the new fonts you want to add. The fonts in the folder will appear in the List Of Fonts box, as shown here. Select the fonts you want to add and choose OK.

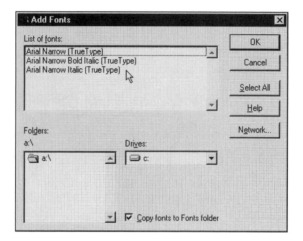

Tip   *Fonts are copied to the \Windows\Fonts folder on your hard drive by default. If you want to use fonts from another location (for example, a Fonts folder on a network server) instead of copying them to your hard drive, clear the Copy Fonts To Fonts Folder check box.*

? What is the *maximum number of TrueType fonts* that I can install on my PC?

Because Windows 95 uses the Registry to store fonts, there is no limit to the number of TrueType fonts that can be installed. You can select and use nearly 1,000 different fonts and styles on any document without any problems.

How do I _preview my fonts_ without actually having to format text in an application?

You can see the fonts without using them in text by doing the following:

1. Open My Computer and double-click Control Panel.

2. Double-click the Fonts folder.

3. Double-click the font you want to see. The font's dialog box will open, as shown in Figure 7-9.

4. Click Print to print the sample fonts, and click Done when you are.

Tip   *To print samples of several fonts in the Fonts folder, select all the desired fonts at once while holding down* CTRL, *open the File menu, and choose Print. (You'll have to click OK in the Print dialog box and Done in the font's dialog box for each of the fonts to complete the printing.)*

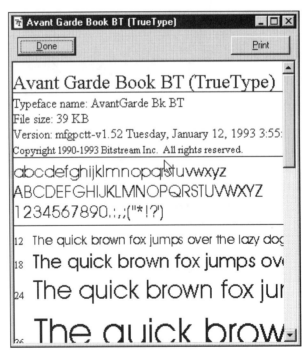

Figure 7-9.   You can see what a font looks like by double-clicking it

? When I _remove a font_, Windows 95 deletes the file and places it in the Recycle Bin. In previous versions of Windows, if font trouble occurred, I could "remove" the font without removing the file from the hard disk. Does this functionality still exist in Windows 95?

Windows 95 accomplishes the same end by moving the fonts to the Recycle Bin. You can then return the font to its folder by opening the Recycle Bin and choosing Restore from the File menu.

chapter

8 Answers!

Networking

Answer Topics!

221

Networking @ a Glance

Computer networking has become more the rule than the exception, and Windows 95 has responded to that by making networking an integral part of the operating system and not an add-on. What Windows 95 has provided is significant. It is both a full and very competent *client* for Novell NetWare and Windows NT servers, and a complete *peer-to-peer networking system* among Windows 95 or Windows for Workgroups computers, with all the features needed for many organizations. In addition, Windows 95 supports networking with several other vendors' software including Artisoft LANtastic, Banyan VINES, and DEC PATHWORKS. Not only can Windows 95 be a client in a client-server network and a full peer in a peer-to-peer network, it can do both at the same time. In all senses, Windows 95 is a networking operating system.

This chapter deals with the various considerations involved in setting up and using a computer on a network. Topics discussed here include the following:

⇨   **Network Compatibility** gives information about several software products that are compatible with Windows 95.

⇨   **Setting Up** covers various problems you might encounter when installing the network software and connecting to a server.

⇨   **Security Considerations** discusses the levels of security, protecting files, assigning passwords, and sharing folders on a network.

⇨   **Using a Network** gives information about general features associated with being on a network, such as how to access a network drive, how to run an application from a network, how to load file and printer sharing, how to run various utilities on a network, and similar concerns.

⇨   **Network Printing** addresses printer problems on a network.

⇨   **Administering and Monitoring Networks** covers administration problems and concerns, such as setting up the network and setting up individual accounts, and monitoring access and network activity.

⇨   **Protocols** discusses what protocols can be used and how they can be used.

NETWORK COMPATIBILITY

❓ Can I use Windows 95 with *Artisoft LANtastic 6.0*?

Yes, you can use LANtastic 5.0 and above with Windows 95. Be sure and have LANtastic installed and running *before* you run Windows 95 Setup. Windows 95 does not supply the LANtastic software—you must get the Windows 95 LANtastic *.INF files from Artisoft. When you do, you must then install them as client software by following these steps:

1. Click the Start button and select Settings | Control Panel | Network.
2. From the Configuration tab, click Add.
3. Click Client and click Add again.
4. Insert the disk with your LANtastic *.INF files into a floppy drive and click Have Disk.
5. Follow the prompts to install the client software.

The LANtastic resources will only be accessible for you through the LANtastic utilities, which you can find by clicking the Start button and selecting Programs and then the LANtastic program group. You will not be able to access LANtastic through Network Neighborhood.

❓ Can I use Windows 95 with a *Banyan VINES network*?

You can, provided you have VINES version 5.52(5) or later. The best way would be to have the Banyan VINES client installed and configured before upgrading to Windows 95. To make your Windows 95 PC work as a client on a Banyan VINES network, you have to have the following components installed in the Network control panel:

⇨ Your network adapter should be set for a real-mode 16-bit NDIS driver (choose this by clicking your adapter in the Network dialog box, the Configuration tab, and then clicking Properties) if you are using an older VINES version.

⇨ Your client software should be Banyan DOS/Windows 3.1 (choose this by clicking Add in the Network dialog box, the Configuration tab, Client, and then clicking Add again).

⇨ Your network protocol should be Banyan VINES Ethernet Protocol (choose this by clicking Add in the Network dialog box, the Configuration tab, Protocol, and then clicking Add again).

Make sure your system files contain the following lines (assume that Banyan VINES is your primary network, that your Banyan files are in the \Vines folder, and that Exp16.dos is your NDIS2 driver):

```
Autoexec.bat:
cd \Vines
ban
ndisban                     ; ndtokban if you are using token ring
redirall
arswait
z:login
c:
cd\
Config.sys:
device=c:\vines\proman.dos /i:c:\vines
device=c:\vines\exp16.dos
Protocol.ini:
[PROTOCOL MANAGER]
drivername=protman$
[VINES_XIF]
drivername=ndisban$         ; ndtokban$ if you are using token ring
bindings=MS$EE16
[MS$EE16]
drivername=EXP16$
interrupt=5
ioaddress=0x300
iochrdy=late
```

Banyan VINES servers will not appear in Network Neighborhood, because Banyan VINES servers do not support browsing. You can use Windows 95's Map Network Drive feature to locate and connect to the Banyan servers.

❓ Does Windows 95 come with support for *DEC PATHWORKS*?

Yes, Windows 95 provides 32-bit protected-mode drivers for DEC PATHWORKS version 4.1 and above. You should use Microsoft's Client for Microsoft Networks and a DEC PATHWORKS protocol, or a 32-bit protected mode driver supplied by DEC. Follow these steps to install the software provided by Windows 95:

1. Right-click the Network Neighborhood icon and choose Properties.

2. On the Configuration tab, click Add.

3. Choose Client and click Add.

4. Choose Microsoft Client For Microsoft Networks and click OK.

5. Choose Protocol and click Add.

6. Click Digital Equipment (DEC); a list of DEC network protocols will be listed, as shown in Figure 8-1.

7. Select the protocol you want to use and click OK.

? I understand Windows 95 ships with _NetWare client software from both Microsoft and Novell_. What's the difference and how do I install my choice?

Windows 95 does include both the Microsoft Client for Novell Networks and the comparable software from Novell (Novell NetWare Workstation Shell for either 3.x or 4.x networks). The Microsoft version is 32-bit protected-mode software versus 16-bit real-mode software from Novell. The Windows 95 file system operates in 32-bit protected mode, so to use the Novell software, the processor is going to have to switch between real and protected mode, which will slow performance. The Microsoft software also supports long filenames and peer resource sharing, neither of which is supported by Novell 16-bit real-mode software. Another option is to use Novell's own 32-bit protected mode software, which must be acquired separately.

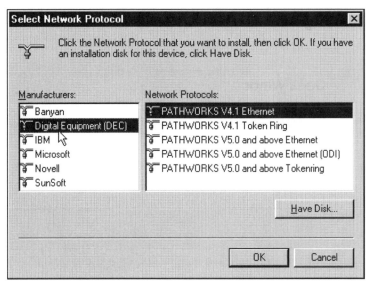

Figure 8-1.   DEC offers several network protocols that can be installed

You can choose and install a NetWare client using the following steps:

1. Click the Start button and choose Settings | Control Panel | Network.

2. In the Configuration tab, select Add | Client | Add.

3. Select Microsoft or Novell from the Manufacturers list, choose the network client you want, as shown in Figure 8-2, and then click OK. Or, if using software from Novell, choose Novell and click Have Disk to install newer 32-bit protected mode files.

? How do I install Windows 95 on a computer that has *networking support from a network vendor other than Microsoft or Novell*?

First, before you install Windows 95, be sure that your network client software is correctly installed under MS-DOS, Windows version 3.1, or Windows for Workgroups, and that the network is running when you start setup.

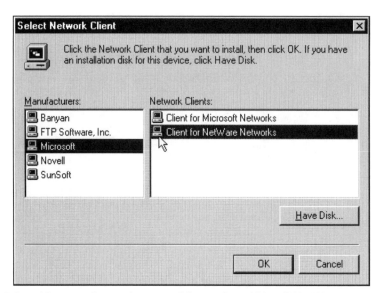

Figure 8-2.   You can choose between Microsoft and Novell NetWare networking clients

During setup, Windows 95 should detect a network adapter and install the Microsoft Client for Microsoft Networks by default. Notice that the Configuration tab in the Network control panel provides the same controls for adding and removing networking components after Windows 95 Setup is complete.

 Tip   *Install any non-Microsoft network* **before** *you install Windows 95, and then install networking support during Windows 95 Setup, not after the fact.*

? Can a Windows 95 computer act as a *Novell NetWare server*?

If you install file and printer sharing for NetWare networks service, the Windows 95 machine can act as a NetWare file and print server. To install this service, do the following:

1. Right-click Network Neighborhood and click Properties.

2. On the Configuration tab, select Add | Service | Add.

3. Select Microsoft and select File And Printer Sharing For NetWare Networks, as shown in Figure 8-3. This will load a virtual device driver (called Nwserver.vxd) that enables Windows 95 computers to process NetWare Core Protocol (NCP)-based requests for file and printer input/output.

? What *types of networking* are supported in Windows 95?

Windows 95 can be a client or a peer in the following networks, but it may need additional software from the particular manufacturer:

- ⇨ **Artisoft LANtastic** version 5.0 and above
- ⇨ **Banyan VINES** version 5.52 and above
- ⇨ **DEC PATHWORKS** version 4.1 and above
- ⇨ **IBM OS/2 LAN Server**
- ⇨ **Microsoft LAN Manager** and **Windows NT**
- ⇨ **Novell NetWare** version 3.11 and above
- ⇨ **SunSoft PC-NFS** version 5.0 and above

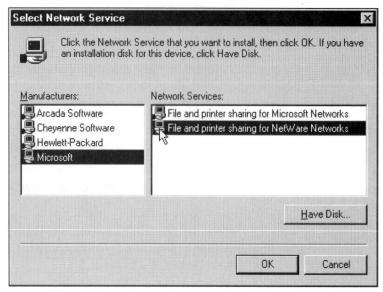

Figure 8-3.   A Windows 95 workstation can share its files and printers over a
NetWare network

SETTING UP

The sidebar, "Tips on Setting Up Windows 95 Networking," provides
some general information about hardware requirements and other
tips for setting up a Windows 95 network.

Tips on Setting Up Windows 95 Networking

To utilize Windows 95 networking, you'll need the hardware
required to set up the applicable Windows 95 components.
Windows 95 makes the software setup easy by leading you
through dialog boxes with lists of alternatives. If your network
adapter is plug-and-play-compliant, setting it up is a snap. Here
are some tips on setting up Windows 95 networking.

   You will need a network adapter card in your computer and
in each computer in your network. The most common adapter
cards are combination Ethernet cards that handle several types of
cabling. Depending on your network adapter card and several

Tips on Setting Up Windows 95 Networking, continued
physical considerations like the distances to be covered and the
number of stations to be connected, you will need one of the
following types of cabling:

⇨ **10Base-T** twisted-pair cabling is the most common today and
   is the most flexible form of network cabling.

⇨ **10Base-2** thin coaxial cable is common in small networks and
   is very cost-effective for them.

⇨ **10Base-5** thick or standard coaxial cable was the original
   networking standard. But it is both expensive and difficult to
   use, so it has been eclipsed by the other forms of cabling.

⇨ **Fiber optic** cabling is appearing for long-distance and
   high-speed networking, but is expensive and probably will
   not replace 10Base-T in the near term.

⇨ **Wireless** networking is beginning to be used where running a
   cable is very difficult. It too is expensive and may encounter
   problems with interference.

If you add networking after Windows 95 has been set up
and without a plug-and-play adapter, you will need to set up the
network manually. You can do this by clicking the Start button
and selecting Settings | Control Panel | Add New Hardware.
You will be guided through the network installation. If your
networking hardware is running prior to installing Windows 95,
Setup will often detect and properly set up Windows 95 to operate
with your hardware. If you install a plug-and-play adapter after
setting up Windows 95, it will automatically set up your network
the first time you start up Windows 95.

How you set up Windows 95 networking depends on
whether you want your computer to be a peer in a peer-to-peer
network or a client in a client-server network. In *peer-to-peer networking*,
generally used in smaller networks, all computers in the network
share their resources equally. In this mode, all computers typically
run either Windows 95 or Windows for Workgroups, although
other possibilities exist. *Client-server*, on the other hand, supports
many computers, known as *clients*, accessing the resources of one
or more designated server computers. The clients can be running

Tips on Setting Up Windows 95 Networking, continued
Windows 95 or other client software, but for Windows 95 clients, the server must be running either Novell NetWare or Windows NT.

To set up or change the Windows 95 networking software configuration, click the Start button and select Settings | Control Panel | Network. The Network dialog box will open, as shown in Figure 8-4. It allows you to install or change four types of networking software components:

⇨ **Clients**, which allow you to access other computers in order to use their resources, are used for both peer-to-peer and client-server networking. Client For Microsoft Networks and the Client For NetWare Networks are the two most common choices.

⇨ **Adapters**, which are the interfaces or drivers between your network adapter cards and Windows 95, are unique to your particular adapter card, and as with a printer, you must select a manufacturer and a model.

Generic NE1000-, NE2000-, and NE3200-compatible adapters are found under Novell/Anthem, and the Dial-Up Adapter is under Microsoft.

⇨ **Protocols**, which are the communication languages used between computers, are determined by the type of networking you will be doing. In a Windows 95 peer-to-peer network or with a Windows NT client-server network, you should use Microsoft NetBEUI. With a NetWare client-server network, you should use Microsoft IPX/SPX or Novell IPX. With dial-up networking to the Internet, you should use Microsoft TCP/IP.

⇨ **Services**, which allow you to share your resources with other computers or to provide other services such as network backup, are primarily needed to provide the server functions in a peer-to-peer network.

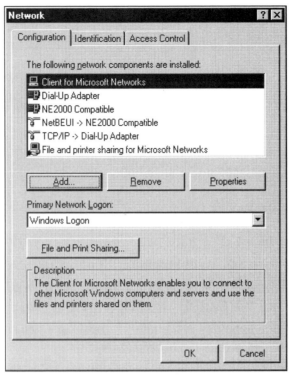

Figure 8-4.   The Network dialog box allows you to select the software components you'll use in networking

? **How do I *change My Computer's name on the Network*?**

This is set in the Network Identification tab. You can set and change it with the following steps:

1. Click the Start button and select Settings | Control Panel | Network.

2. Select the Identification tab.

3. Your computer name should be listed there, as you can see next:

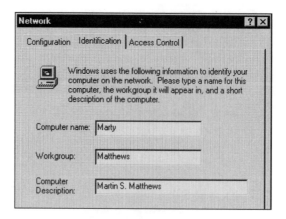

4. Make the change you want, click OK, and follow the prompts to reboot.

? I would like to specify settings normally stored in Net.cfg like the FILE HANDLES variable and such. How can I see and _change settings in Net.cfg using Windows 95 and the Microsoft Client for NetWare_?

In Windows 95, using Microsoft's 32-bit client software, file handles are set dynamically, so you do not have to have a specific setting as you would in Net.cfg. Windows 95 is doing this in the protected-mode redirector (NWREDIR).

? Can I _connect to a Novell server through Dial-Up Networking_?

You need to install the Microsoft Client for NetWare Networks and the IPX/SPX-compatible protocol, which you need to bind to the Dial-Up Adapter driver. To install the client software, see the question later about installing a NetWare client on a Windows 95 machine. The protocol is very likely to already be installed on your computer. Check this by opening your Network control panel and seeing if the following lines are in the list of network components:

```
IPX/SPX-compatible Protocol -> Dial-Up Adapter
IPX/SPX-compatible Protocol -> NE2000 Compatible
```

If the protocol software is not already installed on your computer, follow these steps to install it:

1. From the Network dialog box Configuration tab, select Add | Protocol | Add.

2. Select Microsoft from the list of Manufacturers, and click IPX/SPX-Compatible Protocol, as shown in Figure 8-5.

3. Click OK.

Next make sure the protocol is bound to your Dial-Up Adapter. You can check this with the next set of steps:

1. Double-click your Dial-Up Adapter in the list of Network components on the Configuration tab of the Network dialog box.

2. Click the Bindings tab. Verify that the IPX/SPX-Compatible Protocol is checked, as shown in Figure 8-6. Click OK.

Finally, prepare the dial-up connection for use with a NetWare server using this last set of steps:

1. Open My Computer and the Dial-Up Networking folder, and then right-click the dial-up connection you want to use (if you don't have one, double-click Make New Connection and follow the instructions on the screen).

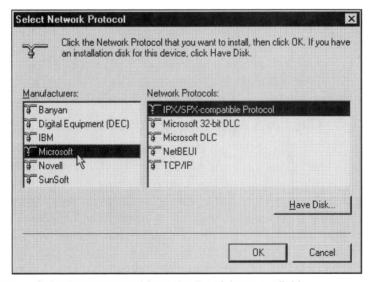

Figure 8-5.   Selecting a protocol from the list of those available

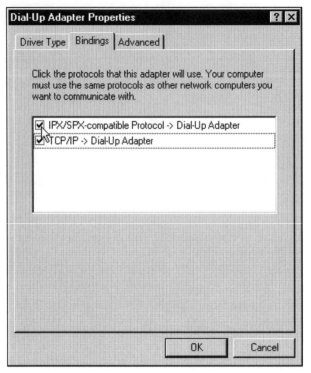

Figure 8-6.   Protocols must be attached or *bound* to network adapters

   2. Click Properties in the pop-up menu and then click Server Type.
   In the Type Of Dial-Up Server list, click NRN: NetWare Connect,
   as you see in Figure 8-7. Click OK twice and close both the
   Dial-Up Networking and My Computer folders.

? Why can't I *connect to Novell servers*?

   One of the first steps is to verify that you have installed the
   IPX/SPX-compatible protocol and set the frame type to AUTO or to
   the specific frame type your server is using. (NetWare 3.11 servers use
   the frame type of Ethernet 802.3, and NetWare 3.12 and 4.0 servers
   use the frame type of Ethernet 802.2.) With the following steps you
   can check the protocol and frame type you are using:

   1. Click the Start button and select Settings | Control Panel | Network.

   2. On the Configuration tab, check that IPX/SPX-Compatible
   Protocol is listed as one of the installed network components.

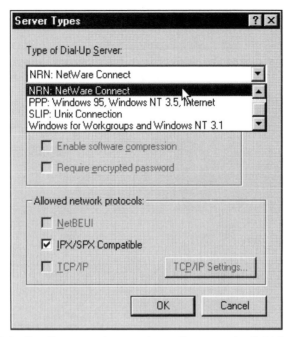

Figure 8-7.   Selecting the correct server type allows you to dial into a
NetWare server

(If not, install it by selecting Add | Protocol | Add | Microsoft |
IPX/SPX-Compatible Protocol. Click OK.)

3. To verify that the frame settings are accurate, click the
   IPX/SPX-Compatible Protocol and click Properties.

4. Click the Advanced tab and then on Frame Type in the Property
   list. Select the type that is appropriate for you, as you can see in
   Figure 8-8.

If this does not solve your problem, use the Network
Troubleshooter in Windows 95 Help to step through possible network
problems. To do this:

1. Click the Start button and choose Help.

2. From the Contents tab, double-click Troubleshooting.

3. Double-click "If you have trouble using the network." The Network
   Troubleshooter will be displayed, as shown in Figure 8-9.

4. Step through the help screens as you are prompted.

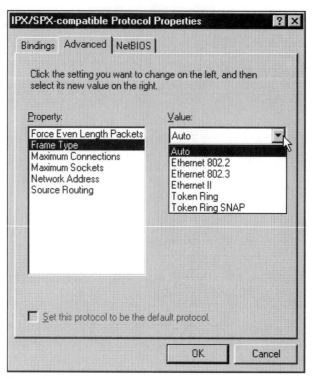

Figure 8-8.   The default Auto frame type is typically the best choice

? Can I *connect two Windows 95 computers* together, or do I need to buy a special peer-to-peer network program?

Windows 95 has built-in networking capabilities. Provided you have the necessary network adapter cards and cables, linking two machines together is no problem. Just make sure both are using the same protocol, for example, NetBEUI.

To verify that both computers are using the same protocol, follow these steps on both computers:

1. Click the Start button and choose Settings | Control Panel | Network.

2. On the Configuration tab, click the protocol and click Properties. Check that the settings in the Bindings tab on both computers are as shown in Figure 8-10.

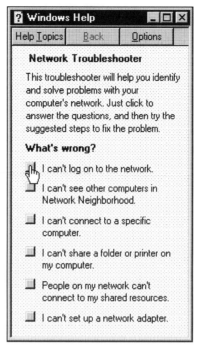

Figure 8-9.   Windows Help provides a Network Troubleshooter to help you identify problems

? *How many users can I have connected to my shared drive?*

The number of users connected to your shared drive is limited by the amount of memory, the speed and the throughput of the server, and the type and speed of the network you are using. Depending on your system, the shared drive should be able to handle as many as a dozen to several thousand users.

? How do I *install a NetWare client on my Windows 95 machine*?

First, you must determine whether to use Microsoft's 32-bit NetWare Client or one of Novell's clients. If your network is running either NetWare 3.*x* or 4.*x*, you can use the 32-bit Windows 95 Microsoft Client for NetWare. To do this:

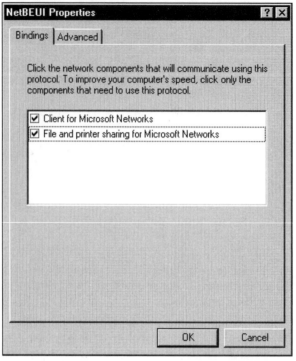

Figure 8-10.   For peer-to-peer networking, all computers need to be using the same protocol and have both a client as well as file and printer sharing for Microsoft Networks

1. Click the Start button and choose Settings I Control Panel I Network.

2. In the Configuration tab, select Add I Client I Add.

3. Select Microsoft and Client For NetWare Networks. This will give you full protected-mode support for NetWare, and you will not be using any conventional memory to load real-mode network drivers. Click OK.

However, if you need to use one of the Novell NetWare 16-bit real-mode clients (NetWare Workstation Shell 3.*x* or NETX), you have to load the Novell NetWare Workstation Shell 3.*x*. To do that:

1. Click the Start button and choose Settings I Control Panel I Network.

2. In the Configuration tab, select Add I Client I Add.

3. Select Novell and then Novell NetWare (Workstation Shell 3.*x*). Click OK.

If you want to use NetWare Workstation Shell 4.*x* (Virtual Loadable Module or VLM), install the Novell NetWare (Workstation Shell 4.*x*) Client in step 3. To use the Novell 32-bit protected-mode client, choose Have Disk in step 3 and insert the Novell disks.

Where do I find *Interlink in Windows 95*?

The Interlink that shipped with MS-DOS 6.*x* is now called Direct Cable Connection. You can use it to connect between PCs via a parallel or serial cable and to share files between the two computers. The Direct Cable Connection is found on the Start menu by selecting Programs | Accessories | Direct Cable Connection. If you don't have this option on your Accessories menu, you will have to install it first. You can do that with these steps:

1. Click the Start button and choose Settings | Control Panel | Add/Remove Programs.

2. Click the Windows Setup tab, select Communications, and then click the Details button for a list of the Communications components.

3. If there is no check mark next to it, click Direct Cable Connection to install it, as shown in Figure 8-11. Click OK twice. (If there is a check mark, it is already installed.)

Will I need new *networking software to connect Windows 95 to my network server*?

No. Windows 95 will continue to run existing real-mode networking components while enhancing the 32-bit protected-mode networking components first delivered with Windows for Workgroups.

After installing Windows 95, I *no longer can connect to my network*. Why?

If your network is supported in Windows 95 with Windows 95 protected-mode drivers (primarily Microsoft and Novell networks), you may have a conflict between real- and protected-mode drivers. Make sure the appropriate client software is installed by opening the

Figure 8-11.   Installing Direct Cable Connection

Network control panel. Then use Notepad to open your Autoexec.bat and Config.sys files, and remark out (put **rem** and a space on the left of the line) all real-mode network drivers (for a Microsoft or a Novell network with the Microsoft client you do not need any statements in your system files that load network drivers).

If the network you have is not supported in Windows 95 with Windows 95 protected-mode drivers, you have to load real-mode client drivers in your Autoexec.bat and/or Config.sys files. If it is an unsupported network, make sure to have the network fully installed and operating *before* starting Windows 95 Setup.

If you think that all of your networking software is correct, make sure that the resources are correctly assigned to your network adapter. Use the following steps to do that:

1. Click the Start button and choose Settings | Control Panel | System.

2. In the Device Manager tab, open Network adapters, select your adapter, and click Properties.

3. In the adapter's Properties dialog box, click the Resources tab, and check on the Interrupt (IRQ) and I/O Address Range, as you

can see in Figure 8-12. The settings you see should match what was set on your adapter card.

4. Make the necessary changes to the IRQ and I/O address and click OK twice.

❓ I'm able to share files from my computer, so why am I _not seen in my workgroup_?

It may be that you are not identified with the workgroup that you think you are. To check or change your workgroup identification, use the following steps:

1. Click the Start button and select Settings | Control Panel | Network.

2. Click the Identification tab and make sure the Computer Name, Workgroup, and Computer Description are correct.

3. Click OK and follow the prompts to reboot.

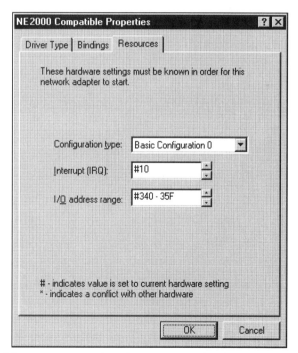

Figure 8-12.   The resource settings in your network adapter's Properties dialog box must match those physically made on the card itself

? I am trying to _run an application from my Novell server_, and I am receiving an error message: "Incorrect MS-DOS version." Why is this happening?

This occurs because either (or both) NetWare or the application were created before Windows 95 (MS-DOS version 7.0), and when they see MS-DOS version 7.0 they mistakenly believe that they can't use it. If you are using NetWare login scripts, you can have a script refer to a variable OSVersion to map a specific NetWare server according to the version of operating system the workstation is running. You will have to update the procedure to have MS-DOS version 7.0 recognized.

You might also have to modify the SETVER table to have the correct version reported to the program.

? What can I do if _Setup does not recognize my network adapter_?

If your network adapter was not identified or installed during Windows 95 Setup, you can, as a first step, run the Add New Hardware Wizard. To do this:

1. Click the Start button and choose Settings | Control Panel | Add New Hardware. To begin, click Next.

2. Allow Windows to detect the hardware and click Next. Click Next again to initiate the search. Chances are that the search will find the adapter card.

   However, if the search again ignores the card, you can manually install it by continuing with these steps:

3. Choose Next | Network Adapters | Next.

4. Select the manufacturer and model of your card from the lists, and click OK.

5. If the card is not listed, click Have Disk, insert the disk that came with your card, make sure the drive letter is correct, and click OK.

6. If you don't have a disk with an Oemsetup.inf file, you will have to quit Add New Hardware and load the drivers through your Autoexec.bat file by following the instructions that came with the card. Having done that, open the Network control panel Configuration tab and select Add | Adapter | Add. This time,

select the Existing ODI Driver from the Network Adapters list, as shown in Figure 8-13, and click OK.

 ## Can I _set up my PC to act as a server to answer calls through Dial-Up Networking_?

To enable Dial-Up Networking to act as a server, you need Microsoft Plus! If you have it, follow these steps:

1. Double-click My Computer and then double-click Dial-Up Networking.

2. Open the Connections menu and click Dial-Up Server. The Dial-Up Server dialog box will open.

3. Click Allow Caller Access and click OK. Your computer can now serve as a dial-up server.

If you don't have Microsoft Plus!, you only use Dial-Up Networking as a client to call out to external servers.

Tip   _You can see if someone is using your dial-up server in the Status box of the Dial-Up Server dialog box._

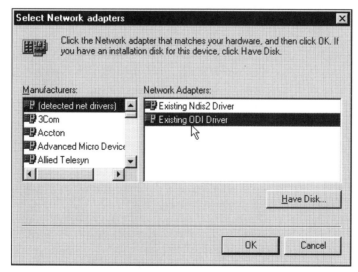

Figure 8-13.   Use the Existing ODI Driver as the network adapter when you load the driver for the adapter in your Autoexec.bat file

I am _using both Microsoft's Client for NetWare Networks and their Client for Windows Networks_. How do I write logon scripts?

Logon scripts run when you log on to either a NetWare or Windows NT Server. If you have supervisor's or administrator's privileges on the servers, you can, in NetWare, type **syscon** and either create or edit logon scripts, or use User Management on the NT Server.

SECURITY CONSIDERATIONS

 What is the _difference between the levels of security—_ share level and user level?

Share-level access is password oriented. With it, a password can be attached to a computer, a printer, or a folder, and anybody on the network who knows the password can have access to the shared resource.

User-level access is user oriented. With it, a security provider is specified, such as an NT domain or a NetWare server. This security provider supplies a list of users from which certain users can be specified for access to the shared resource as well as levels of access (read only, full access, or custom).

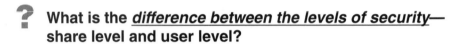

Tip   *User-level security is available only when you are attached to a NetWare or Windows NT Server. In peer-to-peer networking you can only use share-level access.*

 How do I _grant access to others to use my computer's resources_?

To allow others to use your computer's resources, do the following:

1. Open Explorer and select the resource you want to share (disk, printer, folder, or CD-ROM drive).

2. Right-click it and choose Sharing.

3. Select the type of access you want to grant, and type the password if necessary.

If you want others on remote computers to be able to administer your resources, follow these steps:

1. Click the Start button and choose Settings | Control Panel | Passwords.

2. On the Remote Administration tab, click Enable Remote Administration Of This Server, as shown in Figure 8-14.

3. If you are using password-level security, fill in the password, and then confirm it. If you are using user-level security, click Add, and select a person or group from the list on the left.

4. Click Add.

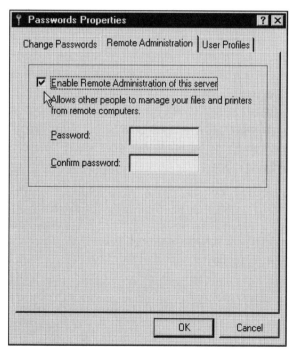

Figure 8-14.   You can enable a remote site to manage your computer's resources

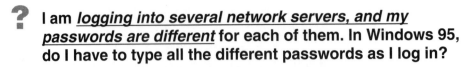

I am _logging into several network servers, and my passwords are different_ for each of them. In Windows 95, do I have to type all the different passwords as I log in?

No. When you log into Windows 95 and its various facilities for the first time after setup, you will be prompted for passwords. You will have an option to save the passwords for future use. If you choose to do this, Windows 95 will store the passwords in the *password cache*. Next time you start Windows 95, you will be prompted only for your primary password. The correct password will unlock the password cache, and you will be connected to all your servers without having to type additional passwords.

My _Net Watcher shows that there is a user connected_ to my machine, but it shows no information about which file is opened from the remote machine. Why?

Some Windows applications do not keep files open. They are designed that way to save file handles. For example, applications like Notepad and WordPad open a file, load it into memory, and then close it. When there is a need to write back to the file, the application will open it again.

I am _not connected to a network on my computer at home; however, it always come up with the "Enter network password" screen when I start Windows_. Why does this happen?

You probably have a network logon selected as your primary logon. To eliminate this, follow these steps:

1. Click the Start button and choose Settings | Control Panel | Network.

2. Under Primary Network Logon, choose Windows Logon, as shown here:

3. Restart Windows. You will no longer be prompted for a network password.

? **I had a _RESTRICTIONS section in the Progman.ini file_ to impose certain restrictions for the users on my network. Do I have to recreate the restrictions, and how do I do that?**

When you install Windows 95 on top of the existing Windows files, a program Grpconv.exe is automatically run. It converts the Windows 3.*x* program groups into Windows 95 folders. All data in the RESTRICTIONS section of the Progman.ini is migrated into the Policies section of the Registry.

If you installed Windows 95 into a different folder, you can convert the groups into folders by using the grpconv /m command (see Chapter 4 for further details). This will also migrate the restrictions.

? **How do I _share a folder_ with another user?**

Open Explorer and find the folder to be shared. Then do the following:

1. Right-click the folder and click Sharing.

2. Choose Shared As and other options will become available, as shown in Figure 8-15.

3. Fill in the Share Name and Comment text boxes, and specify the Access Type: Read-Only, Full (read and write), or Depends On Password. Select whether you want a Read-Only Password, or Full Access Password. Then fill in the Password if needed.

4. Click OK.

USING A NETWORK

? **I often access a network drive. Can't I _define that network drive as a drive on my computer_?**

Yes. This is called *mapping* a network drive. Follow these steps to map a network drive:

1. From Explorer, click the Map Network Drive icon (shown here), or select it from the Tools menu.

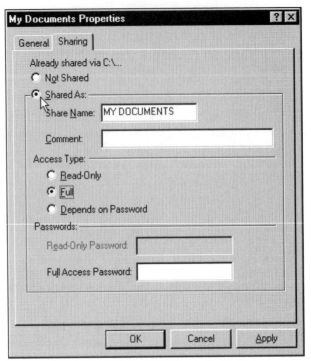

Figure 8-15.   Changing a file or folder to be shared is done from the Properties dialog box

2. In the Map Network Drive dialog box, click the Drive down arrow to find the drive to be mapped. Click it.

3. Using the format *computer**drivename*, enter the path to be mapped to it.

4. Click OK.

Now the network drive will appear not only in the Explorer and My Computer windows, but also in the File Open dialog boxes of all your applications, where you can open it and have immediate access to all the shared files. In Figure 8-16, drives E through H are mapped network drives.

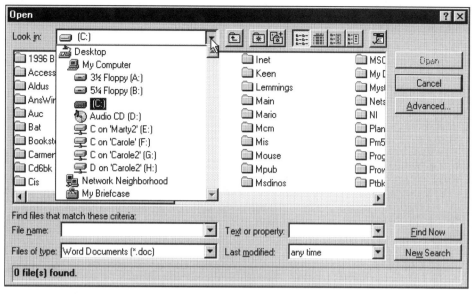

Figure 8-16.   Once you have mapped a network drive to your computer, you can access that drive from within your applications

? Do I have to have a *disk or folder on my server mapped to a drive letter* if I want to access this folder?

No. Windows 95 supports UNC (Universal Naming Conventions), so you don't have to have a drive letter explicitly assigned to a network resource to use it. (You have to have appropriate rights to that resource, of course.) You can, for example, create a shortcut to a network folder right on your desktop. Let's say you want to have a shortcut to a folder WinApps on the volume Drive C on the server Rock. Then use the following steps:

1. Open Network Neighborhood, double-click the Rock server, double-click the Drive C volume, and then right-click the WinApps folder.

2. Choose Create Shortcut. This will create a shortcut to the WinApps folder. You can drag it to your desktop or into another folder in My Computer.

Tip   *If you want to access a network drive or folder from within 16-bit or especially DOS applications, you will need to map the network resource to a drive letter on your machine.*

At work I have an *icon on my desktop called Network Neighborhood, and at home I don't have this icon*. Why?

The Network Neighborhood icon will only appear when you have a network installed. If you are on a stand-alone PC, you will not see the icon on your desktop.

When I have several users accessing one of my shared drives, how can I *improve the performance so that my computer will give priority to shared files*?

The following steps will give priority to shared files:

1. Click the Start button and select Settings | Control Panel.

2. Double-click System and select the Performance tab.

3. In Advanced Settings, click File System.

4. Select the Hard Disk tab, click the down arrow in the Settings box, and select Network Server as shown here:

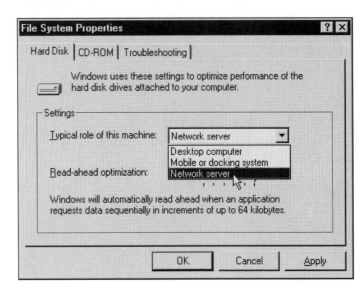

5. Respond to the prompts to reboot.

? **I cannot *load both file and printer sharing for NetWare Networks and file and printer sharing for Microsoft Networks at the same time*. I need to work with both Novell and Microsoft networks. What can I do about this?**

Your Windows 95 machine can only act as one type of server—either the Novell or Microsoft Network server—at a time. You cannot do both simultaneously. You can have multiple clients loaded on the same machine, though. If you have file and printer sharing for Microsoft networks loaded, you can also load Client for NetWare Networks and access your Novell servers.

? **How can I *locate a computer without going through Network Neighborhood or searching through My Computer or Explorer* when I know right where I want to go?**

Rather than use one of the file management programs, use the Find command:

1. Click the Start button and choose Find | Computer.

2. Type in the computer name. You can use wildcards.

3. Click Find Now.

Another trick is to use the Run option. Use the following steps to locate a folder when you know where it is located:

1. Click the Start button and choose Run.

2. Type in the complete path in the form *computername**drive*\ *folder*. For example, the Run command shown next will open the folder window you see in Figure 8-17.

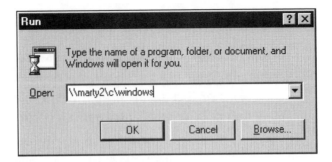

You can also just use the computer name by itself. If you're
looking for a computer, this is a lot faster.

❓ I am only connected to a network occasionally. How can I _prevent Windows 95 from attempting to reestablish the connection if I am not on the net_?

When you are restarting Windows 95, select Cancel at the Network
Password box. This will prevent Windows from reestablishing

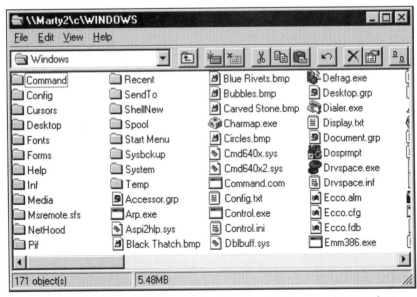

Figure 8-17.   Using Run to find a remote drive and folder can give you fast access

connections. If you are using a Microsoft Network, you have a more elegant way of doing this with these steps:

1. Right-click Network Neighborhood and choose Properties.

2. Select Client For Microsoft Networks, click Properties, and select Quick Logon, as shown in Figure 8-18.

This will allow you to get into Windows without reestablishing connections. The connections will be established only when you need to utilize the network resource, for example, to start a program that resides on the network.

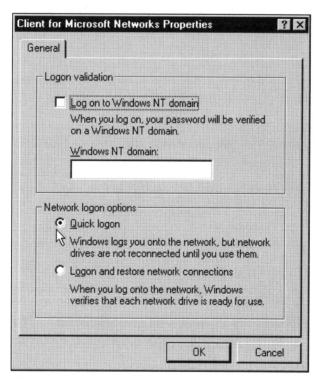

Figure 8-18.   You can bypass the network logon until you want to use a network

? I used the Direct Cable Connection option to get my two computers to talk to each other. The Network Neighborhood icon is now a permanent part of my desktop. How can I *remove the icon from my desktop without disconnecting the direct connect capabilities*?

You can hide the Network Neighborhood icon using System Policy Editor on the Windows 95 installation CD-ROM. Use the following steps to hide the Network Neighborhood:

1. Load your Windows 95 CD and close the Autorun screen.

2. Using Explorer, locate the System Policy Editor in \Admin\Apptools\Poledit\ on the CD.

3. Run the Policy Editor by double-clicking Poledit.exe, open the File menu, and choose Open Registry.

4. Double-click Local User.

5. Open the folders as follows: Local User | Shell | Restrictions.

6. Under Shell Restrictions, click Hide Network Neighborhood so that it has a check mark.

7. Click OK and close the System Policy Editor.

? How can I *run an application from a network drive*?

You can map a network drive to a drive letter on your computer, open that drive in My Computer, locate the application, and run it. You can also create a shortcut to the application and put it on your desktop, on your Start menu, or in a program group in the Programs menu.

? I am running Windows 95 and Novell NetWare on my Windows 95 workstation. How can I *run NetWare system utilities Syscon, Pconsole, and Fconsole*?

To run these utilities, you can go to the DOS prompt, change to the appropriate drive, and type the command. If you will be using these utilities a lot, you can create shortcuts to them. To do this:

1. Right-click the desktop.

2. Choose New and click Shortcut.

3. In the Create Shortcut dialog box, type the full path and the filename of the command and click Next. If you cannot remember what the path and filename are, you can click Browse to find them.

Can I *search for files on a network drive*?

Yes. Use the following steps to search for files on network drives:

1. Click the Start button and choose Find | Files Or Folders.

2. Type the filename you are searching for in the Named box.

3. Type the mapped drive letter and optionally a folder (*drive**folder*) or the UNC path (*computername**drive**folder*) in the Look In box.

4. Click Find Now.

Tip   *You can also look for network files in Network Neighborhood, Explorer, or My Computer.*

Why can't I *see other computers on my network*?

There can be many reasons for this. In essence this is telling you that you are not connected to the network. Here are some things to check in a peer-to-peer network.

⇨ Check the integrity of the cables connecting the computers in the network. This can be done by disconnecting two or three computers from the rest of the network and getting those computers to "talk" to each other, then slowly adding more computers until all the rest of the network is checked out and attached. For each group that you are checking, make sure the cables are properly connected on both ends, are not broken or loosely connected, and that there is activity in the adapter lights in the back of the networking card on the computer you are checking out.

⇨ If you are using thin coax cable (also called thin Ethernet or 10Base-2), make sure you have a grounding resistor properly connected on either end of the network. On *one* end the resistor should have a chain that is connected to the computer case, but the other end should not be connected to the case.

⇨ If you are using RJ-45 twisted-pair "phone" cable (also called "copper pairs" or 10Base-T), make sure the hub to which the computers are connected is itself properly connected, is plugged in, and is working. A quick way to do this is to switch hubs.

⇨ Make sure all computers on the network are using the same protocol. To do this, click the Start button and select Settings | Control Panel | Network. In the Configuration tab, select the network adapter in the list of network components, click Properties, and then in the Bindings tab, ensure that the adapter is bound to the same protocols, as you can see here:

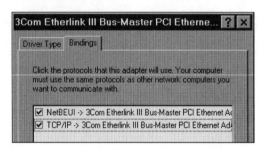

⇨ Make sure the network adapter board is not in conflict with other hardware and that the settings in Windows 95 match those set on the board. To do this, click the Start button and select Settings | Control Panel | System. In the System Properties dialog box, click the Device Manager tab, select your network adapter, and click Properties. Then select the Resources tab and compare the IRQ, I/O port address, and possibly the DMA channel with how the board is actually configured. Make sure you get a "No conflicts" message to show that the board, as shown in Figure 8-19, does not conflict with other hardware.

How do you *start Windows 95 when the network is not running*? It will boot fine when the network is running.

When your computer is set up for client-server networking, it may not start up properly when it is not connected to a network or the network is not up and running. Windows may suggest starting in Safe mode. To restore the normal startup when you are not connected to the network, use the following steps:

1. Go ahead and start in Safe Mode without networking.

2. Click the Start button and select Settings | Control Panel | Network.

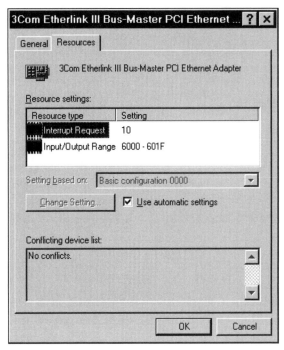

Figure 8-19.   Checking the resource settings and conflict status of a network

3. In the Configuration tab, change your Primary Network Logon from Client For Microsoft Networks (or Client For NetWare Networks) to Windows Logon, as shown in Figure 8-20.

4. Click OK to save your changes and reboot.

This will reboot your computer normally without forcing you to connect to the network. The Windows Logon option is useful not only when the network is not operating, but also when you have a portable computer that is connected to the network only some of the time.

NETWORK PRINTING

My _network printer won't work_. How can I troubleshoot the problem?

There are several factors that have an impact on correctly networking printers. Check the following items:

⇨ In the Network control panel, click File and Print Sharing. Are both of the check boxes checked? If not, check them, click OK, and try your printer.

⇨ Check to see that the shared printer is identified as being shared on its local computer (does its icon have a hand beneath it?). From the Printers folder, right-click the printer and choose Sharing from the pop-up menu. Is the printer Share Name the same as the one on the other computer as found in the next step?

⇨ In the Printers folder on the client machine, right-click the printer and select Properties from the pop-up menu. In the Details tab, check to see that the printer's name in the Print To The Following Port text box is the same as that found in the previous step.

⇨ In the Printers folder, Properties dialog box, Details tab on the client machine, click Capture Printer Port, and select a port other than the LPT1 that the local printer is probably using.

⇨ When you access the printer, be sure to use the port address and not the shared name.

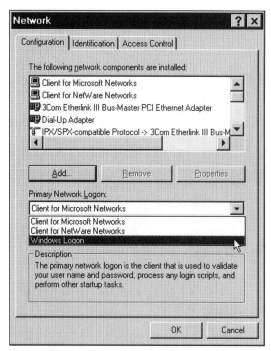

Figure 8-20.   Changing the setting that forces the connection to the network

ADMINISTERING AND MONITORING NETWORKS

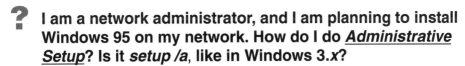 **I am a network administrator, and I am planning to install Windows 95 on my network. How do I do _Administrative Setup_? Is it _setup /a_, like in Windows 3._x_?**

No. In Windows 95, there are many tools for assisting an administrator in setting up Windows 95 throughout his or her network. First, Administrative Setup has been replaced with Server Based Setup, which is a separate program called Netsetup.exe. It is located on the Windows 95 CD-ROM in the \Admin\Nettools\ Netsetup\ folder. (Before running Netsetup, you _must have installed Windows 95;_ you can start Netsetup only from that operating system.) You use Netsetup to create and manage configuration information for each computer in the network. While still using Netsetup, this configuration information is used to create batch files or scripts that will automatically set up Windows 95 on each client workstation. Figure 8-21 shows Netsetup's primary dialog box and the tasks that program performs. Once the batch files are created, you can then set up each workstation by running Setup with the batch file as an argument (**setup msbatch.inf**). See the text files in \Admin\Nettools\ Netsetup\ as well as Chapter 4 of the Windows 95 Resource Kit, or the Resource Kit's Help file on the Windows 95 CD-ROM under \Admin\Reskit\Helpfile\. Also, the CD has sample scripts in \Admin\Reskit\Samples\Scripts\.

How can I have _different users log on to the same PC_?

Not only can you have different users log on to the same computer, but each user can retain a unique configuration. Each user can have different access to the computer's resources, determined by the password used to log on to the computer. To enable this option:

1. Click the Start button and choose Settings | Control Panel | Passwords, and click the User Profiles tab.

2. Select the option Users Can Customize Their Preferences And Desktop Settings, as shown in Figure 8-22.

Now when the computer is booted, Windows 95 will ask for the configuration to be loaded and a password to validate it. Each

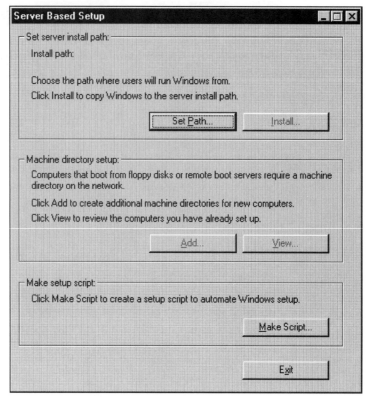

Figure 8-21. Server Based Setup is used to set up diskless and floppy-based
workstations

computer configuration will have its own desktop settings, hardware
configurations, Start menu contents, and shortcuts.

❓ How can I *monitor access to my resources on the peer-to-peer network*?

You can monitor the use of your computer by others with Net
Watcher. You have to have Client for Microsoft Networks installed,
and the file and print sharing options for the network must be
enabled. You also have to have Net Watcher installed. If you don't,
use the following steps to do that:

1. Click the Start button and choose Settings | Control Panel |
   Add/Remove Programs, and click the Windows Setup tab.

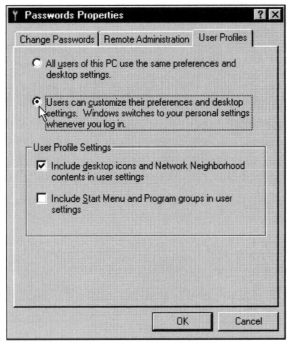

Figure 8-22.   The Passwords Properties dialog box allows you to enable customized configurations for multiple users of one computer

2. Select Accessories | Details and select Net Watcher from the list.

3. Click OK and Finish.

   To start Net Watcher:

1. Click the Start button and choose Programs | Accessories | System Tools | Net Watcher.

2. Open the View menu and click by Connections. In the Net Watcher window, you'll see two panes. On the left are the names of all users currently connected to your PC.

3. Click any user and you will see the full list of resources they are using on the right, as seen in Figure 8-23.

   You can view the network by user, by shared folders, or by shared files using either the View menu or the three tools on the right in the toolbar.

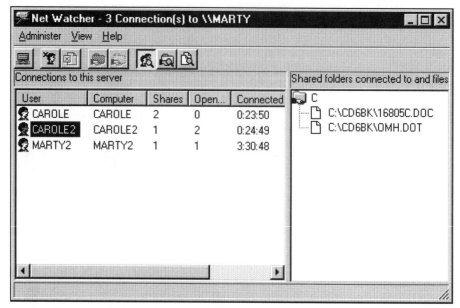

Figure 8-23. Using Net Watcher, you can monitor the users accessing your computer's resources

? How can I *monitor network activity through my Windows 95 PC*?

Windows 95 gives you several useful network monitoring tools. One of them is Net Watcher, discussed in the previous question about monitoring access to resources on the peer-to-peer network. Another is the System Monitor. This application will allow you to monitor the amount of CPU resources used by local applications and by servicing remote requests of other users. If you don't have the System Monitor installed, do it now with these steps:

1. Click the Start button and choose Settings | Control Panel | Add/Remove Programs.

2. Click the Windows Setup tab, select Accessories | Details, and select System Monitor from the list.

3. Click OK twice.

To start and use the System Monitor:

1. Click the Start button and choose Programs | Accessories | System Tools | System Monitor. The System Monitor window will be displayed as shown in Figure 8-24.

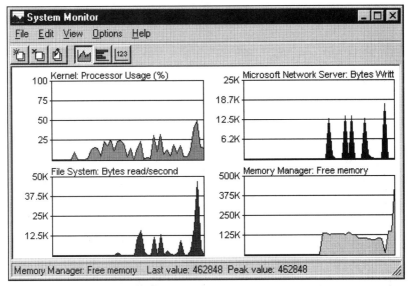

Figure 8-24.   System Monitor allows you to monitor the system resources used on your computer

2. Select the resources to be monitored by clicking the Edit or Add icon, or by selecting that option from the Edit menu.

3. Select from choices of viewing the data as a Line Chart, Bar Chart, or Numeric display. You can either click one of the icons in the toolbar, or select the display option from the View menu.

How do I *set up individual accounts and restrict portions of the system* to my users?

After installation, you can use the System Policy Editor to restrict a user's access to some or all of the features of Windows 95. To utilize the System Policy Editor, follow these steps:

1. On the Administrator's PC, install the System Policy Editor from the \Admin\Apptools\Poledit\ folder on the Windows 95 CD.

2. Open the File menu and choose New File. The Default User and Default Computer icons will appear.

3. Double-click first the Default User and then the Default Computer icon, and edit the policy lists. This will establish a standard or default set of system policies, so that when you go to each machine, all you need to do is enter the exceptions.

4. Once you have created the default policies, open the Edit menu and choose Add User for each user, Add Computer for each computer, and Add Group for each group. For each one you create, make the policy changes for the exceptions.

5. When you are done with the policies, make sure the specific user, computer, and group policies are stored in the NetLogon directory of a Windows NT server, or in the Public directory of a NetWare server. With the policies in these directories, Windows 95 in the remote clients will automatically download the policies during network logon and update the local Registry with the policies.

6. In lieu of or in addition to establishing policies on the server, you can use the System Policy Editor's File menu Connect command to connect to a remote computer and edit that computer's Registry files (User.dat and System.dat). This will establish a set of policies for that one computer.

 Tip   *To set policies on remote computers, you must have administrative privileges for the remote computer, and in that case and when policies are downloaded at logon, the computer must be on a network with both user-level access and Remote Registry enabled.*

PROTOCOLS

I'm using both _TCP/IP- and IPX/SPX-compatible protocols on my networked computer_ in my office, as well as through dial-up networking at home. In the office I get the IPX/SPX-compatible login dialog box immediately after booting. At home this box does not appear because I don't connect at boot time. How can I get this login dialog box? I would like to have one single action that produces the same NetWare access in both my office and my home. Can I invoke the login procedure by running a program?

There is a way to process the login script while in Windows. What you have to do is make sure that you attach to the server first. Use these steps to do this:

1. Go to Network Neighborhood and double-click the NetWare drive on the server you want to connect to. This will prompt you to log in. However, the system login script will not process.

2. After you attach to the network drive, open a DOS window and type the following: **NWLSPROC/SERVER.** *SERVER* is your server name. For example, if my server is NWSERVER1, the command will be NWLSPROC/NWSERVER1. (Make sure to enter the server name in uppercase. If you enter it in lowercase, it will not work.) This will force the script to run. You can make a shortcut to this on your desktop for use whenever you want.

❓ Can I *use the IPX/SPX-compatible protocol to access a Windows NT server*?

Yes, do the following:

1. Right-click Network Neighborhood and choose Properties.

2. Select the IPX/SPX-compatible protocol, click Properties, and click the NetBIOS tab.

3. Select I Want To Enable NetBIOS Over IPX/SPX, as seen here:

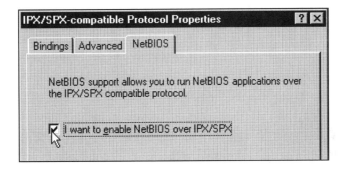

This will allow you to access Windows NT servers with IPS/SPX.

4. Click OK.

❓ Which network protocol should I use with my network?

A *network protocol* is equivalent to a human language; it is the coding scheme used to communicate over a network. Different networks require different protocols. Here are the general rules of thumb:

⇨ Use NetBEUI with Microsoft and IBM networks including Windows 95, Windows NT, Windows for Workgroups, and LAN Manager networks.

⇨ Use IPX/SPX with all Novell networks.

⇨ Use TCP/IP with dial-up networking to the Internet or when communicating on an intranet.

chapter

9 **Answers!**

Communications

Answer Topics!

Communications @ a Glance

While *networking* is connecting computers within a single facility or several closely located facilities, *communications* is connecting computers at remote facilities—anywhere in the world. Communications is primarily conducted over telephone lines connected to modems in the computers at either end. It consists of e-mail, faxes, bulletin boards, the Internet, information services such as CompuServe or Microsoft Network, and the simple transferring of files or information from one remote computer to another. Communications and networking do overlap. You can send e-mail via a network and use communications facilities (modems and phone lines) to do dial-up networking. Windows 95 provides a full complement of communications support, including handling your modem and providing the software for e-mail, faxes, transferring files, connecting to information services and the Internet, and doing dial-up networking.

Here are the areas that contain the most commonly asked questions about communications:

⇨ **Setting Up a Modem** deals with problems with modems that may arise during and after setup. Configuring it properly is a priority subject.

⇨ **Microsoft Network** addresses what Microsoft Network is and how you get started with it, including getting an e-mail address.

⇨ **Microsoft Exchange** answers several questions dealing with setting up and using Microsoft Exchange and its address book component.

267

OSR 2

In OSR 2, Microsoft Exchange is called "Windows Messaging." In this book, we refer to it as Microsoft Exchange, as in Windows 95.

⇨ **Faxing** answers questions on configuring and then using your fax.

⇨ **HyperTerminal** addresses what HyperTerminal is and how you can deal with several problems that can arise in setting it up properly.

⇨ **Phone Dialer** covers questions about how you start the Phone Dialer and use it in the most efficient manner.

SETTING UP A MODEM

? I *cannot dial or connect with my modem*. Why?

There could be several reasons for this. Here are some tips for troubleshooting your modem problems:

⇨ Make sure the modem is set up properly. You should be using Windows 95 drivers, not Windows 3.*x*, which might be incompatible. Open the Control Panel and run the Add New Hardware Wizard to automatically detect the existing modem and load the correct Windows 95 drivers.

⇨ After the modem is installed, verify that your modem is correctly configured with these steps:

1. Click the Start button and choose Settings | Control Panel | Modems.

2. On the General tab, verify that the manufacturer and model for your modem are correct, as shown in Figure 9-1. If not, click Add and use the Install New Modem Wizard. If your modem is not on the list, try the Standard Modem Types and pick the speed of your modem. Make sure to remove any other modem listed as installed.

3. Verify that the modem is enabled. Open the System control panel. In the Device Manager tab, open Modem, select your modem, and click Properties. Make sure that the Device status is "This device is working properly."

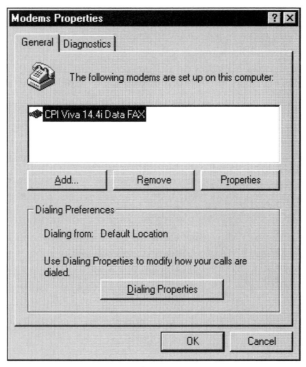

Figure 9-1.   The Modems Properties General tab shows the modems that are installed

4. Verify the port while still in the modem's Properties dialog box by clicking the Modem tab; also verify that the port listed is correct (for example, COM2). If not, select the correct port by clicking the Port down arrow and selecting the port you want. Then click OK.

5. Verify the serial port I/O address and IRQ from the System Properties Device Manager as follows: open Ports, choose the specific port for your modem, choose Properties, and then click the Resources tab. Check the Conflicting Device list on the bottom of the dialog box to see if the modem is using resources in conflict with other devices. If it is, select Change Settings (you may need to remove the check mark from Use Automatic Settings first), and then select a configuration that does not have resource conflicts. For example, if you have a serial mouse or other device on COM1, you cannot use a modem on COM3, because COM1 and COM3 ports use the

same IRQ. The same IRQ addressing applies to COM2 and COM4. Click OK twice to return to the Control Panel.

6. Verify the port settings:

⇨ From the Control Panel, double-click Modems.

⇨ Select your modem, click Properties, and click the Connection tab to check the current port settings, such as data bits, stop bits, and parity.

⇨ Click Advanced to check Error Control and Flow Control. If you are using a Windows 3.*x* communications program, turn off these advanced features. Click OK.

⇨ Now click the Port Settings button to verify the universal asynchronous receiver-transmitter (UART) type. Data transmission problems may occur on a slower 80386-based computer not equipped with a 16550 UART with a baud rate greater than 9600, or when multitasking during a file download. Try lowering the Transmit and Receiver buffers, click OK three times to return to the Control Panel, and then close it.

If you are still unable to connect, use the Troubleshooter for modem problems in Windows Help. Use the following instructions to open the Troubleshooter:

1. Click the Start button and choose Help | Contents tab | Troubleshooting.

2. Choose "If you have trouble using your modem." The window shown in Figure 9-2 will open. Click the appropriate buttons to follow the problem-solving guide.

? **During setup, I _let Windows pick my modem, and it didn't select the correct one_. What can I do about this?**

The modem automatically detected by Windows depends on the chip set and the type of modem. If you are having problems with the type of modem Windows has picked for you, you can manually choose your modem if it is on the list in Windows 95 (there are hundreds), or select a generic modem driver that will allow you to go online. To manually install a modem, follow these steps:

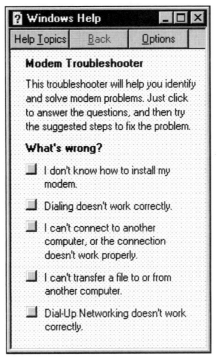

Figure 9-2.   Windows Help can troubleshoot your modem problems

1. Click the Start button and choose Settings | Control Panel | Modems.

2. Click Remove to clear the current installed modem from the system.

3. Click Add to start the Install New Modem Wizard.

4. Click Don't Detect My Modem; I Will Select It From A List and click Next.

5. From the list of Manufacturers, select the manufacturer, and then select your modem model from the Models list. If you don't see your modem, try the same manufacturer and speed if not the exact model. If you don't see your manufacturer, select Standard Modem Types, and from the Models list, select one with the bps modem speed equal to yours, as shown in Figure 9-3. Click Next.

6. Select the port to use with the modem. It is typically COM2 or COM4. Click Next and Windows will install the modem. You will be able to see it in the Modems Properties dialog box.

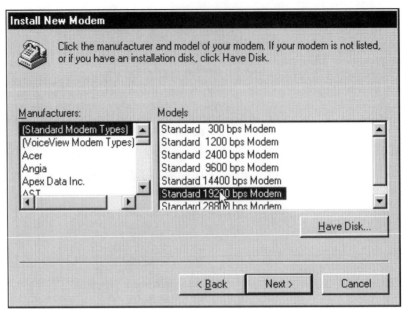

Figure 9-3.   You can choose a modem that is different than the one Windows
selects for you

    Tip   *If you have a 14.4 Kbps modem, you often can run it at 19.2 Kbps.*
If you are using one of the Standard Modem Types, try the 19.2 Kbps model
(Standard 19200 bps Modem) and see if it works.

? My *modem connection fails*! How can I find out what is going wrong?

One possibility is to look at the log file. Do the following to have a log
generated:

1. Click the Start button and select Settings I Control Panel I Modems.
2. From the Modems Properties dialog box, click Properties.
3. In the Modems Properties dialog box, click the Connection tab
   and click Advanced.

4. In the Advanced Connection Settings dialog box, click Record A Log File. This will create a file called Modemlog.txt when you initiate the modem connection.

To view the log, follow these steps:

1. From Explorer, locate the file \Windows\Modemlog.txt.

2. Double-click Modemlog.txt. The Notepad will open and display the log as you can see in Figure 9-4.

My *system freezes when I try to set up my modem*. What can I do about this?

Your problem may be one of conflicting port assignments or interrupt request lines (IRQs). Specifically, you may have either more than one serial device (for instance, your mouse and your modem) assigned to the same port, or an interrupt request line used by two devices. Your

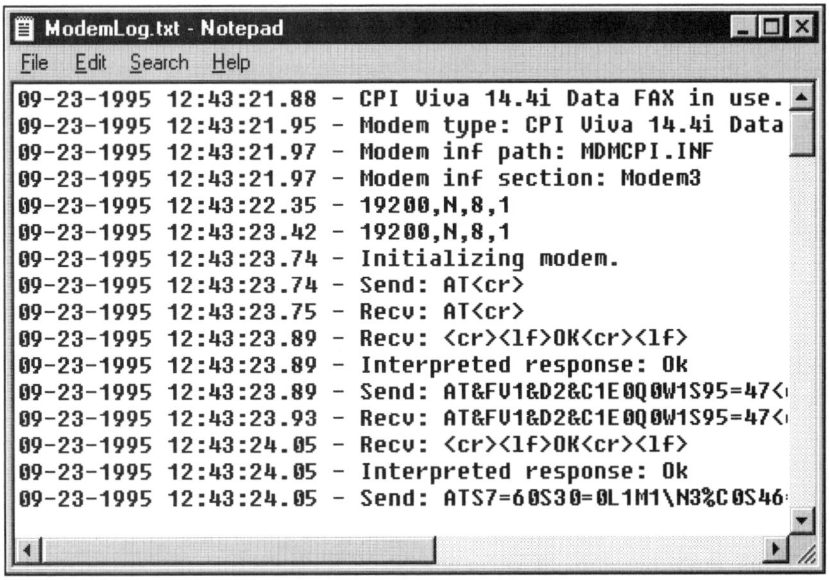

```
ModemLog.txt - Notepad                              _ □ X
File  Edit  Search  Help
09-23-1995 12:43:21.88 - CPI Viva 14.4i Data FAX in use. ▲
09-23-1995 12:43:21.95 - Modem type: CPI Viva 14.4i Data
09-23-1995 12:43:21.97 - Modem inf path: MDMCPI.INF
09-23-1995 12:43:21.97 - Modem inf section: Modem3
09-23-1995 12:43:22.35 - 19200,N,8,1
09-23-1995 12:43:23.42 - 19200,N,8,1
09-23-1995 12:43:23.74 - Initializing modem.
09-23-1995 12:43:23.74 - Send: AT<cr>
09-23-1995 12:43:23.75 - Recv: AT<cr>
09-23-1995 12:43:23.89 - Recv: <cr><lf>OK<cr><lf>
09-23-1995 12:43:23.89 - Interpreted response: Ok
09-23-1995 12:43:23.89 - Send: AT&FV1&D2&C1E0Q0W1S95=47<
09-23-1995 12:43:23.93 - Recv: AT&FV1&D2&C1E0Q0W1S95=47<
09-23-1995 12:43:24.05 - Recv: <cr><lf>OK<cr><lf>
09-23-1995 12:43:24.05 - Interpreted response: Ok
09-23-1995 12:43:24.05 - Send: ATS7=60S30=0L1M1\N3%C0S46
```

Figure 9-4.   Modemlog.txt displays what happened during a communications session

serial ports are COM1 through COM4; your mouse is usually assigned to COM1 or COM3; and your modem, to COM2 or COM4. Interrupt requests are usually assigned so that COM1 and COM3 use interrupt request line 4 (IRQ 4), and COM2 and COM4 use interrupt request line 3 (IRQ 3).

Plug-and-play devices help you avoid this problem, but if you have older equipment that is "hard wired," you will have to search out the problem. To check the use of your ports and IRQs, use the following steps:

1. Click the Start button and choose Settings | Control Panel | System.

2. Click the Device Manager tab. Here you can look at the IRQs assigned to your communications ports and see if there are any conflicts. You can do this in two ways: by looking at each port's properties, and by looking at all the ports in the Computer's properties. Do both of these to see the different information presented.

3. Double-click Ports to expand the list, select the Communications Port used for the modem (usually COM2), and click the Properties button.

4. In the Communications Port Properties dialog box, click the Resources tab, as seen in Figure 9-5. You will see Interrupt Request followed by a setting, usually 03. Also, at the bottom of the dialog box, see that it says "No conflicts." Close the Communications Port Properties dialog box.

5. From the Device Manager tab, click Computer in the list of devices. Then click Properties. In the View Resources tab, click Interrupt Request (IRQ). You'll see a list of ports and the interrupt requests assigned to them, like that shown in Figure 9-6. Here you can see that IRQ 3 is assigned to both COM2 and COM4, and IRQ 4 is assigned to COM1, all as expected. Close the Computer Properties and the System Properties dialog boxes. Next, check to see what is using the COM ports.

6. In the Control Panel, double-click Modems and click the Diagnostics tab to open the Modems Properties dialog box that

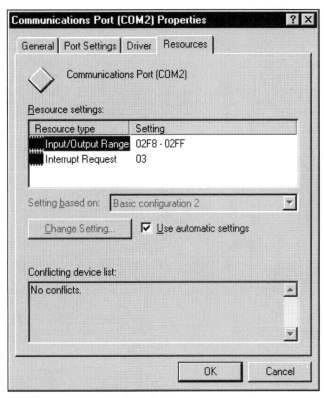

Figure 9-5.   Verify your modem's IRQ in the Communications Port Properties
dialog box

you see in Figure 9-7. Here you can see the assigned usage of each
COM port and make sure that your modem, mouse, and other
serial devices are all assigned to nonconflicting ports.

7. Click your modem port (COM2 in Figure 9-7) and then click
   More Info. You will see a message telling you that the system is
   communicating with the modem. Your modem is being tested.
   The results are then displayed, as you can see in Figure 9-8. If you
   see that the first several of the AT (attention) commands return
   OK, your modem is probably working. If some of the AT commands
   toward the end return ERROR, that simply means that your
   modem has not implemented that command.

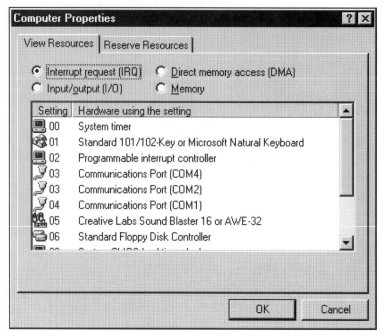

Figure 9-6.   The Computer Properties dialog box will show you all your IRQ assignments in one list

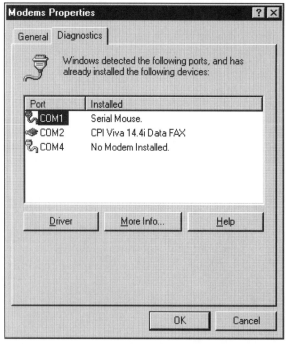

Figure 9-7.   The Modems Properties dialog box will show you what is assigned to each port

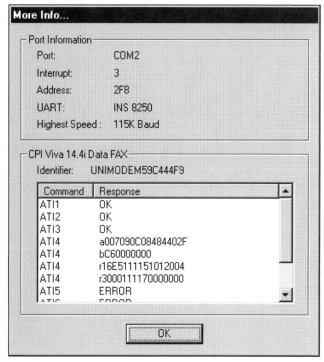

Figure 9-8.   Clicking on More Info tests your modem and then displays the results

8. If you do not see any response to the AT commands, then it is likely that your board is installed incorrectly and that some setting on the board needs to change. You or a technician needs to open your computer and look at the board.

9. Click OK twice to return to the Control Panel.

Setting Up Windows 95 Communications

As with networking, to utilize Windows 95 communications you'll need the necessary hardware and you'll need to set up the Windows 95 communications components you want to use. The Add New Hardware Wizard or Windows 95 Setup leads you through the installation of your modem, and Windows Setup or its subset in Add/Remove Programs provides for the installation of the software components. In any case, communications setup in Windows 95 is considerably easier than in earlier versions. Here are some tips on setting up Windows 95 communications.

Setting Up Windows 95 Communications, continued

The modem hardware that you need for communications can be an adapter card in your computer or an external box that connects to your computer through a serial port. In either case a phone cable will plug into the modem and into a normal RJ-11 jack in the wall connecting you to your phone company and the worldwide telecommunications network beyond it. You can have a dedicated phone line for modem communications, or you may share a phone line between voice and data, or even among voice, data, and fax. With the majority of modems, you can use a phone line for only one type of communication at a time. If, for example, you try to place a voice call while the modem is transmitting data, the data transmission will be interrupted and you'll have to restart it.

Many modems today can handle faxes as well as data. This means that you can send information from your computer to a remote fax machine. For example, if you have a letter that you prepared on your word processor, you can send it to a fax machine across the world with Windows 95 Microsoft Fax.

If your modem or fax/modem is connected to or installed in your computer when you install Windows 95, in many cases Setup will detect your modem and properly set up Windows 95 to use it.

If you install a plug-and-play modem after installing Windows 95, your system will automatically be set up to use the modem. In other circumstances you will need to manually set up your modem. You can do this by clicking the Start button and selecting Settings | Control Panel | Add New Hardware. You'll be guided through the modem installation.

With a modem installed, you can use the following Windows 95 communications tools without having to respecify your modem's characteristics:

⇨ **Dial-Up Networking** connects you as a client to a remote network server and allows the use of all the normal networking resources including file access and transfer, printing, and e-mail. Dial-Up Networking, also called remote access or "razz," is the principal way that you connect to the Internet with Windows 95.

> ### *Setting Up Windows 95 Communications, continued*
>
> ⇨ **HyperTerminal**, which is a full-featured communications package, connects you to a remote computer so that you may send or receive files, or access an information service or a bulletin board.
>
> ⇨ **Microsoft Exchange**, Windows 95's messaging center, allows you to send and receive e-mail and fax messages in one location. You also may access the mail facilities of information services such as CompuServe, Microsoft Network, or Internet mail.
>
> ⇨ **Microsoft Network** is Microsoft's information service. It provides a multitude of services, such as bulletin boards, chat sessions, forums, opportunities to buy products, and information on a wide variety of subjects, including computing, science, business, education, and many others. You can connect to and use the Internet from within Microsoft Network.
>
> ⇨ **Phone Dialer** is used to dial the phone for you so you can talk to someone. You can either enter the number to be dialed or select it from a phone book that Windows 95 will maintain.

MICROSOFT NETWORK

If I sign up on the Microsoft Network, how do I know my *e-mail address*?

Your Internet e-mail address on MSN is your *memberid@msn.com*, or within MSN, just *memberid*. Your *memberid* is the one you use to sign on to MSN.

What is and how can I use *MSN*?

The Microsoft Network (MSN) is both an information service that allows you to search and retrieve information that it provides, as well as an Internet service provider that gives you access to the Internet (see Chapter 10 for numerous questions on the Internet). To use MSN, you need a modem with a phone connection in addition to Windows 95. To set up and use MSN, follow these steps:

1. Double-click the Microsoft Network icon on the desktop.

2. If you have not already signed on, follow the prompts to sign up with Microsoft Network. After you are signed up, click Connect.

3. You may be able to click Getting On The Internet in the MSN Today window. Do that if you wish, or click Close to close the MSN Today window and open the main Microsoft Network screen.

4. If you went to Getting On The Internet, you can learn about Browsing The Web, Internet Newsgroups, and Internet E-mail by clicking those areas at the top of the screen, or you can download the web browser by clicking Upgrade Instructions. When you are done reading the Internet instructions and/or upgrading MSN for the web browser, click Close to return to MSN Today, and then click Close again to return to MSN Central.

5. In MSN Central, click Categories. Then click Internet Center. The Internet folders will be displayed as shown in Figure 9-9. You will see folders about getting on the Internet, the Internet Center, Netiquette, BBS offerings, File Libraries, Internet Newsgroups, World Wide Web access, and much more. If you click Internet Newsgroups and follow on down the chain, you'll move through a series of windows that gives you a more detailed definition of what you want to see until you get to a list of postings on a particular topic. If you double-click one of these postings, it will open for you to read.

6. When you are ready to return to MSN Central, click the house icon on the toolbar from wherever you are. If you are ready to leave MSN, click the broken wire icon to sign out and then click Yes to disconnect.

Note   *You can get free software on CD for a new MSN by accessing* ***http://promotions.msn.com/public/cdorder/cdorder.htm***. *If you sign up for the "old" MSN, you supposedly get a CD sent to you automatically two to four weeks after signing up.*

MICROSOFT EXCHANGE

OSR 2 *Note*   *In OSR 2, Microsoft Exchange is called "Windows Messaging." Here we refer to it as Microsoft Exchange.*

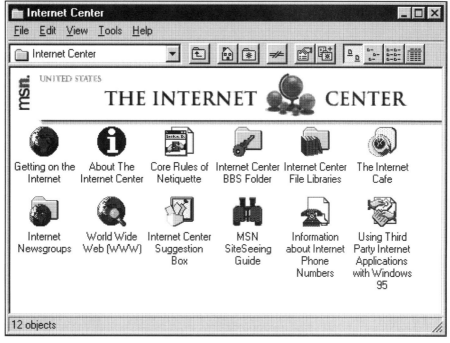

Figure 9-9.   MSN provides access to many Internet services

? How do I *install Microsoft Exchange after Windows Setup has been run*?

To install Microsoft Exchange after setting up Windows 95, use the following instructions:

1. Click the Start button and choose Settings | Control Panel | Add/Remove Programs.

2. Click the Windows Setup tab. A list of components appears.

3. Click the box next to the Microsoft Exchange icon, and then click the Details button.

OSR 2 *Note*   *In OSR 2, Windows Messaging contains three components: Internet Mail Services, Microsoft Mail Services, and Windows Messaging (which is equivalent to Microsoft Exchange). Check all three components if you are planning on using Internet for e-mail.*

4. In the Microsoft Exchange components list, both Microsoft Exchange and Microsoft Mail Services should be checked. Click OK to begin the setup (you'll need your Windows 95 Setup disk(s)). The Exchange Setup Wizard will prompt you through the configuration steps.

OSR 2 *Note*   *You will not need your CD in OSR 2 since the files are already on the disk.*

5. After the wizard is finished, shut down and restart Windows for the changes to take effect.

? How do I *install Microsoft Exchange while running Windows 95 Setup*?

The Custom option in Windows 95 Setup will allow you to install Microsoft Exchange. To accomplish that, follow these steps:

1. Place your Windows 95 first disk or CD in its drive, and start Setup in one of the ways described in Chapter 2. Follow the instructions on the screen. When you are asked in the Setup Options dialog box what type of Setup you prefer, choose Custom and click Next.

2. Continue to follow the onscreen instructions until the Get Connected dialog box, where you can select communications components, appears. At a minimum, click Microsoft Mail as shown in Figure 9-10, and select Microsoft Fax and The Microsoft Network if you wish. Click Next.

3. In the Select Components dialog box that appears next, Microsoft Exchange should already be checked. Click it and then on the Details button where Microsoft Exchange and Microsoft Mail Services should both be checked. Click OK and then continue with the setup by following the instructions on the screen.

4. At the end of setup, the wizards for configuring and adding Microsoft Mail and the other services you choose will guide you in configuring Microsoft Exchange on your computer.

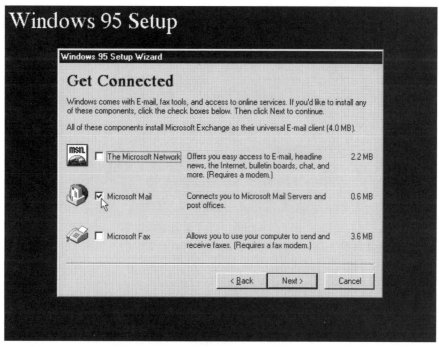

Figure 9-10.   Installing Microsoft Exchange occurs automatically if you install one of its services such as Mail or Fax

In Microsoft Exchange the _Outbox view on the column heading reads "From" and it should be "To."_ How can I change it back to "To"?

Follow these steps:

1. From the View menu, select Columns.

2. Select the From column on the right and click Remove. The "From" will be moved to the left.

3. Select the To field from the Available Columns list on the left and click Add. The "To" will be moved to the right.

4. Select the To column and click Move Up or Move Down until the column is where you want it placed. Figure 9-11 shows one possibility.

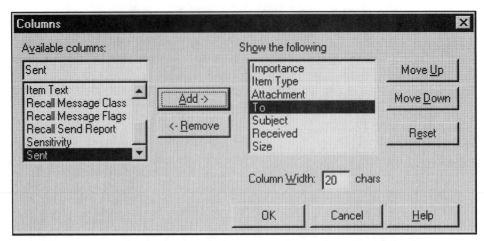

Figure 9-11.   The columns in the views can be changed or resequenced

> **5.** Click OK. The name of the column should be replaced.

 Tip   *If you want to return to the original view, click Reset.*

? How do I *specify the address book* I want to use in Microsoft Exchange?

Microsoft Exchange creates two address books when you install it: a Personal Address Book for all your personal messages and a Post Office Address list for your network, maintained by the post office administrator. You can select an address book from either the Tools menu in Microsoft Exchange or from the toolbar of a new electronic mail message. To select an address book:

1. Click the Start button and select Programs I Microsoft Exchange. (You can also click the Inbox icon on your desktop.)

2. Open the Tools menu and choose Address Book. The Address Book window is displayed as shown in Figure 9-12.

3. In the upper right of the Address Book dialog box, click the name of the address book you want to use in the Show Names From The list box. All the names from the address book you selected are listed.

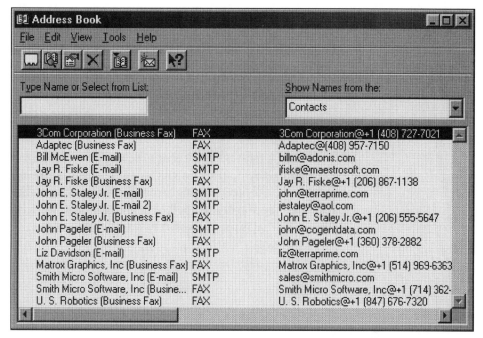

Figure 9-12. The Address Book in Microsoft Exchange provides phone numbers and street addresses as well as e-mail addresses

Tip   *You can choose which address book appears first on the list (and is therefore your default) by opening the Tools menu in Exchange, choosing Options, and clicking the Addressing tab. Then open the Show This Address List First drop-down list and choose which you want. When you're done, click OK.*

❓ How do I *use the Exchange's address book*?

Once you open an address book as described in the previous question, here are some tips on how you can use it:

⇨ To find a particular name in your address book, type the name or a sequence of letters beginning the name in the blank box on the left above the list. The name will be highlighted as you type. Press ENTER to open the entry.

⇨ To add a name to your address book, choose New Entry from the
    File menu, or click the New Entry button on the left of the toolbar.
    Select the type of address you want to enter, and then fill in the
    information.

⇨ To create a message to be sent to selected address(es), select the
    addressees by holding down CTRL while clicking them. Then
    either choose New Message from the File menu, or click the New
    Message button on the toolbar to create a new electronic mail
    message that is preaddressed to the selected people.

FAXING

How do I *attach a predefined cover page to a fax message*?

There are two ways to get predefined cover pages for your faxes.
Windows 95 has some predefined cover pages (Confidential, For Your
Information, Generic, and Urgent). You can choose among these when
you compose a fax from Microsoft Exchange.

Another predefined cover page can be one that you have created
in the Cover Page Editor and then saved. In this case, you can specify
that filename or browse for it when you are asked if you want a
cover page.

How do I *configure Microsoft Fax*?

Use the following steps to configure Microsoft Fax:

1. Click the Start button and choose Settings | Control Panel | Mail
   And Fax.

2. Click Show Profiles, choose a profile to which you want to add fax
   capabilities, and then click the Properties button or click Add to
   create a new profile with Fax in it.

3. In the Services tab, click the Add button to open the Add Service
   To Profile dialog box shown here:

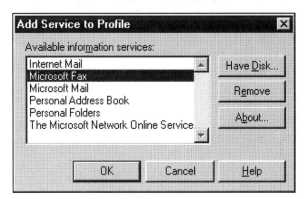

4. Click Microsoft Fax and then click OK. A message asks if you want
   to type your name, fax number, and fax modem now. Click Yes.

5. In the Microsoft Fax Properties dialog box, click the Message,
   Dialing, Modem, and User tabs to verify and enter the following
   information:

   ⇨ On the User tab, enter your fax number. Verify that the other
     information is valid. The information typed in the User tab
     automatically appears on the cover page.

   ⇨ On the Modem tab, the modem information will already be
     entered if your modem has already been installed. If you have
     not installed a modem or want to choose a different modem,
     click the Add button in the modem folder and launch the
     Modem Wizard.

   ⇨ Check the information on the Dialing and Message tabs to see
     if it meets your requirements.

6. Click OK and restart the Microsoft Exchange for the changes to
   take effect.

Tip   *Once you have set up Microsoft Fax, you can also change fax
properties from Microsoft Exchange. Open the Tools menu and from
Microsoft Fax Tools, choose Options.*

? **How do I _create a custom cover page for my faxes_?**

Use these steps to create a custom cover page:

1. Click the Start button and choose Programs | Accessories | Fax | Cover Page Editor.

2. Click OK to bypass the Cover Page Editor Tips.

3. Follow these tips to create your fax cover page:

    ⇨ From the Insert menu, click Recipient | Sender | Message. A submenu with options will be displayed. As you click each field, an edit box with the placeholder will be displayed, as shown in Figure 9-13. Drag each box where you want it on the cover page.

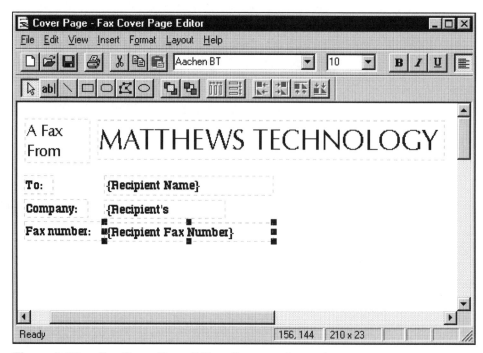

Figure 9-13.   Fax Cover Page Editor allows you to create your own cover page

⇨ If you want an object, such as a graphic for a logo, to be included, select Object from the Insert menu and then drag it where you want it.

⇨ To include your own unique text, click the Text icon. Your pointer will become a set of cross hairs. Drag it to form a rectangle that will contain the text. You can then type, highlight, and format your text with the font, size, and style you want.

⇨ To align objects, select them by dragging a marquee around them, and then select Align Objects from the Layout menu.

⇨ When you are finished, save the cover page by selecting File | Save As and putting it in your \Windows folder with the cover pages that come with Windows 95.

? How do I *create a shortcut to the Fax printer*?

You can place a shortcut to the fax printer on your desktop, drag a document to the shortcut icon, and have it automatically start the Compose New Fax Wizard without going through any menus. Follow the steps listed next to create a shortcut to a fax printer:

1. Click the Start button and choose Settings | Printers to display the currently installed printers.

2. Drag the Microsoft Fax printer icon to the desktop, and click Yes, you want to make a shortcut.

3. If you want to change the name, click the Fax Printer shortcut name and then click it again after a pause.

4. A selection box will surround the name, allowing you to change it. Press ENTER to finalize the name.

When you have a document you want to fax, simply drag it to the Fax icon on the desktop. The Compose New Fax Wizard will be loaded for you to address the document and send it.

? How do I *send a fax from Microsoft Exchange*?

Assuming that you have set up Exchange to send and receive faxes, use the following instructions to send a fax:

1. Open Microsoft Exchange by double-clicking the Inbox icon.

2. From the Compose menu, choose New Fax to launch the Compose New Fax Wizard.

3. Click the Address Book to select a fax recipient from that, or type the name and fax number. Click Next.

4. If you want a cover page, make sure "Yes. Send this one." is selected. Click the type of cover page you want: Confidential, For Your Information, Generic, or Urgent. For additional options, click the Options button. Click Next when you are through.

5. In the Compose New Fax dialog box, type the subject, press TAB, and then type a message. If you want the fax note to be on the cover page, select that option. Click Next.

6. To include a file with your message, type the path to the file, or click Add File and follow the prompts. Click Next.

7. To finish the fax and send it, click Finish.

Tip   *You can also send a fax from many applications by, in a sense, "printing" to the fax—you select Microsoft Fax as the printer you want to use, and the Compose New Fax Wizard will open and lead you through the process as described here.*

? How do I *send a fax using Windows Explorer*?

To use Explorer to send a fax, do the following:

1. Right-click My Computer and click Explore.

2. Locate and right-click the document you wish to fax.

3. Select Send To from the pop-up menu. A submenu will be displayed. Select Fax Recipient. This will launch the Compose New Fax Wizard, which will prompt you for information.

You can also drag the document to a shortcut to the Fax Printer on your desktop, if you have one.

HYPERTERMINAL

? **HyperTerminal _adds a number "1" to a number that I am trying to dial_. The number is in an area code that is different from mine, but it is not a long-distance call for me. How can I bypass this "1" that is added?**

By default, Windows 95 will add a leading "1" if the area code is different from the area code entered by the user as local. This is standard for the United States phone system, but in other countries (for example, Canada) you may not have to dial 1 in some cases. Use the following steps to bypass a number "1" when dialing. Let us say you want to dial (333) 333-3333 from the (555) area code:

1. If you have already created a HyperTerminal connection for this number, double-click its icon in the folder displayed when you open HyperTerminal from the Accessories menu, and click Modify to change the Phone Number.

2. If no connection exists for it, start one by double-clicking Hypertrm.exe. Enter your name and choose an icon. Click OK.

3. In the Phone Number tab or dialog box (depending on whether you're modifying or creating a connection), enter your area code in the Area Code field, and enter the whole number to be called, including the area code, in the Phone Number field. For example, type **555** in the Area Code box, and then **(333) 333-3333** (including the actual area code) in the Phone Number box and click OK.

4. Select Dial. HyperTerminal will not add a 1, because it thinks that the call is local, and it will not dial 555 for the same reason. The number dialed will be (333) 333-3333!

? **How do I get HyperTerminal to _answer an incoming call_?**

This is a major oversight in the design of HyperTerminal, but there is a work-around, as described in the next set of steps:

1. Click the Start button; select Programs | Accessories | HyperTerminal.

2. Double-click Hypertrm.exe, type a name like "AutoAnswer," select an icon, and click OK.

3. Leave the Phone Number blank. Open the Connect Using drop-down list and choose Direct To Com *X*, where *X* is the Com port where your modem is installed, as you can see here:

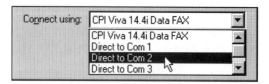

4. Click OK. Correct your port setting, most importantly your speed, and click OK again.

5. In the HyperTerminal window, type **ATS0=2** (that's a zero after the "S," *not* the letter "o"), and press ENTER. Your modem should respond with an "OK" as shown next. This sets up your modem to answer after the second ring. If you want it to answer after the first ring, type **ATS0=1**. If you have an external modem, you will see the AA (autoanswer) light come on.

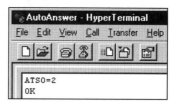

6. When a call comes in, it will be answered and you will see a message "Connected at *x*," where *x* is the speed you set your modem to. You can then type messages between your computer and the one you are connected to, and you can transfer files using the Transfer menu or the Send and Receive buttons on the toolbar.

7. To discontinue autoanswer, type **ATS0=0**, close the connection and the dialog box, and answer Yes to save the session.

? I tried to *connect to a bulletin board service*, and it said to have my parity set to "odd." Where do I do that?

Parity allows the receiving computer to check on the integrity of the data being sent. There are several parity conventions: odd, even, mark, space, and none. To work, both computers must be set to the same convention. The most common is none. To check and possibly change your parity setting, follow these steps:

1. Click the Start button; choose Programs | Accessories | HyperTerminal.

2. Right-click the connection that you want to change, and choose Properties.

3. Click the Phone Number tab, and then click Configure under the Connect Using list box.

4. In the modem's Properties dialog box, click the Connection tab, as shown in Figure 9-14.

5. You will see the Parity under Connection Preferences. Click the down arrow to be able to choose between Even, Odd, None, Mark, or Space. Make your choice and click OK twice.

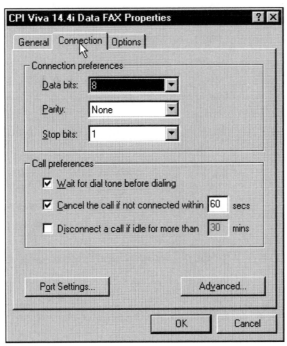

Figure 9-14.   You can set the type of parity in the modem's Properties Connection tab

? ## How do I *dial up a remote computer using HyperTerminal*?

HyperTerminal is a full-featured communications program that can be used with a modem to connect two computers for the purpose of sending and receiving files or connecting to computer bulletin boards or other information services, including the Internet. To create a HyperTerminal connection, use these steps:

1. Click the Start button; choose Programs I Accessories I HyperTerminal.

2. Double-click Hypertrm.exe, which will load the HyperTerminal program.

3. In the Connection Description dialog box, type the name of the connection you want to create, select an icon to associate with it, and click OK.

4. In the Phone Number dialog box, specify the Country Code, Area Code, Phone Number, and Modem Type for this connection, and click OK. If you haven't already installed a modem, you will be prompted for it now.

5. In the Connect dialog box, click Dialing Properties and look at the How I Dial From This Location section, as shown in Figure 9-15. If you need to dial a prefix to get an outside line, to use a calling card, or if you want to turn off call waiting, this is the place to do it. Click OK when you have completed the entries you wish to make.

   If you clicked on Dialing Properties and then checked Dial Using Calling Card, the Change Calling Card dialog box asks for the name and number of your card. If you click the Advanced button, you will see the Dialing Rules dialog box, which allows you to distinguish among calls made within the same area code, long-distance calls, and international calls.

6. When the Connect dialog box reappears, click Dial to do that or click Cancel to avoid dialing the connection (you will still have a chance to save the session). When the connection is made, the computer you are dialing will display its own terminal window as you can see in Figure 9-16.

7. When you are finished with the connection, click the Disconnect (hang up) button on the toolbar, or open the Call menu and select Disconnect.

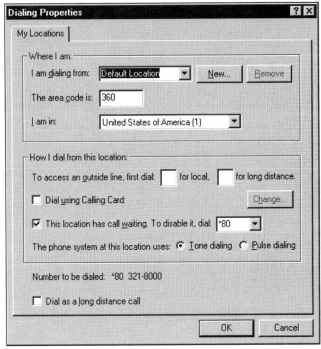

Figure 9-15.   If you have call waiting, turn it off in the Dialing Properties
dialog box

8. When you close the new HyperTerminal window after either
    dialing or canceling, it will prompt you to save your session
    definition. Click Yes and you will see an icon for the new connection
    in the Program Files\Accessories\HyperTerminal folder.

❓ When I use HyperTerminal I often get _disconnected by an incoming call from "call waiting."_ How do I disable that?

You can disable call waiting by placing a code (the code can be *70,
70#, 1170, or *80, depending on the area) that is sent before an
outgoing call (on your phone you would dial the code and then the
area code and phone number). The best way to have the call-waiting
code sent is to do it for all calls made from a given location through
your modem. You do this through the Modems control panel, Dialing
Properties dialog box with the following steps:

1. Click the Start button; select Settings I Control Panel I Modems.

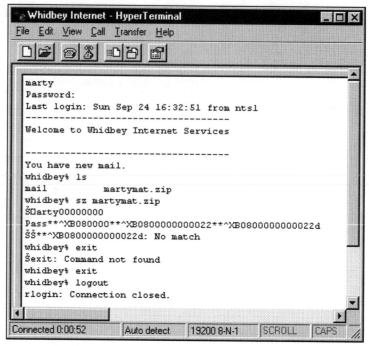

Figure 9-16.   The HyperTerminal window for a particular service, a local Internet provider

2. Click Dialing Properties to open the dialog box as shown earlier in Figure 9-15.

3. Click the check box in the line next to the bottom with the label "This location has call waiting."

4. Open the drop-down list on the right of the call-waiting line, and select the code that is correct for your area. (This code is often listed in your phone book. If not, call your phone company.)

5. Click OK.

❔ What *file transfer protocols* are supported by HyperTerminal?

HyperTerminal supports these file transfer protocols: Kermit, X-Modem, X-Modem-1K, Y-Modem, Y-Modem-G, and Z-Modem.

? **I am trying to type Attention (AT) commands in HyperTerminal, but I keep getting the _New Connection dialog box_. How can I bypass that box?**

In addition to bypassing the New Connection dialog box, you must also set a switch that instructs HyperTerminal to bring up a terminal window before dialing the number. You can then enter your commands before dialing. To do this, follow these steps:

1. Click the Start button; select Programs | Accessories | HyperTerminal. In the folder window, double-click Hypertrm.exe.

2. In HyperTerminal, click Cancel in the New Connection dialog box, leaving you in the New Connection window.

3. Open the File menu and choose Properties.

4. Click the Configure button and then click the Options tab.

5. Select the option Bring Up Terminal Window Before Dialing, as shown in Figure 9-17. This will allow you to type modem commands directly in a terminal window.

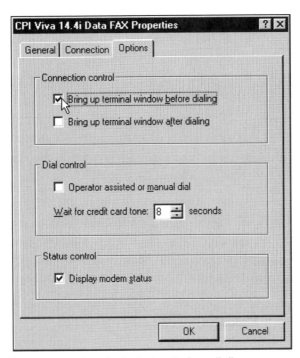

Figure 9-17. If you open a terminal window before dialing, you can set up your modem by typing commands to it

PHONE DIALER

? ### How do I *change my speed-dial settings* in Phone Dialer?

To quickly change one or more speed-dial numbers or names, follow these steps:

1. Click the Start button; choose Programs | Accessories | Phone Dialer.
2. When the Phone Dialer dialog box appears, open the Edit menu and choose Speed Dial.
3. Click the speed-dial button you wish to change.
4. Change or delete the information in the Name and the Number To Dial boxes.
5. When you are done editing, click the Save button.

? ### How do I *create a speed-dial button* to use in Phone Dialer?

To create a speed-dial button:

1. Click the Start button; choose Programs | Accessories | Phone Dialer.
2. In the Phone Dialer dialog box, click the speed-dial button (1 through 8) you want to set.
3. Type the Name that will appear on the button and the phone number to dial.
4. Click Save or Save And Dial to call the number right now. The name you typed now appears on the button.
5. When you want to speed dial the number, click the button and the number will be dialed.

? ### How do I *start the Phone Dialer*?

Use the following steps to start the Phone Dialer:

1. Click the Start button; choose Programs | Accessories | Phone Dialer. A dialog box appears with a telephone pad and speed-dial buttons, as shown in Figure 9-18.

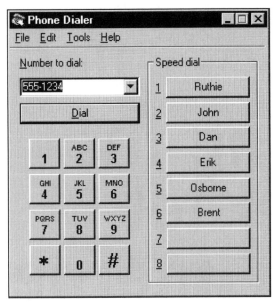

Figure 9-18.   Phone Dialer dials your voice-line telephone calls for you

2. Type a phone number from your keyboard or use the Phone
   Dialer numeric keyboard.

3. Click Dial.

Using the Internet and Internet Explorer

Answer Topics!

Internet Access @ a Glance

In the 21 months between the first and second editions of this book, the Internet and local intranets have gone from being an interesting sidelight to being the central focus of personal computing. For that reason this chapter became a mandatory addition to the second edition. The chapter has three sections:

⇨ **Connecting to the Internet** discusses the types of Internet connection as well as what you need and how to make the connection.

⇨ **Sending and Receiving E-Mail** looks at the differences among e-mail programs, the way e-mail is addressed, how to include files with e-mail, and ways to add more than words to your correspondence.

⇨ **Exploring the Web with Internet Explorer** covers getting Internet Explorer and how to use it without the mouse, securely, in custom ways, and in ways that protects children from unsuitable sites.

CONNECTING TO THE INTERNET

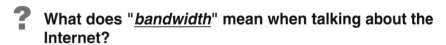 **What does "_bandwidth_" mean when talking about the Internet?**

> _Bandwidth_ refers to the data-carrying capacity of your connection to the Internet or any Internet link in terms of the number of bits per second (bps) that can be carried. Normal dial-up service today is either 28.8 Kbps or 33.6 Kbps, with 56 Kbps gaining ground. ISDN (Integrated Services Digital Network) dial-up service is either 64 Kbps or 128 Kbps. Direct connection service ranges from 64 Kbps for a

single channel ISDN direct service, to a 1.54 Mbps T-1 line and a 44.74 Mbps T-3 line. The common discussion relating to bandwidth is the need to increase it from today's standard of 28.8 Kbps to at least 1.54 Mbps.

 ## How do I *connect to the Internet*?

The simple answer is to double-click The Internet icon shown on the left. This answer, though, has a number of assumptions implicit in it that may not be correct for you. For that reason a comprehensive sidebar on connecting to the Internet has been included in this chapter.

• • • • • • • • • • •

Connecting to the Internet

How you connect to the Internet depends on the version of Windows 95 you have and on the method you choose to connect to the Internet (see the question on the methods of connecting to the Internet). You also may need certain information from the organization you are going to use to connect to the Internet before you try to connect (see the question on information needed from an Internet service provider or ISP).

Windows 95 Versions

In the "Versions of Windows 95" sidebar in this book's Introduction, four versions of Windows 95 are described. From the standpoint of the Internet, there are three major versions of Windows 95:

⇨ The original retail version of Windows 95, where the software is separately purchased for existing computers

⇨ The original OEM (original equipment manufacturer) version on new computers

⇨ The OSR 2 (OEM service release 2) version shipped on new computers beginning in fall 1996

The Service Pack 1 upgrade versions of either of the original versions did not change how Window 95 works with the Internet.

Connecting to the Internet, continued

The reason for the distinction is that the OSR 2 version has an Internet Connection Wizard as well as a folder called "Online Services" with programs to connect to several information services such as AOL and CompuServe. The original retail version did not have either of these, and the original OEM version had an early version of the Internet Connection Wizard.

To compensate for the lack of Internet support in the original retail version, you can get Microsoft Plus! Companion for Windows 95, which was included in the original OEM version. This provides the Internet Connection Wizard and Internet Explorer, as well as other software, but does not provide the software to connect to information services except for MSN. Alternative software to Microsoft Plus! is available from most ISPs and information services.

Method Used to Connect

There are three methods that you can use to connect to the Internet:

⇨ Using a modem and phone lines to connect to an information service such as MSN, CompuServe, or AOL.

⇨ Using a modem and phone line to connect to an independent Internet service provider.

⇨ Using a local area network (LAN) to connect to an Internet provider procured by someone else. This can be your company's own Internet node, an independent service provider, or an information service.

Using an Information Service

If you want to use an information service other than MSN, such as CompuServe or AOL, as your Internet link, you will need software provided by those firms. This is included in the OSR 2 version of Windows 95—simply open the Online Services folder on the desktop, as shown next, and then double-click the service you want to use and follow the instructions. After installing the software, start the program and you'll be prompted on what to do as a new user.

Connecting to the Internet, continued

If you do not have OSR 2, find one of the millions of copies of the software to connect to either AOL or CompuServe distributed via magazines and direct-mail campaigns. If you don't have it, ask your friends. It is highly likely that someone in your immediate acquaintance has a copy of this software. If not, there are toll-free numbers available where you can ask to have the software sent to you (CompuServe is 800-848-8199 and AOL is 888-265-8002).

If you want to use MSN, all versions of Windows 95 have an MSN icon on the desktop for this purpose. Simply double-click this icon and follow the instructions to get online with MSN. See Chapter 9 for more on setting up MSN.

Using an Independent Internet Service Provider

If you want to use an independent Internet service provider (ISP) and you have either the OEM version or the retail version with Microsoft Plus!, all you need to do is double-click the Internet icon on your desktop. If this is the first time you have done that, the Internet Connection Wizard will open. (If Internet Explorer appears instead of the Internet Connection Wizard, then the wizard has already been run and you may not need to do so again. If you do want to run the wizard, then use Windows Explorer to open the C:\Program Files\ICW-Internet Connection Wizard folder and double-click the Icwconn1.exe file.) In the

Connecting to the Internet, continued

Internet Connection Wizard click Next. You'll be asked if you want to use an Automatic or Manual method to set up.

If you don't know an ISP to use, choose the Automatic option; you'll be asked about your area code and the first three digits of your phone number, and then the Wizard (using an 800 number) will search a database for ISPs that you might use. Your computer may be rebooted, and then you'll be shown a list of ISPs. Select the one you want by clicking the check mark on the far right of that ISP's listing. That ISP will be automatically called (again using an 800 number), and you'll be asked a series of questions that ISP needs for you to sign up. If you are asked for a credit card number, it will be over a secure link. In most cases, when you are done, you should be able to immediately use the Internet. Remember that the list of ISPs presented by the Internet Connection Wizard may not all be a local phone number to you. You need to check if they are local, long-distance, or 800 numbers for which you'll be billed extra.

If you do know of an ISP you want to use or if you are connecting over a LAN, click Manual. You are asked if you want to use a LAN or a phone line to connect. If you choose a phone line, you are asked if you want to use MSN or an account with a different ISP. For an ISP, you are asked the name and telephone number of that ISP, your user name and password, and the IP, DNS, and e-mail information for the ISP. If you use a LAN to connect, you only need to enter your e-mail information. In most cases, when you are done, you should be able to immediately use the Internet.

Testing an Internet Connection

With an Internet connection set up, you can test it in two ways: by using Internet Explorer to explore the Web and by using either the Internet Explorer or the Exchange (Inbox) to send and receive e-mail. First, double-click the Internet icon again. This time, instead of the Internet Connection Wizard, you'll see the Connect To dialog box open. If all the information is correct, click Connect. You should hear your modem dialing. After connecting, the Internet Explorer will open asking you to register Internet Explorer. You can register if you wish, or you can enter another web site by typing the web address or URL in the Address box.

Connecting to the Internet, continued

For example, if you type **http://www.cnn.com** and press ENTER, CNN Interactive will open, as you can see in Figure 10-1. You can also use the File Open dialog box as an alternative to typing in the Address box.

From CNN you can click a link to go to other web sites, or you can enter another URL. When you are done, click the Close button in the upper right of the window. You should remain connected to the Internet.

 The second thing you can do to test your web connection is to send and receive e-mail. Have a friend use your e-mail address to send you some mail. Then double-click the Inbox icon. If asked, choose the profile supporting Internet mail and click OK. The Inbox will appear. Open the Tools menu and choose Deliver Now. If you are not connected to the Internet, you will be directly connected. If you have mail, the Deliver Messages dialog box will be displayed, as shown in Figure 10-2, while the mail is downloaded. If you got mail from your friend, you can open it, and after reading it, click the Reply button in the toolbar to send a message back to that person.

If you are connected to the Internet just to get mail, you'll be automatically disconnected when you are done downloading it. If you remain connected from Internet Explorer, you'll need to manually disconnect. Do that by clicking the Connect To task in the Taskbar, or in OSR 2, clicking the Connect icon in the status area on the right and then clicking Disconnect.

❓ How do I *find an Internet service provider* (ISP)?

Probably the best sources for a local ISP recommendation are your friends and acquaintances. Ask people if they are on the Internet and if so, how they are connected. See how happy they are with the service. How often do they get a busy signal, how often is it really slow (this may be the fault of the Internet itself and not the ISPs), and how good is the support? If the friends and acquaintances approach doesn't work, go into a couple of computer stores and ask them who the good local ISPs are. Ask which ISP the store uses.

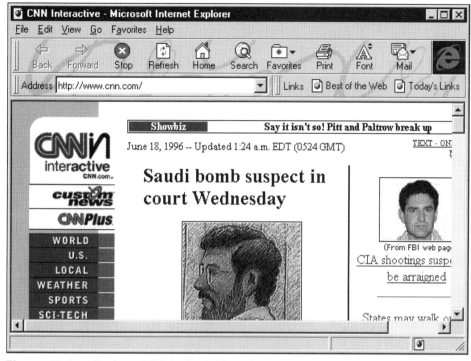

Figure 10-1.   Typing a URL in the Address box and pressing ENTER opens that web site

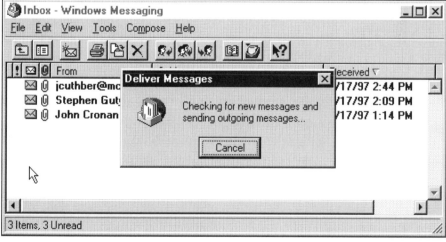

Figure 10-2.   Checking for e-mail

Other sources are the yellow pages and newspaper ads. Some areas have computer-related newspapers, which not only have ads for ISPs, but may also rate them.

❓ I have heard people talk about a *firewall* in relation to the Internet. What is it and how is it used?

The purpose of a *firewall* is to protect an intranet within an organization from being accessed across the intranet's connection to the Internet. A firewall is most often a separate computer that sits between an intranet and the Internet. This computer stops and validates any request made from outside to inside the intranet. If it passes the inbound tests, then the firewall computer itself makes the request of the intranet and makes sure that any information going out meets certain criteria. Only after the outbound tests are passed is the information given to the Internet requester.

❓ What *information do I need from my Internet link* before I can connect to the Internet?

Depending on how you choose to connect to the Internet, you may need to talk on the telephone with the organization that will act as your link and get certain information that you will use as you are setting it up. With AOL, CompuServe, and MSN, the information you need is generated and given to you as you are signing up. With some Internet service providers (ISPs), you need only a phone number (see the earlier question on how to find an ISP). All the other information is generated during sign up. In other cases you must talk to them on the phone and get the following information:

⇨ **Phone numbers** you are to use with various modem speeds.

⇨ **User name or ID and password**, for example, "georgem" and "owl*4567." (Can you use the same user name/ID and password for both logging on to the Internet and for e-mail, or do you need different ones, and what are they?)

⇨ **Provider's domain name**, for example, "provider.com."

⇨ **Provider's primary and alternate DNS** server numbers, for example, 123.12.34.56.

⇨ **Your e-mail address** and your Internet mail server, for example, "georgem@provider.com" and "provider.com."

Ask your ISP if they require a terminal window for authentication (most do not). If so, have them explain how to set up a script to handle that. Also ask if they automatically assign you an IP number (most do), or if they give you a permanent number and what that number is.

? What should I *look for in an Internet service provider* (ISP)?

An *Internet service provider* (ISP) is your link to the Internet. You go through them for all that you do on the Internet. This includes your Internet e-mail, your exploring or "surfing" of the World Wide Web (the Web), and the posting of your own web pages for others to see. Therefore the primary issue is easy, unobstructed access. This translates to the following criteria:

⇨ **Local phone lines** Phone lines without long distance charges where you are (or will be if you travel much with a computer).

⇨ **A high ratio of incoming lines and modems to the number of users** One line and modem for seven users is a good standard, one for ten is tight, and anything lower than that (say one line and modem for 12 users) is not acceptable.

⇨ **A large enough connection to the rest of the Internet to handle the ISP's users** A T-1 line will max out if a little over 50 users at 28.8 Kbps are all trying to access the Internet at exactly the same time. The key is the last part of that statement, "all trying to access the Internet at *exactly the same time*." With "average usage," many firms believe that between 1,000 and 1,500 users can be accommodated on a single T-1 line. But the next two considerations significantly affect this.

⇨ **Redundancy in their connection to the Internet** An ISP needs to have at least two separate links to two separate Internet nodes, so that if one goes down, they still have the other. While they could use a fractional T-1 or an ISDN line, for an ISP of any size (a thousand or more users), they should have at least two T-1 lines connected to different Internet nodes.

⇨ **Load balancing among the outgoing lines and their Internet nodes** An ISP with two or more outgoing lines needs to be able to balance the load among those lines and be able to switch away from a node that is becoming a bottleneck. Such equipment is available in the routers currently on the market, but it is newer and expensive.

In addition to easy and unobstructed access to the Internet, there are a number of other factors to consider when choosing an ISP. Among these are

⇨ **Attractive pricing and services**   The price of Internet access is obviously related to the services that it buys. A low price that doesn't provide the services you need is worthless, while a full-service price that gives you more than you need is a waste of money. You have to look at an ISP's offerings and decide if the price is commensurate with the services being provided. This requires that you look at and compare several ISPs. An industry norm is $19.95 per month for unlimited access (although not a full-time connection) up to 33.6 Kbps (many ISPs are now offering 56 Kbps at the same or slightly higher price) and generally includes a personal web page and one or more megabytes of storage. You often can get a discount if you pay for a year in advance, but make sure you want to stay a year.

⇨ **A "busy-free" service policy**   If you get a busy signal very often when you connect to your ISP, you have lost the access that you wanted. This is normally controlled by the ratio of lines and modems to users, but it can be enhanced by an ISP guaranteeing not to exceed a certain number of busy signals monthly—or even no busy signals. The guarantee has to mean something, like a credit on your monthly bill, for it to be worthwhile.

⇨ **Users complementary to your use**   If you are a business user, you want an ISP geared to business users, with a large percentage of business customers. If you are a home user, you want an ISP that is geared to that market. This generally addresses the type of services that are available, the pricing, and the type and amount of support.

⇨ **Plentiful and easy to reach support**   The optimum support is a toll-free line staffed 24 hours a day, seven days a week, with a guarantee that they will get back to you in three hours or less if they are busy when you call. Very few ISPs provide this service, and many charge extra if you want it. Is the probably less than optimum support good enough for you; does it supply what you need? If you only use the Internet in the evening and weekends, and service is only available during business hours, it's not what you need.

⇨ **Web page services commensurate with your needs** If you want to put your own web page up on the Internet, does your ISP provide what you need? Consider factors such as the amount of disk space you can use and the amount of traffic you can have on your page before they start charging you. ISPs normally provide limits on both of these. If you want to use a web page authoring program such as Microsoft FrontPage to create your web page (and it's probably the easiest way to do so), then you want your ISP to support the FrontPage server extensions.

I have the original retail version of Windows 95 without the Microsoft Plus! companion disk. How do I _manually set up a dial-up Internet connection_**?**

If you don't have Microsoft Plus!, you can manually set up a connection for using the Internet in two major steps. First, you must install and configure a modem, as described in Chapter 9. Then you have to install Dial-Up Networking. To install Dial-Up Networking, follow these steps.

Tip   *Once connected to the Internet with a dial-up connection, you will need browser software such as Microsoft Internet Explorer or Netscape Navigator to actually search and retrieve information on the Internet, and to send and receive Internet mail. You can often get this software from your ISP.*

1. Open My Computer and double-click Dial-Up Networking. If you do not have a dial-up connection, the Make New Connection Wizard welcome message will be displayed. Click Next.

2. If you already have a dial-up connection, the Dial-Up Networking folder will be displayed. In that case, double-click Make New Connection. The Make New Connection Wizard will be displayed.

3. Type a name for the computer you will be dialing, and verify that the modem is properly configured by clicking Configure. It will display the Modems Properties dialog box as described in Chapter 9.

4. Click the Options tab. If you need to enter your user name and password when you sign on to the Internet, then click Bring Up

Terminal Window After Dialing. When you are satisfied with the modem properties, click OK and then click Next.

5. Enter the Area Code, Telephone Number, and Country Code as needed. Click Next.

6. Click Finish to complete the installation.

7. In the Dial-Up Networking dialog box, right-click your new connection and click Properties. The connection's Properties dialog box will open.

8. Click Server Type. The Server Types dialog box will open, as shown in Figure 10-3.

9. Make sure that PPP: Windows 95... is selected as the Type Of Dial-Up Server. If NetBEUI and IPX/SPX protocols are enabled, click them to disable those protocols. TCP/IP should be enabled (checked).

10. Click TCP/IP Settings. The dialog box that opens has very important settings that only your Internet provider can tell you how to set. Discuss these settings with your Internet provider and

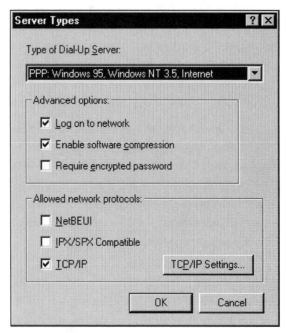

Figure 10-3.   Setting up a dial-up connection to an Internet server

set them accordingly (see the earlier question on what to ask your ISP).

11. When you have made the TCP/IP settings, click OK three times to return to the Dial-Up Networking folder.

Tip   *Remember the TCP/IP Settings dialog box, reached from your dial-up connection's Properties and then Server Types dialog boxes. The TCP/IP Settings dialog box contains a number of settings that can cause you grief. In particular, if your Internet provider does not have a strong opinion on whether to use IP Header Compression (second from the bottom check box), disable it by removing the check mark.*

The PPP protocol is installed by default because it is the most flexible, being able to work over NetBEUI, IPX/SPX, and TCP/IP. Now use the connection with these steps:

1. From the Dial-Up Networking window, double-click the Internet connection you just created. The Connect To dialog box will open.

2. Enter your User Name and Password, check on the correctness of the Phone Number, and click Connect. You should hear your modem dial and will see a message that the system is trying to connect to your Internet provider. If the Terminal window opens, you will need to enter your user name and password again, possibly type **ppp**, and then press F7 to close the terminal window. Finally, you should see a connected message like this:

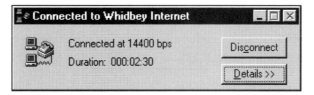

Once you have gotten the connection message, you can start your web browsing and Internet mail packages. With Microsoft Plus!, you can use Microsoft Exchange for Internet mail, and Internet Explorer 3.0 and beyond includes Internet mail.

If you did not get connected, look at the Windows 95 Help Troubleshooter for your modem and for Dial-Up Networking. If that does not help, go over all of your settings with your Internet provider.

❓ What are the differences among the _methods to connect to the Internet_?

There are a number of choices that you have when you look at connecting to the Internet. Among your choices are the following:

⇨ **A LAN connection or a telephone connection**   (In the near future, a TV cable or satellite connection will be added to this list.) If you are on a local area network (LAN) with a connection to the Internet, you can go through your LAN to connect to the Internet. That is probably the fastest and least expensive way to connect to the Internet, barring the availability of a TV cable or satellite connection. Without a LAN, TV cable, or satellite connection, you must use a telephone connection.

⇨ **A dial-up telephone connection or a direct dedicated-telephone connection**   A dial-up connection is the standard modem connection to any phone jack. A direct dedicated connection is a dedicated phone line open all the time between you and the organization linking you to the Internet. It is normally terminated on your end with a _router_ that can be connected to a LAN or directly to several computers. A direct connection is definitely faster, but it is also a lot more expensive. Therefore, unless you share a direct connection with a number of people, which reduces some of the speed benefit, a direct connection is normally too expensive.

⇨ **Information services or independent Internet service providers (ISPs)**   _Information service providers_ such as America Online (AOL), CompuServe, and Microsoft Network (MSN) provide Internet access as well as their own value-added content, generally at a higher price. Independent ISPs only provide Internet access at lower prices. One other benefit of information services is that they have local phone service in many cities in the world, so that if you travel a lot, you are more likely to find a local phone connection.

❓ What do I _need to access the Internet_?

You need to have

⇨ **A physical connection to the Internet**   This can be a local area network (LAN) connection, a dial-up connection using a modem and phone lines, or a direct connection through a router and one or more dedicated phone lines (see the earlier question on methods to connect to the Internet).

⇨ **An organization to act as your link to the Internet** This can be an information service such as AOL or CompuServe, or an independent Internet service provider (ISP). (See the earlier questions on methods to connect to the Internet and what to look for in an ISP.) In the case of larger organizations (companies, universities, or government agencies), they may have the equipment and act as their own link to the Internet.

⇨ **Software to establish the connection either over a LAN or a modem, software to handle your e-mail, and software to browse the Web** In Windows 95 the connection software is supplied by the networking and dial-up networking components of the operating system. The e-mail can be handled by the Microsoft Exchange Client that is included with Windows 95 as the Inbox. (See the question in the next section on differences among e-mail clients.) You must get the web browser separately if you are using the retail version of Windows 95 by either getting Microsoft Plus! for Windows 95, or by using some other way (many ISPs offer a free browser on a disk when you sign up with them). If you buy a new computer with Windows 95 installed on it, it should have the Internet Explorer 3.0*x* browser already installed, as well as its integrated Internet mail.

SENDING AND RECEIVING E-MAIL

I keep getting messages with *acronyms like ROFL and odd little faces* like :-7 that I don't understand. Where can I find out what these mean?

ROFL stands for "rolling on the floor laughing" and viewed sideways the little face, called a "smiley," indicates a wry statement. The best sources on acronyms and smileys are the acronym and smiley dictionaries at **http://magicpub.com/netprimer**.

What are the *differences among e-mail programs*?

With Windows 95 you get a free e-mail client program called Microsoft Exchange that has as its icon the Inbox. It provides a full-featured facility for creating, sending, receiving, and storing e-mail that is sent and received over the Internet, over a LAN, or with one or more information services such as CompuServe. Microsoft Exchange provides an address book, the means to easily reply and forward mail, to attach files to a message, and to set up a folder system for storing mail, as you can see in Figure 10-4.

If you use either Microsoft Internet Explorer or Netscape Navigator, there is a mail program that is available and provides almost the same services that are available in the Exchange. The only difference is that the Exchange can also be used for LAN mail and for some information services mail.

There are also a number of other mail programs available on the Internet. Probably the most widely used is Eudora. There is a free version, Eudora Light 3.01 for Windows. A more full-featured version, Eudora Pro 3.01 for Windows, costs $89 in a box from a retailer or $69 if you download it (doesn't include disks or paper manuals). You can also download a 30-day demo version of Eudora Pro for free from **http://www.eudora.com/demos**. Eudora Pro 3.01 for Windows has all of the features of Microsoft Exchange, as shown in Figure 10-5, and is

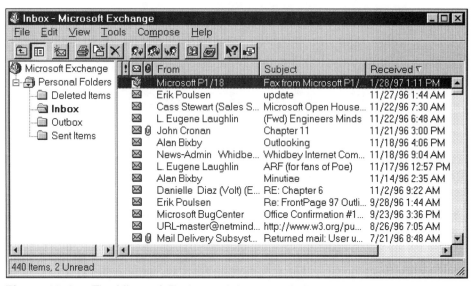

Figure 10-4.   The Microsoft Exchange Inbox e-mail client

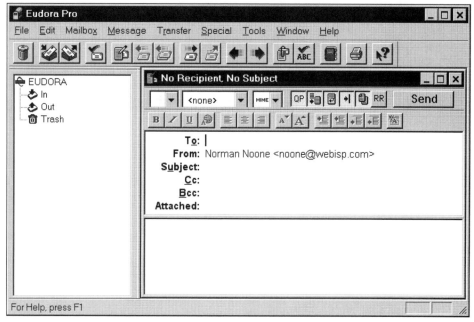

Figure 10-5.   Eudora Pro 3.01 for Windows e-mail client

arguably easier to use. The only question is whether Eudora Pro is worth its price in comparison to a free product.

Microsoft Office 97 includes Outlook, which beautifully handles e-mail from and to many sources. It also provides scheduling, contact lists, task lists, and a number of ways to automatically create journal entries, all integrated with e-mail, as you can see in Figure 10-6. Outlook is the author's choice for e-mail, because it allows you to use Microsoft Word to create and read e-mail, and because it provides the ability to do group scheduling and task assignments with the mail system.

 Note   *See* The Microsoft Outlook Handbook, *by Martin Matthews, published by Osborne/McGraw-Hill.*

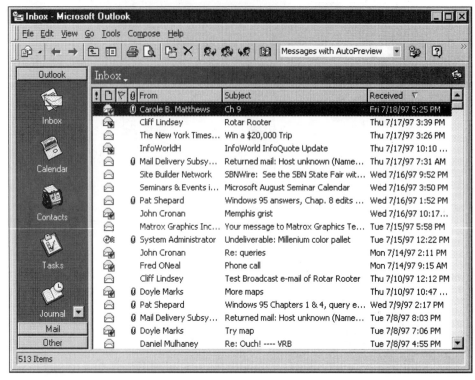

Figure 10-6.   Microsoft Outlook—e-mail and a lot more

? How do I *get an e-mail address, and what form does it take*?

The organization through which you connect to the Internet will
assign you an e-mail address. Your address will be of the form:
youraccountid@domainname.domaintype. The "domaintype" in the
United States is one of six three-letter suffixes: .COM for commercial
accounts, .NET for Internet infrastructure organizations such as ISPs,
.GOV for federal government organizations, .MIL for military
organizations, .EDU for educational organizations, and .ORG for
other organizations not covered by the other suffixes. Outside of the
United States, the suffix is a two-letter identification of the country,
such as .CA for Canada, and .UK for the United Kingdom. The
"domainname" identifies the organization providing the connection to
you. For example: McGraw-Hill is *mcgraw-hill.com*, the United States
Department of the Treasury is *ustreas.gov*, and NCF Communications,
Inc., an ISP, is *ncfweb.net.* The "youraccountid" depends on your
Internet connection. If you are connected using CompuServe, this

is a number; if you are connected through an ISP, they may prescribe an account ID such as "johnc" or "jclark," or they may allow you to pick your own.

❓ Can I _get my own domain name_, and if so, how?

Yes. A _domain name_ is the part of the e-mail and web address that ends in ".com" or ".net," for example, "microsoft.com" or "whidbey.net." The easiest way to get a domain name is to ask your ISP. For a fee, normally a one-time payment of a couple hundred dollars and a much smaller monthly amount, they can set you up with your own domain name so you can be "_you@yourdomain_.com." You don't need your own domain for either e-mail or a web page, but if you want to promote something, putting that in your domain name can be beneficial.

Domain names are all registered in the United States with InterNIC, a cooperative activity of the National Science Foundation, AT&T, and Network Solutions, Inc. You can go directly to InterNIC (**http://rs.internic.net/rs-internic.html**) to obtain a domain name. The fee is $100 for the first two years and then $50 per year thereafter, but you will need to have a host such as an ISP for the name, so you might as well go to your ISP to start with.

An important service provided by InterNIC is the online directory of registered domain names at **http://rs.internic.net/cgi-bin/whois**. By using this directory, you can check out a domain name to see if it is being used, as shown in Figure 10-7. If you do not find an existing user of the domain name, you will get the message "No match found for _domainname_.com." Otherwise the search results will be displayed like this:

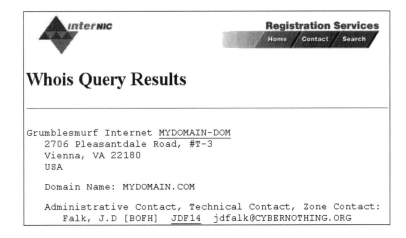

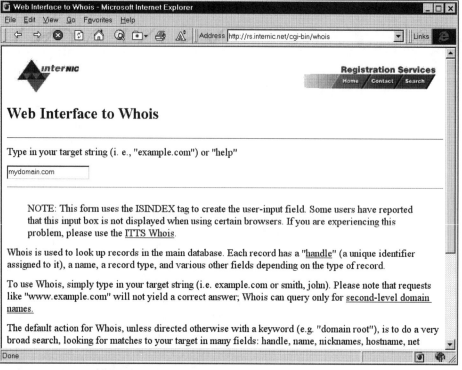

Figure 10-7.   InterNIC's Whois web page, which allows searching for existing
domain names

    Note   *In Canada, domain name registration is through Cyberspace*
Research, in North York, Ontario, at http://www.csr.ists.ca/w3can/
forms/registration.html.

I would like to *include a document with an e-mail*
***message*. I know I can copy and paste it in the message,**
but is there a way to send the file?

    Yes. You can attach any file to an e-mail message and send it with
the message. In Microsoft Exchange Client, Outlook, and Internet
Explorer 3.0 Internet Mail, this is accomplished while you are creating
a message (the New Message window is open) by clicking the Insert
File button in the Standard toolbar. When you click this button, the
Insert File dialog box will open where you can select the drive, folder,
and file that you want to send.

EXPLORING THE WEB WITH INTERNET EXPLORER

? **I have a hard time using a mouse, but web pages are so "mouse-centric." Is there a way to *access the web content without using the mouse*?**

Yes, the Internet Explorer has several accessibility options that provide optional ways to access and view web content. These include using your keyboard in place of the mouse, enlarging the font that is used in a page, and viewing alternative text in place of images.

The most important set of keys to navigate a web page are TAB and SHIFT-TAB. These keys scroll a web page forward and backward from the Address block at the top of the Internet Explorer window to the first hyperlink on the page, to the next hyperlink, and so on. As each hyperlink is selected, a narrow border appears around it. You can then activate the hyperlink by pressing ENTER. See Table 10-1, for other possibilities.

Table 10-1. Keyboard Alternatives for Web Navigation

Key	Function
BACKSPACE or ALT-LEFT ARROW	Go back to the previous page
CTRL-N	Open another Internet Explorer window
CTRL-O	Open a new Internet address, file, or folder
CTRL-P	Print the current page
CTRL-S	Save the current page
CTRL-TAB	Go from one frame to the next
ENTER	Activates the selected hyperlink
ESC	Stop downloading the current page
F5	Refresh the current page
SHIFT-BACKSPACE or ALT-RIGHT ARROW	Go forward to the next page
SHIFT-CTRL-TAB	Go backward from one frame to the next
SHIFT-F10	Open a hyperlink's context menu
SHIFT-TAB	Go up the page from one hyperlink to the next
TAB	Go down the page from one hyperlink to the next

You can change the size of the font used by the Internet Explorer by opening the View menu, choosing Fonts, and selecting the size you want to use, as shown next. Finally, most web authors include alternative text with the graphic images they place on a web page. If you move the mouse pointer over the image, a tooltip will appear displaying the alternative text, as you can see in the second illustration.

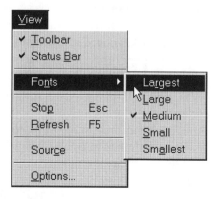

? My company would like to send some proprietary information over the Internet, but we are concerned about security. What can we do to _assure that information sent over the Internet is secure_?

Assuring the security of Internet information has three elements, all of which must be handled satisfactorily for you to achieve your objective. The elements are

⇨ Authenticating the sender, the receiver, and the data transferred, so both parties know that the other party and the information are as represented

⇨ Securing the transmission of information so that it cannot be read by an unintended recipient

⇨ Limiting access to web pages and the server containing them so the pages aren't changed

Much of what needs to be done to implement web security must be done at the web server. This is especially true with the limiting of access. To handle the server-side questions, you'll need to work with your network administrator or Internet service provider (ISP). If you want to set up your own Windows NT server, an excellent reference is Tom Sheldon's *The Windows NT Security Handbook*, published by Osborne/McGraw-Hill. Another good source is the Microsoft Security Advisor at **http://www.microsoft.com/security**.

The security features that you can control are described in the sidebar "Internet Explorer Security Features."

Internet Explorer Security Features

The security features in the Internet Explorer that you can control are in the Options dialog box Security and Advanced tabs, which you can open from the View menu. In the Security tab, shown in Figure 10-8, you can

⇨ View and change the certificates on your computer for yourself and for software publishers, and the certification authorities that you will accept. If you have your own certificate, then others will know that you are who you say you are. If you accept the certification authorities, then you can see the certifications of information and programs you download.

Your personal certification requires that you be certified by a certification authority. In other words, a *certification authority* will certify that you are who you say you are. With Internet Explorer, you can get a free Class 1 certification or "Digital ID" from VeriSign, Inc. at **http://digitalid.verisign.com/ms_client.htm**. At this site you can see what the difference is between a Class 1 and Class 2 certification and the associated costs.

Internet Explorer Security Features, *continued*

⇨ Control the type of software that can be downloaded and run on your computer. A number of web sites have small ActiveX and Java programs that they download and run on your computer. You can prevent various types of programs from being downloaded, or prevent the running of those programs.

⇨ Determine the level of security that you want. As shown next, you have a choice of three levels that give various degrees of protection and warnings.

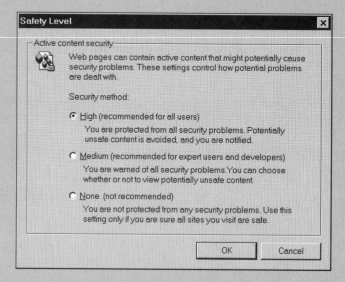

In the Advanced tab that you can see in Figure 10-9, you can

⇨ Determine what kinds of security conditions you want to be warned about. While the warnings are worthwhile to keep you informed, they also can get annoying if they are not telling you something you care about.

⇨ Make cryptography settings. This dialog box, shown next, determines the type of encryption that you will allow. This enables Internet Explorer to automatically encrypt and decrypt information transferred between you and a secure server using the https service. Under most circumstances, all three protocols are valid means of securely transmitting information.

Internet Explorer Security Features, continued

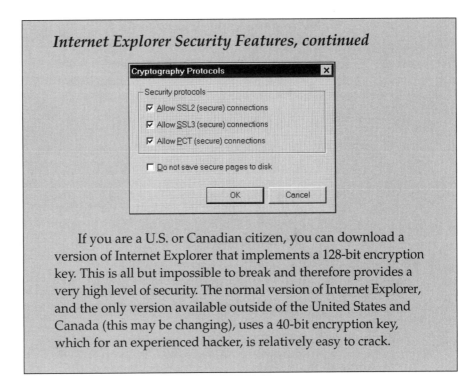

If you are a U.S. or Canadian citizen, you can download a version of Internet Explorer that implements a 128-bit encryption key. This is all but impossible to break and therefore provides a very high level of security. The normal version of Internet Explorer, and the only version available outside of the United States and Canada (this may be changing), uses a 40-bit encryption key, which for an experienced hacker, is relatively easy to crack.

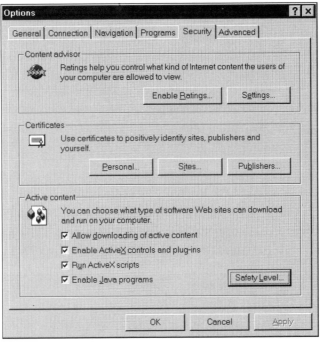

Figure 10-8.   Security tab of the Options dialog box

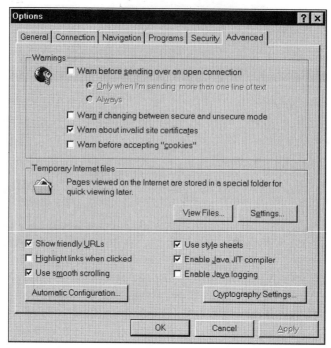

Figure 10-9.   Advanced tab of the Options dialog box

? Can I _control what my children see on the Web_?

Yes. Internet Explorer 3.0 has a ratings feature that allows you to
control access to web sites based on the PICS Internet rating system.
This allows you to choose the level of language, nudity, sex, and
violence that you feel is acceptable. You can also block access to sites
that aren't rated, and set passwords that allow access to blocked sites.
To set the level of material that users are allowed to see, follow these
instructions:

1. In the Internet Explorer (3.0 and above), open the View menu,
   choose Options, and click the Security tab.

2. Click Enable Ratings, enter and confirm a password that must be
   used to change the ratings, and click OK.

3. The Content Advisor dialog box will open. (If you have previously set the password, you'll need to click Settings to open the Content Advisor.) Click one of the four content areas (Language, Nudity, Sex, or Violence), and a five-position slider bar will appear, as you can see in Figure 10-10.

4. Move the slider to the highest level of content that you want to allow users of the computer to be able to see. If you want more information of the meanings of each level, click the More Info button at the bottom of the Content Advisor dialog box.

5. Click each of the other content areas and set the desired level.

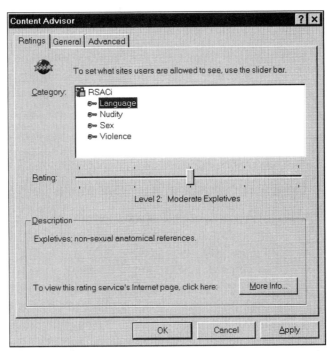

Figure 10-10.   Setting the level of content that can be viewed in the Internet Explorer

6. When you have completed setting the desired levels, click the General tab shown here:

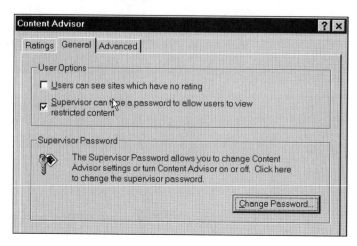

7. Determine if you want users to see sites without ratings and if you want to use a supervisory password to allow users to see sites that would otherwise be blocked. You can also change the supervisory password.

8. When you have made your settings, click OK twice to close both the Content Advisor and Options dialog boxes.

? What are "*cookies*" and are they harmful?

Cookies are small pieces of information that are placed on your computer by a web site to identify your computer to that site. When you first visit a web site, you may be asked for identifying information such as your name, company name, and so on. The web site then places this information in a cookie and stores it on your computer. The cookie also contains the domain name and path of the web page that created it, as well as an expiration date and security flag. The next time you visit that web site, the Internet Explorer first looks to see if you have a cookie for the site, and if you do, it will send the information to the site as it is connecting to it.

As a general rule, cookies are not harmful and are actually helpful in that they can save you the time of identifying yourself every time you visit the site. If you would like to be warned before accepting cookies on your computer, you can accomplish that with these steps:

1. In Internet Explorer, open the View menu, choose Options, and click the Advanced tab.

2. Click Warn Before Accepting "Cookies," as shown here:

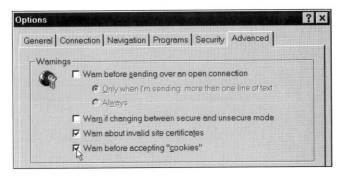

3. Click OK to close the Options dialog box.

❓ I would like to change some of the ways the Internet Explorer looks and behaves. What *customization capabilities are available in Internet Explorer*?

There are a number of changes that you can make to customize the Internet Explorer, including changing the size, position, and contents of the toolbar; organizing the list of favorite sites; and setting up your start page and links. Here are some things that you can do directly:

⇨ Place the mouse pointer on the bottom of the toolbar area below the Address box and drag that area up and down. You can see how you can enlarge the toolbar, as shown in the first illustration next, or shrink it to a single row without labels, as you can see in the second illustration.

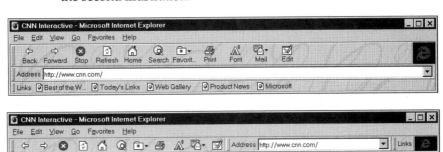

⇨ Click the ridged area on the left of the Address or Links bar to maximize and minimize these bars.

⇨ Place the mouse pointer on the Address or Links labels, and drag those bars to place them in various positions.

⇨ Place the mouse pointer on the ridged area of the Address, Links, or toolbar, and drag those bars to make them smaller or larger.

⇨ Remove, restore, and customize the Standard toolbar, and the Address and Links bars by opening the View menu, choosing Options, and selecting the options you want in the lower part of the General tab.

⇨ Change what web site is automatically opened when you start Internet Explorer by displaying the web site in the Internet Explorer, opening the View menu, choosing Options, clicking the Navigation tab, selecting Start Page in the Page drop-down list, and clicking Use Current.

⇨ Change the web sites that are pointed to on the Links bar by opening the View menu, choosing Options, clicking the Navigation tab, selecting Quick Link #1 through #5, and entering the Name and Address of the URL that you want to use.

⇨ Organize how web sites are displayed in your Favorites list by opening the Favorites menu, choosing Organize Favorites, and then moving, renaming, deleting, and placing in new or existing folders the web sites that are listed.

❓ How can I *get the latest version of Internet Explorer*?

At the time this is written (summer 1997), the latest English language version of the Internet Explorer for Windows 95 and Windows NT 4.0 is Version 3.02. It is available for download from **http://www.microsoft.com/msdownload/ieplatform/iewin95.htm**.

❓ I have *several web sites that I want to be able to quickly open*. What is the best way to do that?

Probably the easiest way to handle this is to put shortcuts on your desktop to these web sites. Then all you need to do is double-click the shortcut to open Internet Explorer and display the web site, if you are connected to the Internet. Use these steps to create the shortcuts:

1. Connect to the Internet and start Internet Explorer.

2. Enter the URL or address of the site for which you want to create a shortcut and press ENTER. Your site should be displayed in Internet Explorer.

3. Open the File menu and choose Create Shortcut. A message will appear telling you that a shortcut is about to be created. Click OK. A shortcut to the web site will appear on your desktop, like this:

I have several foreign e-mail correspondents. Does Internet Explorer *support international character sets*, and if so, how?

Yes, Internet Explorer supports a large number of international character sets by default, and you can download additional support packs for Chinese (Traditional or Simplified), Japanese, and Pan Euro for Eastern European support. To view e-mail and web pages with the special characters in French, German, Spanish, and the Scandinavian languages, you don't have to do anything special—the characters will automatically be displayed. For the Eastern European and Far Eastern languages, you must download support packs. Do that with these steps:

1. Open the Microsoft Internet Explorer download page at **http://www.microsoft.com/ie/download/**.

2. Select the operating system you are using (probably Windows 95 and Windows NT 4.0) and click Next.

3. In the drop-down list, choose Internet Explorer 3.0 Multilanguage Support, as shown here, and then click Next.

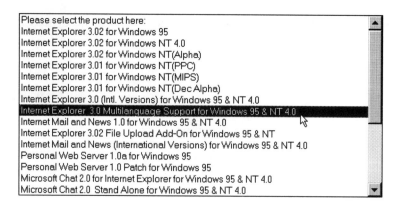

Please select the product here:
Internet Explorer 3.02 for Windows 95
Internet Explorer 3.02 for Windows NT 4.0
Internet Explorer 3.02 for Windows NT(Alpha)
Internet Explorer 3.01 for Windows NT(PPC)
Internet Explorer 3.01 for Windows NT(MIPS)
Internet Explorer 3.01 for Windows NT(Dec Alpha)
Internet Explorer 3.0 (Intl. Versions) for Windows 95 & NT 4.0
Internet Explorer 3.0 Multilanguage Support for Windows 95 & NT 4.0
Internet Mail and News 1.0 for Windows 95 & NT 4.0
Internet Explorer 3.02 File Upload Add-On for Windows 95 & NT
Internet Mail and News (International Versions) for Windows 95 & NT 4.0
Personal Web Server 1.0a for Windows 95
Personal Web Server 1.0 Patch for Windows 95
Microsoft Chat 2.0 for Internet Explorer for Windows 95 & NT 4.0
Microsoft Chat 2.0 Stand Alone for Windows 95 & NT 4.0

4. Select the language you want to use, for example, for Korean, choose Korean - Internet Explorer 3.0 Multilanguage Support, and then click Next.

5. Choose the server that you want to use, and follow the instructions that are provided.

To use the new language support, click the globe in the lower right of Internet Explorer and select the desired language. Doing this with the Korean language is shown in Figure 10-11.

Korean (KSC-5601)

 Tip   *You can get many full-language versions of Internet Explorer (where all the labels and menus are in another language) in addition to the ability to support another language in the English language version.*

❓ I have been using Eudora to handle my e-mail and would like to switch to Internet Explorer. How can I *transfer my address book and message file to Internet Explorer*?

Release 3.02 of the English language version of Internet Explorer for Windows 95 and Windows NT 4.0 will automatically detect and ask if you want to import your Eudora Light, Eudora Pro, or Netscape address book and existing mail messages when you open Internet

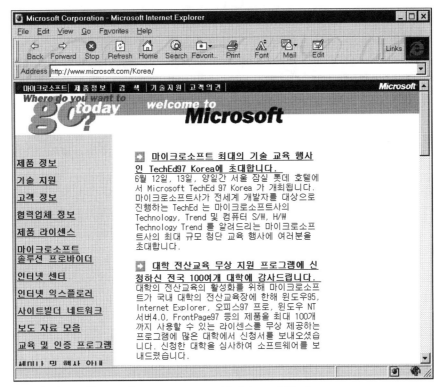

Figure 10-11.   Korean language support in Internet Explorer

Mail and News for the first time. You'll be given a choice of importing messages or the address book from Eudora or Netscape Navigator. You can also import your mail messages and the address book after the first startup of Internet Mail and News by opening the File menu and choosing Import.

chapter

11 Answers!

Multimedia

Answer Topics!

Multimedia @ a Glance

Multimedia is to computing as spice is to food—it may not fill you up, but it sure improves the taste. *Multimedia* is the addition of sound and video plus the use of CD-ROMs in a computer environment. Windows 95 provides a substantial enhancement to the support for multimedia that has been available at the operating system level. Windows 95 includes built-in programs to record, edit, and play back digital audio, and to play back digital video. Windows 95 also includes a substantial enhancement in the playback of full-motion video, has built-in support for many audio and video compression schemes, allows sharing a CD-ROM over a network, and includes a new media control interface for controlling different types of media devices. Windows 95 is the first multimedia operating system.

To make full use of multimedia and really, of Windows 95, you need a CD-ROM drive (2x, or double speed, and above), an audio or sound board (preferably 16-bit), and a pair of speakers. You also need to install the multimedia components that come with Windows 95. You can install them during setup or by using the Add/Remove Programs control panel. When installed, the programs are available by choosing Start | Programs | Accessories | Multimedia. Here are the most common multimedia applications that come with Windows 95:

CD Player plays your CD audio disks. It allows you to play CD music or other files. You can start, stop, fast forward and rewind, and skip to the beginning or end. You can play a CD continuously or in random order, and select which tracks you want to play. You can also build and maintain a database of the selections on your CDs.

Media Player is a general-purpose multimedia player that plays all types of multimedia files: audio, video, and animation. It allows you to control the play of a clip, create a new clip by inserting one file into another, and edit an existing clip.

Sound Recorder allows you to digitally capture sound from either a microphone or the CD. With it you can record, stop, go to the beginning or end of the recording, insert other files into it, and perform special tasks, such as increasing the volume for specific parts of the recording, adding an echo, or mixing two recordings so both are heard.

Volume Control controls the volume and balance of your audio files by providing a slider for each function. Depending on your equipment, you will have a dialog box for volume and balance of all multimedia, line-in, synthesizer, CD, wave, and microphone devices.

This chapter discusses the following topics:

⇨   **Sound** covers such items as assigning sound to events, how to get sound from speakers even if you don't have a sound card, and adding a sound card to your computer.

⇨   **CD-ROM** includes information about changing the configuration of your CD-ROM, how to play a music CD on your computer, how to correct problems that may occur with your CD-ROM after installing Windows 95, the effects of plug-and-play on your CD-ROM drivers, and shortcuts to use with the Windows 95 CD player.

⇨   **Media Player** defines Media Player and covers how to use this feature. This section also shows you how to find out if you have an MPEG driver installed.

⇨   **Volume Control** gives information about problems that may occur and how to remedy them, and how to put Volume Control on the Taskbar.

⇨   **Sound Recorder** shows you how to use the recorder, and how to deal with problems when no Wave driver is installed.

SOUND

 I have _added a sound card to my PC_. What is the easiest way that I can set it up for use with Windows 95? The disk that came with the card is for Windows 3.x. Should I use it?

Don't use the disk with the card, because the driver provided was written for Win3.x. You should let Windows 95 do the setup for you. If your card is plug-and-play compliant (you will find that information in the card's label or user's guide), all you have to do is plug in the card and start Windows 95. If the card is not plug-and-play, do the following:

1. Click the Start button; choose Settings | Control Panel | Add New Hardware.

2. Click Next and then click Yes for the question "Do you want Windows to search for your new hardware?"

3. Click Next and after several seconds, Windows 95 will automatically detect the card and load the appropriate 32-bit driver. Follow the prompts on the screen.

4. If Windows 95 did not automatically detect the card, manually select the manufacturer and model by first selecting Sound, Video And Game Controllers.

5. You will be shown a group of possible resource settings that you can print. Windows has considered the needs of the board and the available resources, and determined these are the best. If these settings do not match what is set on the board, you can either open the Device Manager in the System control panel, or you can change the settings on the board. In either case, click Next and follow the instructions to complete the installation.

? How can I *assign sound to program events*?

Events, such as opening files, completing a job, or encountering an error, can have sounds assigned to them if you have a sound card. Use the following steps to do this:

1. Click Start; choose Settings | Control Panel | Sounds. The Sounds Properties dialog box will open.

2. In the Events list, select the event you want to assign a sound to. (You can scan the list and see what events currently have sounds assigned to them, such as starting Windows. Events with sounds assigned are identified by a speaker icon, as shown in Figure 11-1.)

3. In the Name list, select the sound you want to hear when the event occurs. If you don't see the sound in the list, click Browse and locate the sound. Windows 95 has several sound schemes that come with it. More are available on the CD-ROM, although you might have to install them, because they are not installed by default.

4. You can create a scheme that is used with your own chosen sounds and save it by clicking Save As and naming the sound scheme.

5. Click OK when you are finished.

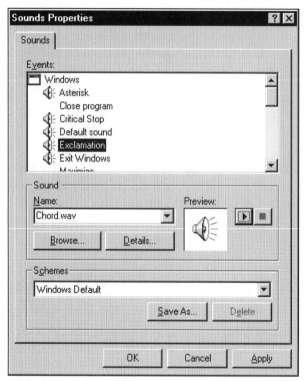

Figure 11-1.   Assign a sound to an event by clicking the event and then selecting a sound

Can I *get sound from my PC speaker if I don't have a sound card*?

Yes, if you have the PC speaker driver file Speaker.drv. You can obtain this from the Microsoft web site. Start at **http://www.microsoft.com/ WindowsSupport**; search for article Q138857, read the article, and then download file Speak.exe. After you download the file (you should do it into an empty directory), double-click it to extract Speaker.drv and the other files. Read the text files by double-clicking them. When you are ready, use the following steps to install Speaker.drv.

Tip   *You won't get very high-quality sound out of your PC speaker, and depending on your equipment, you may not get sound that you want to listen to. That's why Microsoft did not include it in Windows 95.*

1. Click the Start button; choose Settings | Control Panel | Add New Hardware.

2. Click Next to start the Add Hardware Wizard.

3. Choose No to avoid having Windows 95 search for new hardware. Click Next.

4. Select Sound, Video And Game Controllers from the Hardware Types list. Click Next.

5. Click Have Disk and then Browse to where you have your PC Speaker driver file. (The system looks for an .INF file. It will find the Oemsetup.inf file, which Windows 95 will use to set up the speaker driver.)

6. Choose OK to install. When it is done, you'll be asked if you want to restart your computer to complete the installation. Click Yes.

To modify the settings for PC Speaker:

1. Click the Start button; choose Settings | Control Panel | Multimedia.

2. Click the Advanced tab. Double-click Audio Devices and you will see Audio For Sound Driver For PC Speaker.

3. Click it to select it, and then click Properties to verify or change the settings. (If the Settings button is not available, the settings cannot be changed.)

4. Click OK three times to finalize it, and close all the dialog boxes. If you now go to the Sounds control panel, you should be able to click a sound and hear something.

CD-ROM

With the plug-and-play features of Windows 95, _are the drivers that came with my CD-ROM necessary_? Will Windows 95 already have drivers built in?

Windows 95 provides the drivers for the majority of CD-ROMs, so you don't need any drivers that come with your CD-ROM. You may need the drivers for use with the previous versions of MS-DOS if you are using a dual-boot system with an option of booting into a previous version of MS-DOS or Windows 95.

OSR 2 Note   With OSR 2 you can no longer dual-boot with Windows 3.1/DOS.

? I have installed Windows 95 and now my *CD-ROM no longer works*. How can I get it to work?

The problem could be because Windows is using the real-mode drivers from your Config.sys file. See the discussion on this subject in Chapter 2. If your CD-ROM is a Sony, Mitsumi, Panasonic, Toshiba, or a number of others, Windows 95 will install the appropriate drivers. After removing the Config.sys statements, try running the Install New Hardware Wizard in the Control Panel and let the system autodetect the hardware.

If the system fails to detect the CD-ROM, you'll have to manually select the manufacturer and model.

? How can I optimize the performance and *change the configuration of my CD-ROM drive*?

You can optimize the performance of the CD-ROM drive by setting up a cache large enough to contain an entire multimedia stream. To do that, follow these steps:

1. Click the Start button; choose Settings | Control Panel | System icon.

2. In the System Properties dialog box, click the Performance tab and click the File System button in the lower left.

3. Click the CD-ROM tab in the File System Properties dialog box, as shown in Figure 11-2.

4. Open the Optimize Access Pattern For drop-down list, and select the speed of the CD drive that you have.

5. Drag the Supplemental Cache Size slider to a setting according to these guidelines. (These settings are based on 8MB of RAM or more.)

    ⇨ **Single speed**, set to Small

    ⇨ **Double speed**, set to one-third across from the left

    ⇨ **Triple speed**, set to two-thirds across from the left

    ⇨ **Quad speed**, set to Large

6. Click Apply | OK | Close when you are finished.

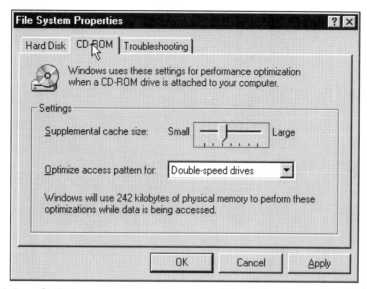

Figure 11-2.   Optimize your CD-ROM from the File System Properties dialog box

7. Answer Yes to "Do you want to restart your computer now for changes to take effect?"

Can I *play a music CD on my PC*?

You sure can. In fact, Windows 95 has an AutoPlay feature that begins playing the audio CD disk as soon as you insert the disk into the CD-ROM drive. (To prevent automatically playing the CD, hold down the SHIFT key when you insert it.) To permanently disable the AutoPlay feature so that it does not begin playing the CD automatically, follow these steps:

1. Double-click My Computer, open the View menu, and choose Options.

2. Click the File Types tab.

3. Select AudioCD and then click Edit. The Edit File Type dialog box will be displayed, as shown in Figure 11-3.

4. Click Set Default to toggle AutoPlay off. If the Play command is in boldface, the CD will play when it is inserted; if "Play" is not bold, it will not.

5. Click OK when you're satisfied.

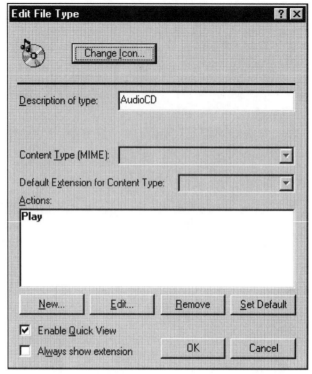

Figure 11-3.   You can vary the default to automatically play a CD

❓ Are there any *shortcuts or tricks that I can use with the Windows 95 CD player*?

Yes. You can play or change songs using a variety of techniques. Try some of the following:

⇨ Open the Explorer and click your CD-ROM drive with an audio CD in it. In the right panel you will see Track01.cda, Track02.cda, and so on, as shown in Figure 11-4. If you right-click a track, you can play it automatically by choosing Play from the pop-up menu. If you already are playing a track, it will be changed.

⇨ If you double-click a track displayed in Explorer, it will play automatically.

⇨ Try right-dragging a track onto your desktop and creating a shortcut. Rename the track's shortcut to the song's real name, as

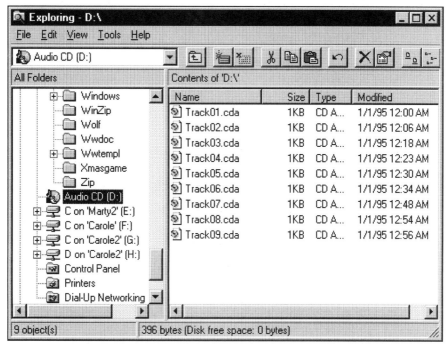

Figure 11-4. Viewing the tracks on a CD with Explorer allows you to pick which one you want to play

shown here. Whenever you have the CD in the drive, you can now double-click its icon on the desktop to play it.

⇨ You can also drag tracks to your hard drive and put them in your Start menu, or create a folder with CD tracks in it.

Tip   *When you drag a "copy" instead of a shortcut to your hard drive, you are not really copying the music file, only a pointer or link to it similar to a shortcut. To get the music on your hard disk, you must record it, although you should note that the .WAV file sizes are quite large (a 48-second piece in 16-bit stereo is over 8MB).*

I connected everything, but _Windows 95 does not seem to recognize my CD-ROM drive_. How do I install it?

Make sure that your controller is recognized. Use the following steps to do this:

1. Right-click My Computer and choose Properties I Device Manager.

2. Locate the SCSI or IDE controller in the device tree. (If you do not immediately see it, it is probably hidden under the hard disk controller's device.)

3. Open the branch for your SCSI or IDE controller by clicking the plus (+) sign at the left. Click the controller and then click the Properties button.

4. On the General tab, verify that the Device Status message states, "This device is working properly," as shown in Figure 11-5, and that the Device Usage check box is enabled for the Original Configuration. Click OK to return to the Device Manager.

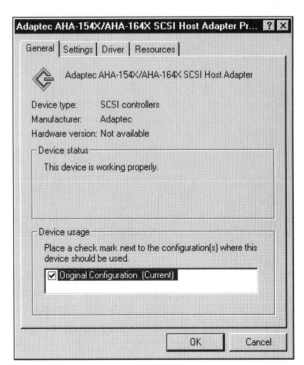

Figure 11-5.   From the Device Manager, you can verify that Windows 95 thinks the device is operating correctly

OSR 2 *Note   OSR 2 displays two check boxes here instead of the list of configurations in retail Windows 95.*

If you have several devices connected to the controller, and any of the SCSI or IDE devices does not have a Windows 95 driver, you can only use the devices connected to the controller with real-mode drivers.

MEDIA PLAYER

How can I find out if I have an *MPEG driver installed on my system*?

1. Click the Start button; select Programs | Accessories | Multimedia.

2. Click Media Player and then open the Device menu as shown here. If an MPEG device such as ActiveMovie is one of the devices listed, you have it. If not, you do not have MPEG installed.

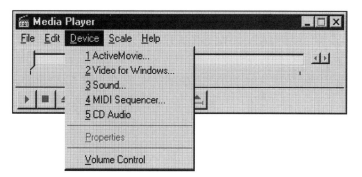

What is Media Player?

Media Player is a multimedia application that allows you to play MIDI, video, and CD-Audio files. Unlike the Sound Recorder, this is a playback-only device. To access Media Player, you must have a sound card installed. If you have it installed, do the following:

1. Click the Start button; choose Programs | Accessories | Multimedia | Media Player. You will see the Media Player window open, as shown here:

To play a file, first select the device, as follows:

1. Click Device and choose the type you will be using: for example, Video For Windows, Sound, MIDI, or CD Audio. The options you see will depend on the hardware you have installed.

2. Select the file for playback and click Open.

3. Click the Play button.

 Tip   *Sound files usually have the extension .WAV; video files, .AVI; MIDI files, .MID; movie files, .MPEG; and CD audio files, .CDA.*

VOLUME CONTROL

Why can't I *get the Volume Control utility included with Windows 95 to work with my sound card*?

Volume Control will only work if you install one of the sound drivers included with Windows 95 or a Windows 95-specific driver for your sound card. The Sound Blaster driver included with Windows 95 should work fine with Sound Blaster-compatible cards. To install that driver:

1. Click the Start button; choose Settings I Control Panel I Add New Hardware.

2. The Add New Hardware Wizard will be displayed. Click Next to get it started. Choose No when it asks you if you want Windows to search for your new hardware. Then click Next.

3. From the list of Hardware Types, select Sound, Video And Game Controllers, as shown in Figure 11-6. Click Next.

4. Choose Creative Labs for the manufacturer and Creative Labs Sound Blaster as the model. Click Next.

Figure 11-6.   Select the sound device from the list of hardware types

5. You will be shown the default settings that will be used for the new device. You have the opportunity to print the settings, and it is a good idea to do so. Click Next.

6. Files will be copied at this point, so you may be required to insert the Windows 95 installation CD-ROM or floppy disks. Follow the onscreen instructions.

Can I put *Volume Control on the Taskbar*?

A Volume Control icon on the Taskbar is very handy for controlling the volume and turning the sound on and off (for example, during phone calls!). You can do this using the following steps:

1. Click the Start button; choose Settings | Control Panel | Multimedia.

2. Click the Audio tab, and select the option Show Volume Control On The Taskbar. Click OK.

Tip *In the Audio tab, if the Show Volume Control On The Taskbar option is unavailable, make sure it is installed. Do this by opening the Control Panel, double-clicking Add/Remove Programs, and selecting Windows Setup tab. Select Multimedia in the Components list, click Details, and check Volume Control in the Components list.*

3. To use Volume Control, double-click the icon on the Taskbar to open the Volume Control dialog box, shown in Figure 11-7 (your Volume Control dialog box may look different, depending on your sound card), or click this icon to open the Volume Control slider, shown here:

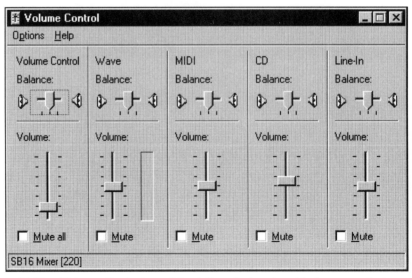

Figure 11-7.   Volume Control provides full audio level and balance control

SOUND RECORDER

? **I tried to start Sound Recorder, and there is _no Wave driver installed_. What do I do?**

The prerequisite is to have a sound card (or at least the Speaker.drv file described earlier). Then you can do one of the following:

⇨ Install or reinstall the sound card using Add New Hardware as described in several instances before.

⇨ If the sound card is Sound Blaster compatible, use the Sound Blaster driver that ships with Windows. (See the question under CD-ROM for how to install that driver.)

⇨ If the correct driver for the type of sound card being used is not listed, try using Windows 3.1 drivers for the specific card.

? **How do I _use the Sound Recorder_?**

If you have a microphone or a CD connected to your computer, you can record sound. Use the following steps to do this.

1. Click the Start button; choose Programs | Accessories | Multimedia | Sound Recorder. The Sound Recorder window will be displayed, as shown here:

2. Click the red Record button on the right.

3. Click the Stop button to end recording.

4. Open the File menu, choose Save As, and type a filename for this .WAV file.

chapter

12 Answers!

Windows 95
DOS

Answer Topics!

Windows 95 DOS @ a Glance

Why does a Windows 95 book talk about DOS? There are two good reasons.
First, because there are thousands of DOS programs out there, especially games,
that people are not willing to quit using, and second, because DOS and its
command language *are* a very real and important part of Windows 95. Why in
this point-and-click world would someone want to type DOS commands?
Because certain tasks are easier for longtime DOS users to perform with
commands, and because some debugging tasks can only be performed at a DOS
prompt. You therefore can look at DOS from two different, although related,
standpoints: using DOS to run DOS programs and using its command language.

Here are the areas explored by this chapter:

⇨   **How Do I Do This in DOS** describes how some DOS tasks are handled in
    the new environment.

> ⇨ **Improving Performance** answers questions arising about response time, optimizing and customizing DOS, and otherwise improving the performance of DOS with Windows 95.
>
> ⇨ **Running DOS Programs** describes situations that can arise with trying to run DOS programs, such as accessing specific drivers.
>
> ⇨ **Managing Autoexec.bat and Config.sys Files** covers how Windows 95 uses (or doesn't) these DOS files and how they can be modified.
>
> ⇨ **Between DOS and Windows** answers questions about how DOS and Windows 95 interact—to pass parameters or data, for example.
>
> ⇨ **Effects of Long Filenames** covers how this new feature in Windows 95 can raise questions in DOS.

HOW DO I DO THIS IN DOS?

? **I have MS-DOS 3.3 on my system, and I _cannot boot into the previous MS-DOS version_. I edited Msdos.sys as suggested, added BOOTMULTI=1, and it still does not work. How can I solve this problem?**

Unfortunately, you've just encountered a "no-solution" problem. To boot into the previous DOS version, you need DOS version 5.0 or greater.

? **Can I _change the way my MS-DOS window looks_?**

To change the DOS window, do the following:

1. Right-click the Start button and choose Open.

2. Double-click Programs, find the MS-DOS Prompt, and right-click it.

3. Choose Properties from the pop-up menu.

   ⇨ On the Font tab, you can select between font types of Bitmap Only, TrueType Only, or Both Font Types. You can also change the point size for the font for your DOS window. As you choose a Font Size, you can see how it will look by its effects on the Window Preview and the Font Preview, as shown in Figure 12-1.

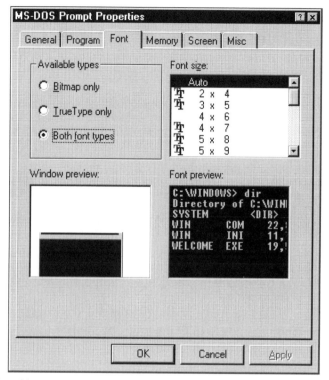

Figure 12-1. You can see how font changes will affect the DOS window

⇨ On the Screen tab, you can choose to run the program full screen or in a window, set an initial size or number of lines in the screen, and specify whether to display the toolbar.

Has the _DOS Replace command been removed_ from Windows 95?

Yes, it has been removed from the DOS in Windows 95. However, you can use the new version of Xcopy that comes with Windows 95 with the /y switch to overwrite existing files without prompting, or with the /-y switch to prompt before overwriting. This duplicates the functionality of Replace.

Caution _You may find that Replace is on your CD-ROM in the \Other\Oldmsdos folder. These DOS commands are from version 6.2, even though they are dated with Windows 95. They are_ not _long-filename aware and can cause damage if they are used with long filenames._

? In MS-DOS mode, I cannot access a new folder I have created called "My Letters"! When I type CD \My Letters, I get an *error message: "Too many parameters - Letters."* Is MS-DOS mode not compatible with long filenames?

You just have to vary your command format. To switch to your new folder, type **CD \"My Letters"**. Enclosing the name of the folder in quotes makes MS-DOS read the name of the folder as one block of text.

? Can I *run a Windows program from the DOS prompt*, or do I have to start it from the Windows 95 desktop?

You can start both Windows and DOS programs from the DOS command line using the new START command. For example, to start Microsoft Excel from the DOS command line, type this:

START [drive letter]:\[full path] excel.exe.

For example: START C:\Excel\Excel.exe

You can add the following switches to the START command, for example: START/m.

⇨ **/m** runs application minimized in the background

⇨ **/max** runs application maximized in the foreground

⇨ **/r** runs application restored in the foreground (default)

⇨ **/w** stands for wait; will not return control to the user until another program exits

? How can I *specify a working folder for a DOS application*?

A *working folder* is what the application uses as a default folder to store its output. You can specify a working folder in the properties for the program stored with its shortcut. Use the following steps to access the properties for a DOS application and specify a working folder:

1. Click the Start button and select Programs | Windows Explorer.

2. Open the folder with your application, and then right-click the application.

3. Choose Properties and then click the Program tab. You can specify the working folder in the Working box, as shown in Figure 12-2. Click OK.

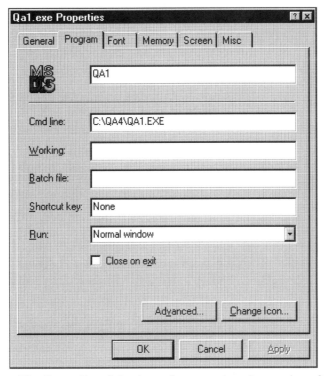

Figure 12-2.   The Properties dialog box allows you to set a number of parameters for a DOS program

Tip   *From the Properties dialog box you can establish a batch file that will run before starting a DOS program. Type in the name of the batch file just below the working folder name. For example, if you want to use DOSKEY without loading it with Autoexec.bat, you can enter **DOSKEY** as the startup batch file. You'll save some conventional memory that way.*

Can I *start Windows 95 in the DOS mode at all times*?

Yes. You can boot in DOS, and then start Windows 95 from DOS when you're ready for it. To do so, follow these steps:

1. Using Explorer, open your root folder, right-click the file Msdos.sys, and choose Properties. (If you don't see the file, open the Explorer's View menu, click Options, in the View tab click Show All Files, and click OK. Now try to right-click Msdos.sys.)

2. In the Msdos.sys Properties dialog box, if Read-Only and Hidden in the bottom of the dialog box are checked, click them to remove the check marks, and then click OK. This allows you to edit Msdos.sys and save your changes.

3. Right-click Msdos.sys and choose Copy. Right-click an empty area of the right pane of the Explorer window and choose Paste. This creates a copy of Msdos.sys that you can use if you make a mistake while editing it.

4. Right-click Msdos.sys again and choose Open With | Notepad.

5. Locate the section entitled [Options], as seen in Figure 12-3.

6. Change the line *BootGUI=1* to **BootGUI=0**.

7. Save the changes and reboot.

8. The PC will now always start in DOS mode.

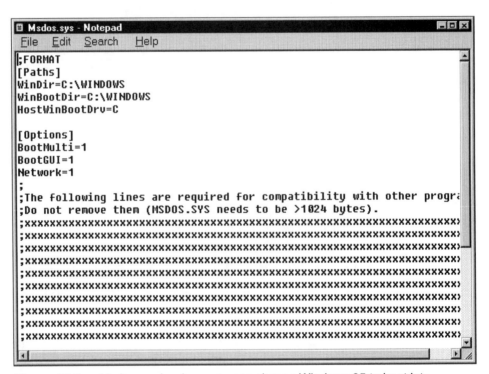

Figure 12-3.   Msdos.sys is where you can change Windows 95 to boot into DOS mode

9. To go into Windows 95, at the command prompt type **WIN**.

10. When you're satisfied with the changes, you can reset the Hidden and Read-Only attributes of Msdos.sys to prevent overwriting, and delete the copy.

More About DOS and Windows 95

In most cases Windows 95 will run DOS programs better and more easily than any prior version of DOS. This is true because Windows 95 takes less conventional memory (that below 640K) than prior versions of DOS, and because Windows 95 does a better job of providing memory and disk resources than was the case in the past. Windows 95 also gives you a number of ways to start DOS programs. Among these are

⇨ Locating the program in Explorer or My Computer and double-clicking it

⇨ Placing a shortcut to the program on the desktop where you can double-click it, or putting a shortcut on the Start menu where you can click it. (The Windows 95 shortcut replaces the .PIF files used in previous versions of Windows.)

⇨ Typing the path and filename for the program in the Run Option dialog box

⇨ Opening a DOS window or booting into DOS, and typing the path and filename for the program

While this last method describes two classical DOS approaches to starting DOS programs, the first three methods are classical Windows. The second, using shortcuts, is all Windows 95. As a matter of fact, shortcuts do more for DOS programs than for Windows programs. A shortcut for a DOS program allows you to specify a number of settings about how you want the program to run, including whether you want the program to run

⇨ in DOS mode

⇨ in a window

More About DOS and Windows 95, continued

⇨ full screen

⇨ without detecting Windows

(If a DOS program tells you it can't run under Windows 95, try telling it to not detect Windows in its shortcut.)

⇨ by shutting down Windows and starting DOS by itself

A shortcut for a DOS program can be created in the same ways as with other programs: dragging a program's .EXE file to the desktop or Start menu, or choosing Create Shortcut from either the File menu or pop-up menu. You can also create a shortcut to a DOS program by opening the Properties dialog box for the program. Since the program didn't come with properties, a shortcut is created for the program. It is the shortcut's properties that you will be looking at.

The DOS commands in Windows 95 are a mixture of some new commands and some old (and familiar) DOS commands. The old commands remaining in Windows 95, while they have the same name and the same structure, have been rewritten to work in the 32-bit world and with long filenames. Windows 95 has also deleted some previous DOS commands. You can look up the commands not included in Windows 95 (see Figure 12-4) as well as all those that are in the Windows 95 Resource Kit help file located in the \Admin\Reskit\Helpfile\ folder on the Windows 95 CD-ROM. (Double-click Win95rk.hlp and then open Appendixes | Command-Line Commands Summary | Native Windows 95 Commands | Commands Not Included In Windows 95.) You can also check on a command's existence and see what parameters and switches are used with it by typing the command followed by /? either in the Run command, or at the command prompt in a DOS window.

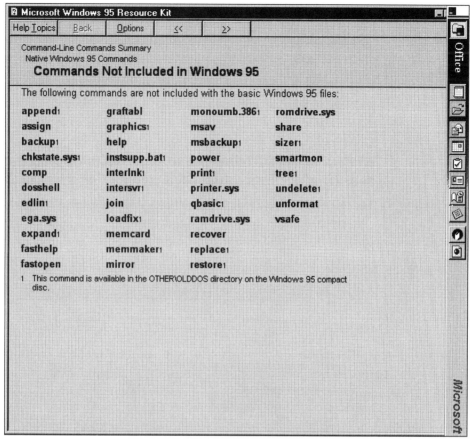

Figure 12-4.   The Windows 95 Resource Kit lists the old DOS commands not in
Windows 95

IMPROVING PERFORMANCE

? **How _can I speed up my MS-DOS application_? It slows
down to a crawl when it runs in the background.**

You can adjust the speed of the application by doing the following:

1. Right-click the Start button and choose Open | Programs.

2. Right-click the MS-DOS Prompt icon.

3. Choose Properties, and then click the Misc tab, as shown in Figure 12-5.

4. Move the Idle Sensitivity slider to Low.

5. In the Background area, make sure that Always Suspend is not selected.

? Will Windows 95 allow me to _customize/optimize my "DOS sessions"_ for individual DOS applications as OS/2 does?

Yes, you can do that with the Properties dialog box for the DOS program. Here are the steps to follow:

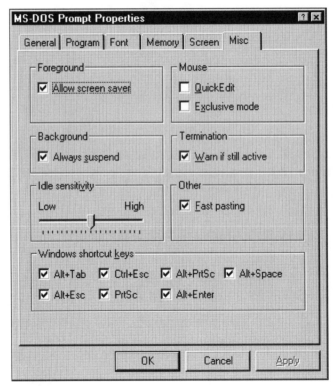

Figure 12-5.   MS-DOS Prompt Properties can be modified for improved performance

1. Using Explorer, find the program file (.EXE file) of the DOS program, and drag it to the desktop. That creates a shortcut to the DOS application.

2. Right-click the shortcut and choose Properties from the pop-up menu. The program's Properties dialog box will be displayed. Here you can change and modify the settings for the application. The functions of each of the tabs are as follows:

   ⇨ **General tab** displays the statistics and attributes about the program and allows you to set the attributes for Read-Only, Archive, Hidden, and System.

   ⇨ **Program tab** displays the program name, path to find it, working folder, batch file, shortcut key, and with which type of window (Normal, Minimized, or Maximized) it will begin. The Advanced button allows you to set whether the program can detect Windows and if you want the program to run in DOS only mode, as shown in Figure 12-6.

   ⇨ **Font tab** is used to set the type and size of fonts used in the DOS window.

   ⇨ **Memory tab** controls the settings for Conventional Memory, Expanded Memory, Extended Memory, and MS-DOS Protected-Mode Memory.

   ⇨ **Screen tab** controls whether the DOS program will run full size or in a window, what size it will be, whether a DOS toolbar is displayed, and whether to use Fast ROM Emulation or Dynamic Memory Allocation.

   ⇨ **Misc tab** controls miscellaneous settings for foreground and background operations, using the mouse, terminating the program, shortcut keys, and more.

❓ I am running Windows 95 as my operating system now. I would love to _delete my old DOS to save some disk space_. Do I still need it?

You only need your old DOS folder if you plan to use the F4 option to boot into the previous DOS version. If you don't think you will ever be doing that, you can safely delete the DOS folder. The new versions

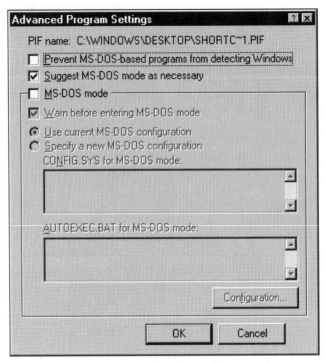

Figure 12-6.   The Advanced Program Settings dialog box allows you to prevent a
DOS program from seeing Windows

of DOS files that some applications might need are now in the
\Windows\Command folder.

**? When typing the MEM /C command in an MS-DOS window
to find out what free memory I have, I am told that I have
zero kilobytes free memory in the upper memory area
(UMA). How can this be? _Isn't Windows 95 supposed to
be better at allocating memory_?**

Windows 95 is, indeed, managing the memory very effectively. MEM
/C reports zero kilobytes because after loading all the real-mode
drivers during startup, Windows 95 reserves all global upper memory
blocks (UMBs) for Windows 95's own use or for expanded memory
support.

RUNNING DOS PROGRAMS

❓ I realize that Windows 95 can do a lot for DOS applications in shortcuts, but what if my _DOS application needs specific drivers_?

You may find that you have certain DOS applications that still need to see specific drivers being loaded. Windows 95 can and will use a Config.sys file if the file is created. Also, in the Advanced settings of the program's Properties dialog box, an MS-DOS mode can be specified, in which case, you can load specific drivers only when launching that program. To set MS-DOS mode to be loaded, follow these steps:

1. Open Explorer and find your DOS program.

2. Right-click the DOS application's icon, and choose Properties from the pop-up menu.

3. Click the Program tab and click the Advanced button.

4. Then select MS-DOS mode. Other options will then become available. If you select Specify A New MS_DOS Configuration, as shown in Figure 12-7, you can type in your desired configuration changes.

5. An easier way to change the configuration is to use a configuration checklist displayed when you click the Configuration button. Do that now and the Configuration Options dialog box in Figure 12-8 will open.

6. Click the options necessary for your program and then click OK.

7. Make any changes to the configuration that you need, and then click OK twice more.

❓ My _DOS application will not load because Windows is running_. How can I run this under Windows 95?

Some DOS-based programs are written not to load if they detect that Windows is running. So you must trick them a bit. Try this to run the program:

1. From Explorer, right-click the program.

2. Choose Properties from the pop-up menu.

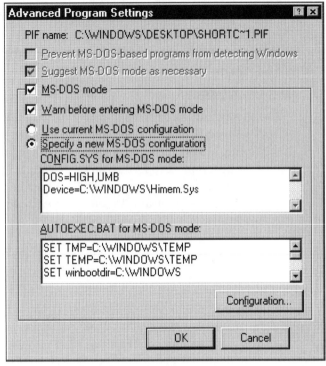

Figure 12-7.   You can specify a specific Config.sys and Autoexec.bat to run only when you run a specific DOS program

3. Click the Program tab and then click the Advanced button.

4. Click Prevent MS-DOS-Based Programs From Detecting Windows, as you saw earlier in Figure 12-6, and click OK.

5. Click OK again. This will return a code to these applications that says Windows is not running.

? Why does the *DOS window remain open with the text "Finished - application name"* appearing on the title bar when it is finished?

The DOS window remains open so you can see any error messages that the DOS application may have displayed. You can change the program properties for the MS-DOS-based application so that it does close by following these steps:

1. From Explorer, right-click the icon for the DOS application.

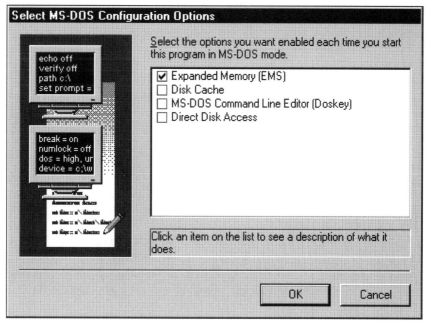

Figure 12-8.   A Configuration Options dialog box gives you a checklist of
possible options

2. Choose Properties from the pop-up menu and click the Program tab.

3. Select the Close On Exit option and click OK.

What can I do with *programs that won't run even in MS-DOS mode*?

Many legacy DOS programs, especially those that needed a boot disk,
will only run in MS-DOS mode under Windows 95. Sometimes, even
when you specify that the program run in MS-DOS mode (see a
previous question for how to do this), the program will not run or will
not run correctly. If you are using the current MS-DOS configuration
for Config.sys and Autoexec.bat, beware that by default, Windows 95
gives you a "clean boot" configuration. Your DOS program may need
specific device drivers and other settings not loaded by default in
order to work. Finding and loading these drivers and settings
manually can be quite a hassle. An easy way to do this is to copy
the old Autoexec.bat and Config.sys files into the new ones that
Windows 95 will use. Follow these steps to do this:

1. Find the appropriate boot disk the program used to work with.

2. Copy the Autoexec.bat and Config.sys files to your hard drive with identifying names (Darkfrce.aut and Darkfrce.cfg, for example).

3. From Windows 95, right-click the program shortcut icon and choose Properties. Click the Program tab and then the Advanced button. Select the MS-DOS mode and then click Specify A New MS-DOS Configuration.

4. While the Advanced Program Settings dialog box is open, click the Start button and select Programs | Accessories | Notepad.

5. Open the configuration files (Darkfrce.aut and Darkfrce.cfg in this case) one at a time.

6. Select all the contents of the file, copy them to the Clipboard using CTRL-C, click the Advanced Program Settings dialog box, and paste the Clipboard contents, using CTRL-V, into the Autoexec.bat and Config.sys text boxes, respectively.

7. Clean out any duplicate lines from the text boxes. Notice that some of the drivers from the old DOS folder should now be accessed from the Windows folder. Delete any of the default lines if necessary.

8. When you are finished, click OK twice.

When I am running a program in MS-DOS mode, *why can't I press ALT-TAB to go back to Windows*?

When you are running a program in MS-DOS mode, the application has exclusive access to the system, and all other applications are terminated, including Windows 95 Explorer, which is the Windows 95 shell. You are effectively shutting down Windows to run this application. Windows will restart when you exit.

MANAGING AUTOEXEC.BAT AND CONFIG.SYS FILES

How do I *add a "path" in Windows 95 similar to what existed in Autoexec.bat with PATH=*?

Run Sysedit.exe and add a path statement to the Autoexec.bat file. It is still there and it is still used by non-Windows applications.

? Do I need *Autoexec.bat or Config.sys in Windows 95*?

Windows 95 doesn't need Autoexec.bat or Config.sys. In fact, it speeds up your computer if you don't have them and may even make your DOS programs run better because Windows 95 does a better job of managing memory than if you try to do it in those files. The reason they are there is twofold: First, for compatibility—some programs look at these files and their contents. Second, you may need a driver that has no Windows 95 equivalent, in which case you can load them in real mode with Config.sys and Autoexec.bat.

? If Windows 95 doesn't need Autoexec.bat or Config.sys, how does it *load my necessary real-mode drivers, such as Himem.sys and Dblspace.bin*?

In Windows 95, the functionality of Autoexec.bat and Config.sys is replaced by a new file, Io.sys. The drivers that are loaded by default through Io.sys are the following:

⇨ Himem.sys

⇨ Ifshlp.sys

⇨ Setver.exe

⇨ Dblspace.bin or Drvspace.bin (if found on the hard disk)

In addition to these drivers, the following values are set by default with Io.sys:

⇨ DOS=high

⇨ Files=60

⇨ Lastdrive=z

⇨ Buffers=30

⇨ Stacks=9,256

⇨ Shell=command.com /p

⇨ Fcbs=4

Io.sys is not an editable file, but an entry in Config.sys will take precedence over the Io.sys settings. For example, Io.sys does not load Emm386, so if you have an application that loads data into the high memory area, you can load Emm386.exe in Config.sys.

Tip   *Contrary to what is said in the Windows 95 Resource Kit, Windows 95 does provide ExPanded memory without you having to load Emm386. See for yourself by removing the Emm386 statement and then looking at Mem /c in a DOS window.*

❓ *Windows 95 removes several lines in my Autoexec.bat file that I need to run specific DOS applications.* Does it mean that the commands are illegal? Why is that?

Setup remarks out lines starting with "Rem" that are no longer needed with Windows 95 although they are not illegal. After the setup is complete, you can use any text editor, such as Notepad, to edit Autoexec.bat and reenable the lines. However, if you don't run these applications often, you might consider running them in MS-DOS mode with their own Autoexec.bat and Config.sys files and allowing Windows to run the way it set itself up.

BETWEEN DOS AND WINDOWS

❓ Can I *cut and paste between MS-DOS applications and Windows applications, or between two MS-DOS applications*?

Yes, if the applications are running in separate windows. To paste from a DOS window to a Windows application, do the following:

1. If the DOS program is running full screen, press ALT-ENTER to switch to window mode, click the MS-DOS icon on the left of the title bar, choose Properties, and select Toolbar (if not selected).

2. Click the Mark button on the toolbar, select the lines to be copied, and click the Copy button.

3. Press ALT-TAB to switch to the Windows application, open the Edit menu, and choose Paste.

To paste from a Windows application to a DOS window:

1. Select and copy the lines from the Windows application.

2. Switch to the DOS application.

3. Click the Paste button.

? When I open a DOS window from Windows 95, I get an error message: *"Parameter value not in allowed range."* What did I do wrong?

Check to see if your MS-DOS Prompt settings are correct. Take a look at the properties for your MS-DOS Prompt. Make sure there are no additional settings that might confuse the system. To do this, follow these steps:

1. Click the Start button; choose Program | MS-DOS Prompt.

2. Then click the Properties button in the toolbar. (Or if you have a shortcut to MS-DOS Prompt on your desktop, right-click it and choose Properties.)

3. Check on the settings and verify that they are OK.

? How can I *pass parameters to my DOS application*?

You can do this in three ways. First, you can start the program by typing its name and the parameters in the Start menu Run option. Second, if you want to have a permanent set of parameters passed to the application every time you start it, you can enter those parameters in the Cmd line (command line) in the program's Properties dialog box Program tab. Finally, if you want to manually enter parameters when you run the program, you can add the ? prompt to the end of the command line in the program's Properties dialog box Program tab,
so that you will be asked to enter the parameters when the program starts. To add the prompt, follow these steps:

1. Using the Explorer, find your DOS program shortcut and right-click the icon. From the pop-up menu, choose Properties, and then click the Program tab.

2. Add a ? (question mark) to the end of the Cmd line (command line), as shown here:

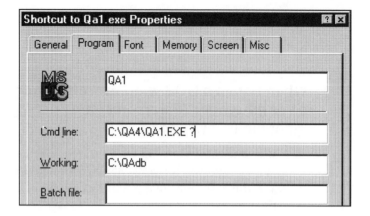

When you run the DOS program, you will be prompted to enter parameters in a little dialog box.

? **I was looking through the \Windows\System folder and have come across a *program called Mkcompat.exe*. Is this how you make old DOS programs compatible with Windows 95? How do I use it?**

Mkcompat.exe is used to make older Windows applications work with Windows 95. You use it by double-clicking it, opening the File menu, and specifying a program you want to work on. You then select the functions you want set, save your settings, and exit Mkcompat. Relatively few programs require the use of this program. The vast majority of both DOS and Windows programs work with Windows 95.

? ***What does Windows 95 Setup do to the DOS commands?***

Windows 95 deletes and upgrades a number of DOS files during setup. You can get a list of these files in the Windows 95 Resource Kit help file on the Windows 95 CD in the \Admin\Reskit\Helpfile\ folder. See Figure 12-4, shown earlier, for related information.

? ***Will Windows 95 run all my MS-DOS programs?***

Windows 95 is designed to run MS-DOS programs. If you have problems with a specific MS-DOS program, try these steps in order (all of the settings are made in the program's Properties dialog box):

⇨   Turn off the screen saver (Misc tab), and run Full-screen (Screen tab).

⇨ Prevent the program from detecting Windows (Program tab | Advanced Program Settings).

⇨ Force the program to run in an MS-DOS mode using the current configuration, which gives a program exclusive access to system resources but with the standard setup (Program tab | Advanced Program Settings).

⇨ Force the program to run in an MS-DOS mode using a custom configuration, which gives a program exclusive access to system resources and its own setup (Program tab | Advanced Program Settings | Configuration Options).

Tip   *When you run a program in MS-DOS mode, it will shut down Windows 95 and will load the program exclusively in an MS-DOS environment. When the program completes, it will automatically reload Windows.*

EFFECTS OF LONG FILENAMES

Why, when I am in a DOS window within Windows 95 or when I boot Windows 95 to a command line, is the *ability to create long filenames limited to 127 characters*?

The default command-line character limitation is 127 characters. In this default configuration, the DOS environment does not allow more than 127 characters to exist in a given command line. The command-line character can be increased to its maximum by placing the following line in the Config.sys file: **shell=c:\windows\ command.com /u:255**

When at a DOS prompt, I see *many of my files have been renamed using a ~ character*. Why is this?

While Windows 95 DOS does handle long filenames so that they are not lost or corrupted, it displays the 8.3 filename alias using a ~ (tilde). It takes the first six characters, adds the ~, and starts numbering consecutively, starting with 1. So, for example, if you have "Saturday's paper.doc" and "Saturday afternoon.doc," these will display as "Saturd~1.doc" and "Saturd~2.doc."

chapter

13 Answers!

The Registry and Microsoft Plus!

Answer Topics

Advanced Windows 95
Customization @ a Glance

There has been a lot of discussion of the largely successful attempt by Windows 95 to make personal computing easier to use with a more user-friendly interface. Another, but little discussed, success of Windows 95 was providing a powerful set of capabilities for customizing the way Windows looks and acts. Two sources of advanced customization capabilities are the Microsoft Plus! Companion for Windows 95 and the Windows 95 Registry, along with the tools that allow you to change the Registry: the Control Panel, the System Policy Editor, and the Registry Editor (also called Regedit). This chapter will cover advanced customization as follows:

⇨ **The Registry and Its Tools** looks at questions on how to access the Registry, what the files related to the Registry are and how they are used, how to find settings in the Registry, and how to solve problems related to the Registry.

⇨ **Using the Microsoft Plus! Companion** covers what is in Microsoft Plus!, how many of the components are used, and what some of the solutions are to possible problems.

⇨ **Other Customization Areas** includes a variety of questions that didn't fit easily elsewhere in the book.

373

THE REGISTRY AND ITS TOOLS

 Caution   *The answers to some of the following questions suggest that you make changes to the Registry. Improper changes to your Registry can cause your system to perform erratically. You should therefore make the suggested changes very carefully and **only after** making a backup copy of your Registry files, System.dat and User.dat. See the question, "What is the easiest way to make a copy of my Windows 95 Registry?"*

How do I *access the Registry settings*?

You can access the Registry settings in four ways. These, in the order of their ease and safety (with the first being the easiest and the safest), are as follows:

⇨ Using the **Control Panel** items allows you to change many of the settings in the Registry. The dialog boxes associated with the Control Panel give you a lot of information about what you are doing and are generally easy to use. To use the Control Panel, click Start | Settings | Control Panel, and then choose the area you want to access.

⇨ **File type** associations (the associations between document types and the programs that can open them) are a major component in the Registry. To create an association for a file type (generally indicated by the three-letter file extension) that does not have one, simply double-click the file, and the Open With dialog box will appear. Here you can enter a description and identify the program you want used to open the file. If you want to change, delete, or add new file associations, open the View menu in either Explorer or My Computer, choose Options, and then click the File Types tab, which is shown in Figure 13-1.

⇨ The **System Policy Editor**, which is hidden in the \Admin\ Apptools\Poledit folder on your Windows 95 CD-ROM, provides access to many areas of the Registry to allow the implementation of policies on the use of computers within an organization. The Policy Editor's settings, of course, can also be used to make desired Registry changes on a single machine. See the example in Chapter 4. To use the Policy Editor with your local Registry, insert your Windows 95 CD and use Explorer to open the \Admin\Apptools\Poledit folder.

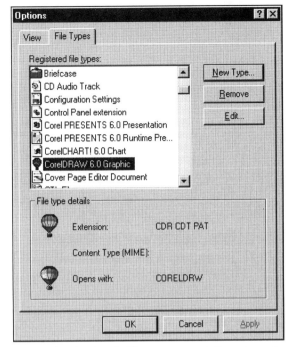

Figure 13-1. Change the Registry's file type associations from the Explorer's View menu Options dialog box

Then double-click Poledit.exe, open the File menu, and choose Open Registry.

⇨ The **Registry Editor's** Regedit.exe program in your \Windows folder gives direct access to all of the Registry's settings. The problem is that there is no information about what your options are or what the effect of a change will be. You simply select a setting and make a change, as shown in Figure 13-2, hoping the change will give you the desired results. You can access and use Regedit with the following steps:

1. Click the Start button, choose Run, and type **regedit**. (If you will be using it a lot, create a shortcut to it on your desktop or under Programs.) This will bring up the Registry Editor.

2. To display settings, double-click the folder and its subfolders for the key you want to access until you see the value you want to change on the right.

3. Right-click the value you want to change to bring up the pop-up menu shown in Figure 13-2. Alternatively,

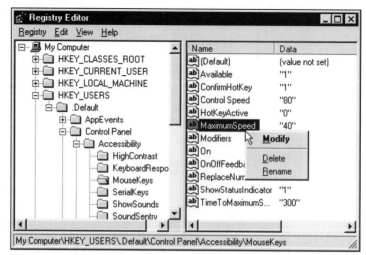

Figure 13-2.   Regedit provides direct access to the Registry but little help in changing it

double-click the value if you just want to modify it. This will bring up the Edit String dialog box shown here:

 Caution   *Make sure you back up the Registry's User.dat and the System.dat files in your \Windows folder **before** making modifications to the Registry.*

? What are the *files System.dat, System.da0, System.1st, User.dat, and User.da0*?

The System.dat file is your system Registry. This file stores all information about your computer and software. The System.da0 file is a backup copy of System.dat, which is created whenever you start

Windows. If Windows finds that your Registry is damaged, it attempts to use System.da0 from the previous session of Windows instead of System.dat.

The System.1st file is a copy of System.dat from the first time your computer booted successfully after the last installation of Windows 95. Unlike all the Registry files, which are in your \Windows folder, System.1st is in your root directory.

User.dat contains specific user information. A copy of User.dat always exists locally. When User.dat is placed in the user's logon folder on a server, a copy of that file is made on the user's local computer when the user logs on. User.da0 is a backup copy of User.dat. Like System.da0, it is created every time you start Windows and is automatically used if Windows thinks User.dat is corrupted.

Caution   User.dat and System.dat are very important to your system. Even though the system maintains a backup, it is only as old as the last time Windows 95 was started. You should make your own backups of these files periodically.

How can I *find a specific setting in the Registry*?

You can use Regedit to locate a setting:

1. Click the Start button, choose Run, type **regedit**, and click OK.

2. Open the Edit menu and choose Find.

3. Type a string to look for. For example, if you want to find the settings associated with a modem, open the Edit menu, choose Find, and type **modem**, like this:

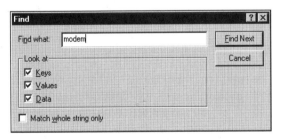

4. Click Find Next. To find another instance of the same string, press F3.

? **How can I *get rid of an application name in Add/Remove Programs* that is still there even though I have removed the application?**

You can accomplish this by making changes in the Registry. Use the following instructions for that purpose:

1. Open the Start menu, choose Run, type **regedit**, and press ENTER.

2. Select HKEY_LOCAL_MACHINE and click on the plus sign to expand the tree in this order: Software\Microsoft\Windows\CurrentVersion\Uninstall. The Uninstall folder has all the 32-bit programs you've installed.

3. Select the one(s) that you want to remove and press DEL. Confirm that you do want to remove the application(s) from the list.

4. When you are done, close Regedit. If you then look at Add/Remove Programs, the program(s) will be gone from the list.

? **What do the different *keys in the Registry* contain?**

The Registry keys are described next.

⇨ **HKEY_CLASSES_ROOT** contains information similar to that in Reg.dat in Windows 3.*x*—information about file associations and OLE parameters. All the file association information is here, as are drag-and-drop rules. Windows 95 has added information on shortcuts and some information on the user interface.

⇨ **HKEY_CURRENT_USER** contains user-specific information that is generated when the user logs on and is based on information for that user in HKEY_USERS.

⇨ **HKEY_LOCAL_MACHINE** contains information about the computer being referenced. It includes the drivers loaded on the system, what kind of devices are installed, and the current configuration of installed applications. This is machine-specific, not user-specific, information.

⇨ **HKEY_USERS** contains information about all users of the PC, plus a description of a default (generic) user. The information stored here concerns applications configuration, desktop settings, and sound schemes, among other things.

⇨ **HKEY_CURRENT_CONFIG** contains information about the current configuration of the workstation. This is used when you create different configurations for the same workstation—for example, laptop versus docked configuration.

⇨ **HKEY_DYN_DATA** contains dynamic status information for system devices used in plug-and-play. The device information includes its current status and any detected problems.

Is there a way I can *make a change to the Registry take effect without rebooting*?

Yes, you need to reload the Registry without rebooting. You can do this by pressing CTRL-ALT-DEL to bring up the Windows 95 Close Program window. Select Explorer and click on End Task. When Windows asks if you want to shut down, select No. Then you have to wait a couple of seconds, and at the next dialog box click End Task. This will refresh the Registry.

What is the easiest way to *make a copy of my Windows 95 Registry*?

Your Registry is made up of two files, System.dat and User.dat, in your C:\Windows folder. You can copy them in the same way you would copy any other files. Open the Windows 95 Explorer, open the Windows folder, find and select the files, right-click on one of them, and choose Copy from the context menu. Then select the disk and folder where you want the copies, right-click on any blank area in the right pane of the Explorer, and choose Paste. Copies of the two files will appear in the folder you choose, as shown here:

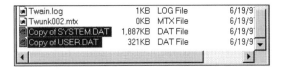

Twain.log	1KB	LOG File	6/19/9
Twunk002.mtx	0KB	MTX File	6/19/9
Copy of SYSTEM.DAT	1,887KB	DAT File	6/19/9
Copy of USER.DAT	321KB	DAT File	6/19/9

Note   *Windows 95 automatically makes a backup of your Registry files, System.dat and User.dat, and calls those files System.da0 and User.da0. The backup files are placed in the Windows folder with the original files.*

If you can't find the two Registry files, open the Start menu, choose Find | Files Or Folders, type **system.dat user.dat**, and click on Find Now. The result should look like Figure 13-3. Once you have found the two files, you can copy them as described earlier right from the Find dialog box.

Caution   *The files displayed in the Find dialog box are not copies but the original files. If you move or delete these files, you are moving or deleting the original files.*

? Why am I *missing my Network Neighborhood* icon from the Windows 95 desktop?

The Hide Network Neighborhood option may be enabled in your system policy. You can edit your system policy with the System Policy Editor (Poledit.exe), which is on your Windows 95 CD in the \Admin\AppTools\Poledit folder. Use the following instructions to turn the Network Neighborhood back on:

1. Load your Windows 95 CD. With the Windows 95 Explorer, locate and start the System Policy Editor.

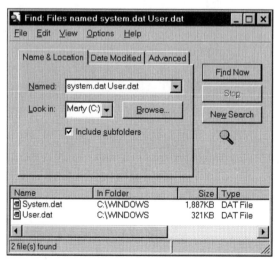

Figure 13-3.   Finding the Registry files

2. If the Open Template File dialog box automatically appears, double-click on Admin.adm to use that as the template.

3. Open the File menu and select Open Registry. Two icons will appear, Local User and Local Computer, as you can see here:

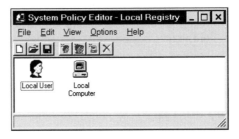

4. Double-click on Local User to open the Local User Properties dialog box. Click on Shell and then Restrictions to open their components, as shown in Figure 13-4.

5. Click on the Hide Network Neighborhood check box to clear it, and then click on OK to close the Properties dialog box and close the System Policy Editor.

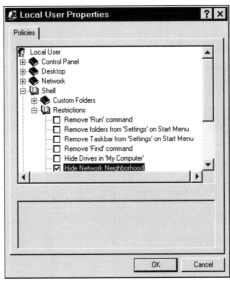

Figure 13-4.   Making changes in the system policy

? **How do I recover if I ever corrupt or have a _problem with the Windows 95 Registry_?**

The short answer is to copy System.da0 and User.da0 to System.dat and User.dat, respectively. The problem is that these are hidden, read-only files. Also, you probably won't be able to start Windows, so you must use DOS. If you are in Windows, shut down and restart in MS-DOS mode. Here are the DOS commands to type:

```
C:\WINDOWS>
C:\WINDOWS>Attrib -h -r -s system.da?
C:\WINDOWS>Attrib -h -r -s user.da?
C:\WINDOWS>copy system.da0 system.dat
C:\WINDOWS>Copy user.da0 user.dat
C:\WINDOWS>
```

When you have completed the previous steps, reboot your computer and start Windows 95 normally. If you still have problems and you have an additional backup other than .DA0, replace the .DA0 files in the previous instructions with your other backup files.

The instructions for recovering the Windows 95 Registry files are also contained in the Registry Help file. To see and possibly print them, start Regedit as described in the questions earlier, choose Help | Help Topics | Restoring The Registry, and click Display. To print the topic, click Options | Print Topic, as you can see in Figure 13-5.

? **Windows 95 stores the _recent history of RUN commands_ somewhere. Where can I find it?**

The recent contents of the Run Open drop-down list are in the Registry under HKEY_CURRENT_USER\Software\Microsoft\Windows\CurrentVersion\Explorer\RunMRU. The contents are listed under Data opposite the names a, b, c, and so on.

? **How can I change my _registered owner name_?**

This is maintained in the Registry, and you can change it there, as follows:

1. Open the Start menu, choose Run, type **regedit**, and press ENTER.

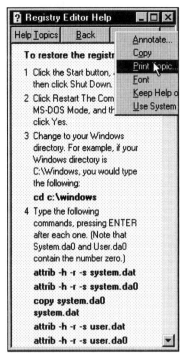

Figure 13-5.   Print the Help topic for restoring the Registry

2. Select HKEY_LOCAL_MACHINE and click on the plus sign to expand the tree in this order: Software\Microsoft\Windows. Then open CurrentVersion by clicking on it.

3. In the right pane locate the "RegisteredOwner" entry and double-click it.

4. In the Value Data box of the Edit String dialog box, shown next, change the name and click OK.

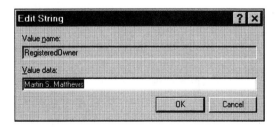

You can repeat the procedure for the "RegisteredOrganization" entry.

? **Can I _remove the shortcut arrows_ in shortcut icons on the desktop?**

Yes. From the Start menu choose Run, type **regedit**, and press ENTER. When the Registry Editor opens, click on the Edit menu, choose Find, type **IsShortcut**, and click on Find Next. The Registry will be searched and the first instance of IsShortcut will be found, like this:

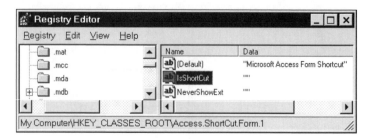

By pressing DEL and answering Yes that you really want to delete the value, you can remove the shortcut designation and arrow from this item. You can continue finding additional instances of IsShortcut by pressing F3. When you have removed all instances of IsShortcut, you'll get a message that you are finished searching the Registry. Close Regedit, select the desktop, and press F5 to refresh it. There will be no more shortcut arrows.

USING THE MICROSOFT PLUS! COMPANION

? **Why would I want to _buy Microsoft Plus!_?**

The Microsoft Plus! Companion for Windows 95 provides six additional features or capabilities for Windows 95. As shown in Figure 13-6, these are

⇨ **DriveSpace 3** provides enhanced disk compression over DriveSpace that is in Windows 95. This includes a Compression Agent that allows you to choose how you want to compress or not compress individual files and folders, and whether for the entire disk you want to use the minimum amount of disk space or have the maximum system speed and use more disk space (or balance the two). DriveSpace 3 also includes a driver that is optimized for Intel Pentium processors.

⇨ **System Agent** allows the scheduling and automatic running of system-maintenance tasks and other programs, such as scanning and defragmenting disk drives. At the scheduled time, the System

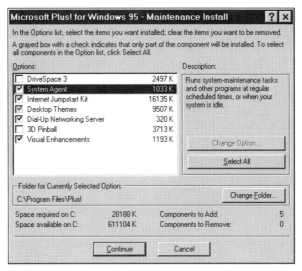

Figure 13-6.   Components of Microsoft Plus!

Agent will see if the computer has been idle for 10 minutes. If so, it will try to run the task. If the computer is busy, the System Agent will watch for idle time of 10 minutes or more and, when found, will try to run the task.

⇨ **Internet Jumpstart Kit** provides the Internet Connection Wizard for making easy connection to the Internet—the Internet Explorer for browsing the Web—and adds Internet Mail to the Microsoft Exchange/Windows Messaging client (Inbox). See the discussion in Chapter 10.

⇨ **Desktop Themes** provides 12 themes that you can use to customize your desktop, including the wallpaper, icons, mouse pointer, and sounds.

⇨ **Dial-Up Networking Server** allows you to set up your computer so you can access it remotely using your modem and phone connection.

⇨ **3D Pinball** provides an arcade game with super graphics and sound.

⇨ **Visual Enhancements** provides five enhancements for your screen that you can turn on or off using the Plus! tab of the Display Properties dialog box. Most important of these is the smoothing of screen fonts and showing the contents of windows as they are moved.

Only you can determine if these features and capabilities are worth the cost (under $50) and time to install (less than 5 minutes). From the viewpoint of the authors, the Internet Jumpstart Kit is worth the cost and time all by itself, and all the rest of Microsoft Plus! is a bonus.

OSR 2 *Note   All of the Internet Jumpstart Kit and most other features of Microsoft Plus! come with OSR 2.*

❓ How can I _change the name and icon for the Recycle Bin_?

You cannot change the name of the Recycle Bin, and you can only change its icon with the Microsoft Plus! Companion for Windows 95 or some other icon editor. The following instructions describe how to use Microsoft Plus! to do this, assuming you have Microsoft Plus! already installed:

1. Right-click on the desktop to open the context menu, choose Properties, and click on the Plus! tab, which will open as you can see in Figure 13-7.

Figure 13-7.   You can change system icons with the Plus! tab of the Display Properties dialog box

2. Click on Recycle Bin (Full), and then on the Change Icon button. The Change Icon dialog box will open displaying the Cool.dll icons.

3. Using the scroll bar, look at the icons that are available. If you don't see an icon you want to use, click on Browse.

4. In the C:\Windows\System folder (assuming a default installation), you'll find a file named Shell32.dll. Select this file and click on Open.

5. Again using the scroll bar, look at the icons that are available. About two-thirds across the scroll bar you should see three alternative recycle bins, like this:

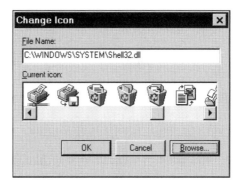

6. Select one of the alternatives, and click on OK twice to return to the desktop, where you should see your new Recycle Bin after a couple of seconds.

When I run programs in DOS mode, I get *insufficient memory errors* that I did not get prior to Microsoft Plus! installation. How come and how do I fix this?

This is probably caused by DriveSpace 3, which in DOS mode is using a large real-mode driver in conventional memory. First, make sure you are using the correct protected-mode driver in Windows. You can check this by opening the Control Panel and the System icon. Then look in the Performance tab, and see if the Disk Compression status says "MS-DOS compatibility mode." If it does, you are using the DOS real-mode driver and need to change that. Do so with these steps (drive C is assumed to be your primary compressed drive, drive D is your CD-ROM drive or it could be your floppy drive, and drive H is your noncompressed boot drive, also called the *host drive* for C):

1. Using Windows 95 Explorer, look in the \Windows\System\ Iosubsys folder and see if you have the file Drvspacx.vxd. If you do not find this file, extract it from the Plus_1.cab file on the Microsoft Plus! CD-ROM or Disk 1 by opening the Start menu Run command and typing the following command:

   extract /l c:\windows\system\iosubsys d:\plus_1.cab drvspacx.vxd

Note *The second string should be a:\... instead of d:\... if you are extracting from floppy Disk 1.*

2. Again using Windows 95 Explorer, drag the file Drvspace.bin from the C:\Windows\Command folder to the root directory of your host drive, H:\.

3. Open the root directory of the host drive (H:\) in Windows 95 Explorer, right-click on Drvspace.bin that you just dragged there, and choose Copy from the context menu. If asked, click Yes that you want to copy over any existing copy of this file.

4. Right-click on a blank area of the right pane of Explorer while it is displaying H:\ and choose Paste. Rename this new file **dblspace.bin**. If you are told you can't rename the new file because there is an existing file with that name, delete the existing file named dblspace.bin, and them rename the copy you just made.

5. Restart your computer and then open the Control Panel and the System icon, and in the Performance tab confirm that the Disk Compression status no longer says "MS-DOS compatibility mode." If it does and you didn't bring in a new copy of Drvspacx.vxd, then do that and try again.

With DriveSpace working correctly in Windows, the next step is to reduce the amount of conventional memory used by DriveSpace in DOS mode. To do this, you need to have the DOS real-mode driver loaded into upper memory. This can be accomplished by editing the Config.sys file that is used for DOS mode; normally this is called Config.dos when you are running in Windows. Assuming that is its name, open Config.dos in Notepad and make sure that the following lines are present in the order shown (there may be other lines in between and following those shown):

```
DEVICE=C:\WINDOWS\HIMEM.SYS
DEVICE=C:\WINDOWS\EMM386.EXE NOEMS
DOS=HIGH,UMB
DEVICEHIGH=C:\WINDOWS\COMMAND\DRVSPACE.SYS /MOVE
```

When you are done editing Config.dos, save it and reboot your system into DOS mode. You should now have enough memory to run your DOS programs. If you still have problems, look at Config.dos (in Windows or Config.sys in DOS mode) and see if there are any other drivers loaded with DEVICE (except Himem.sys and Emm386.exe) that you can put in upper memory with DEVICEHIGH. Also look at Autoexec.dos (in Windows or Autoexec.bat in DOS mode) and see if there are any memory-resident programs that you can start with LOADHIGH. You of course should also delete any device drivers and memory-resident programs that you don't need.

I installed dial-up networking from the Microsoft Plus! CD, but I don't see an icon for it anywhere. How do I _set up and control dial-up networking_?

Caution   The dial-up networking server allows you or anyone else with a computer and a modem to access your computer using phone lines and your modem. You can set up password protection for signing on to your computer, and you can individually share or not each folder, drive, and printer. Nevertheless, it is an access point to your computer, and you need to consider if it is worth the risk.

To set up the dial-up server you need to:

⇨ Install dial-up networking and the dial-up networking server from the Windows 95 and Microsoft Plus! CDs, respectively

⇨ Install and set up your modem (see Chapter 9 for how to do this)

⇨ Set up the networking properties on your computer using the same protocols that will be used on the remote computers (see Chapter 8 for how to do this)

⇨ Determine the disk, folder, and printer resources that you want to share, and set the appropriate sharing status on each resource

⇨   Enable and set the properties of the dial-up server with these steps:

1. Open the Dial-Up Networking folder in My Computer.

2. Open the Connections menu, choose Dial-Up Server, and click Allow Caller Access, as shown here:

3. Click Change Password if you want to set a password that must be entered by the remote user, enter the old password and the new password twice (if you have never set up a dial-up server, then your old password is blank—no password), and click OK.

4. Click OK to close the Dial-Up Server dialog box.

To utilize the dial-up networking server, you need to set up a dial-up networking client on a remote computer. To do that you must:

⇨   Install dial-up networking from the Windows 95 CD

⇨   Install and set up the modem (see Chapter 9 for how to do this)

⇨   Set up the networking properties on the remote computer using the same protocols that were used on the server (see Chapter 8 for how to do this)

⇨   Enable dial-up networking with these steps:

1. Open the Dial-Up Networking folder in My Computer, and double-click Make A New Connection.

Office

2. Enter a name for the computer you want to connect to, and select the modem that is installed in the computer, as shown in Figure 13-8. Click Next.

3. Enter the Area Code and Telephone Number of the server, click Next, and then Click Finish. A new dial-up connection icon will appear in the Dial-Up Networking dialog box, as shown on the left.

Once you have set up both a server and a remote client, you can initiate a dial-up networking session by following these steps:

1. Start the server and its modem and leave them running.

2. Start the remote computer and its modem. On that computer, open My Computer, double-click Dial-Up Networking, and double-click the dial-up networking connection icon you just created.

3. Enter any necessary password and click Connect. You should connect to and be able to use the server computer with any application or utility the way you can use any other computer on a network.

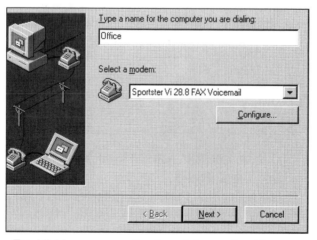

Figure 13-8.   Establishing a connection to a dial-up networking server

392 Chapter 13: The Registry and Microsoft Plus!

 How do I _set up and control the System Agent_—I don't see it in the Control Panel?

 You should see a new icon in the notification area on the right of the Taskbar next to the clock. If you double-click on this icon, the System Agent will open as you can see here:

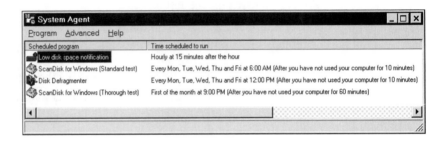

🔑 ***Tip*** *If the System Agent icon doesn't appear in the Taskbar, it was probably turned off. To turn it on, open the Start menu and choose Programs | Accessories | System Tools | System Agent.*

You can change the default scheduled programs by double-clicking on each of the scheduled items and making changes in the Properties dialog box that opens. You can add new programs to the System Agent's schedule by opening the Program menu and selecting Schedule A New Program. You can remove an existing item by selecting it and pressing DEL.

❓ **When I tried to run Microsoft Plus! Setup a second time, I got a _Setup error message 943_ that Setup files may be damaged. What does this mean and how do I correct it?**

This is probably caused by the Setup.stf in the Program Files\Plus!\ Setup folder being corrupted in some way. Correct it by deleting the entire Program Files\Plus!\Setup folder and then rerunning Microsoft Plus! Setup.

Note   *The same cause and solution are associated with Setup Error 723 that says that processing of top-level information has failed.*

? I have carefully set up a dial-up networking client and a server, and I still can't get the two to communicate. What are some suggestions for *troubleshooting dial-up networking*?

Troubleshooting any form of networking is difficult because of the number of variables involved. Dial-up networking has all the networking variables and adds to it the many communications variables. A key point to remember is that the remote client and the server *must be set up the same,* both in networking and communications. In other words, the networking and communications settings must be the same in both computers except for hardware differences. With that in mind look at the following points:

⇨ During a test of the dial-up networking, observe what is happening and see if the computers are connecting modem to modem—from what you hear from the computer and see on the screen you should be able to determine if the two modems are connected.

⇨ If the computers aren't connecting modem to modem, check that the modems in *both* the server and the remote client are communicating with some other computer. This could be an information service such as CompuServe, an Internet service provider (ISP), or just another computer.

⇨ If one computer is not connecting, compare the modem settings (Start menu | Settings | Control Panel | Modems) on both computers. Does the modem selection match the modem installed? In the Connection tab are connection preferences the same (normally 8 data bits, no parity, 1 stop bit)? In the Advanced Connection Settings (Advanced button in the Connection tab) are Use Error Control, Compress Data, Use Flow Control, and Hardware all selected, as shown here?

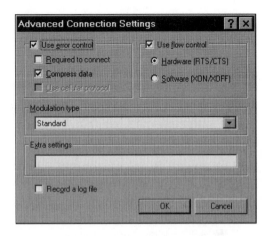

➪ If one computer is still not connecting, switch modems, either between the two computers if they use the same type of modem, or with another modem of the same type. If the problem goes away with a different modem, then the modem may be bad.

➪ If you believe that the computers are connecting modem to modem but you are unable to access the disk or printer of the server, observe, if possible, how each computer is working on a regular local area network (LAN), not dial-up. Are all the normal network functions working properly?

➪ If one of the computers is not functioning on a LAN, compare the network settings in both computers (Start menu | Settings | Control Panel | Network). Is the identified network adapter the same as the installed adapter, and are the network protocol selection and setting the same as the rest of the network?

➪ If a computer is still not functioning on a normal LAN, check the physical cable. If they are OK, switch network adapters with a computer that you know is working (make sure to change any affected settings for differences in the adapter cards—look at the settings in the computer that is working).

➪ If you find a network adapter that you believe is working in another machine but not in the server, compare the system resources assigned to the adapter with those set on the adapter itself. You can look at the assigned resources through the Device Manager tab in the System Properties dialog box (Start menu | Settings | Control Panel | System | Device Manager | Network

Adapters | *your adapter* | Properties | Resources), as shown in Figure 13-9.

⇨ Once you have both computers working on a normal LAN, but not working on a dial-up network, make sure that the dial-up adapters on both computers are bound to the correct protocol (in the Network dialog box select the dial-up adapter, click Properties, and look in the Bindings tab), and that the protocol includes NetBEUI or IPX/SPX.

⇨ In the Network dialog box on both the server and remote client select the protocol and make sure that the bindings include File And Printer Sharing For Microsoft (or NetWare) Networks on the server and Client For Microsoft (or NetWare) Networks on the remote client.

⇨ Also in the Network dialog box on both computers open the Identification tab and make sure that the Workgroup name is the same and that the Computer name is unique, no more than 14 characters long, and doesn't contain spaces or / \ * , . and ".

⇨ Finally, make sure that the dial-up server is enabled, as described in an earlier question.

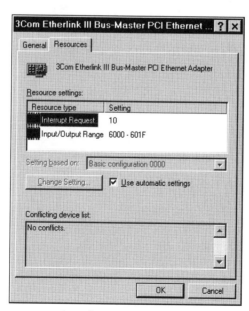

Figure 13-9.   Resources assigned to a network adapter

? **I installed Microsoft Plus! including several desktop themes, but I can't find them. Once they're installed, how do I _use the desktop themes_?**

If you open the Control Panel (Start menu ┃ Settings ┃ Control Panel), you'll see an icon labeled "Desktop Themes." If you double-click on this icon, the Desktop Themes dialog box will open, as you can see in Figure 13-10. By opening the Theme drop-down list, you can choose a theme and have it previewed in the dialog box. By clicking on the respective button, you can also see or hear what the screen saver, pointers, and sounds will be with a particular theme. Finally, you can choose what parts of the theme to apply with the check boxes under Settings. If you like a theme you have chosen, you can install it on your desktop by clicking on OK.

Figure 13-10.   Preview desktop themes including sounds and screen savers

OTHER CUSTOMIZATION AREAS

? My computer had been used by someone dealing in foreign currency, and all my applications display amounts of money in that currency. How do I _change the currency display to my country's currency_?

This is controlled in the Regional Settings. Open the Start menu, choose Settings | Control Panel | Regional Settings. In the Regional Settings tab select your country and answer Yes to let the system restart your computer. After restarting, reopen the Regional Settings dialog box and open the Currency tab. Your currency should be displayed. If it isn't, you need to reload Windows 95 from the CD or floppy disk.

? How do I _enable daylight saving time_ so my system will automatically adjusts the time twice a year?

This is done in the Date/Time control panel. Open the Start menu and choose Settings | Control Panel. Double-click Date/Time and in the Time Zone tab put a check in Automatically Adjust Clock For Daylight Saving Changes. Click OK.

? I deleted the Briefcase icon from my desktop; how do I _get the Briefcase back_?

Right-click on the desktop, choose New from the context menu, and then click on Briefcase.

? The active window I am using is outside what the monitor displays, and I can only see the lower half of it. I can see neither the toolbars nor the menus. How can I _get the window back in the middle of the screen_?

Hold down ALT, press SPACEBAR, and then while continuing to hold down ALT, press the M key. This activates the Move feature. Now use the arrow keys to move the window back toward the center of the screen. Once you have the window where you want it, press ENTER.

? **I just got a new computer with Windows 95 already installed. When I'm away from my computer for a period of time and come back to use it, there is an annoying delay. What causes this _startup delay_ and can I change it?**

OSR 2 You must have the OSR 2 version of Windows 95 (see the discussion in the Introduction to this book on OSR 2). OSR 2 has a power-management feature that in newer computers can tell the disk drive to power down (*spin down*) if it has not been used for a period of time as an energy conservation measure. You can turn this feature on and off, and you can control the length of time the machine must be inactive before the disk is shut down (spun down). You can do this through the Power control panel (Start menu | Settings | Control Panel | Power). In the Disk Drives tab if the When Powered By AC Power option is checked, then the drive will spin down after the length of idle time set.

OSR 2 *Note*   *If you have a portable computer with OSR 2 and a PC card modem, you can control whether the modem is powered down if it is not used in the PC Card Modems tab of the Power control panel.*

Installation
Components

The following table shows you which components are installed in the various types of installations for the retail and original OEM versions of Windows 95 (additional components provided in the OSR 2 version are listed at the end). The files are available on both floppy disk and CD-ROM unless there is a "Yes" in the CD-ROM Only column.

	Available on			
Component	Typical	Portable	Compact	CD-ROM Only
Accessories				
Accessibility Options	Yes	No	No	No
Briefcase	No	Yes	No	Yes
Calculator	Yes	Yes	No	No
Character Map	No	No	No	Yes
Clipboard Viewer	No	No	No	No
Desktop Wallpaper	No	No	No	No
Document Templates	Yes	No	No	No
Games	No	No	No	No
Mouse Pointers	No	No	No	Yes
Net Watcher	No	No	No	Yes
Object Packager	Yes	No	No	No
Online User's Guide	No	No	No	Yes
Paint	Yes	No	No	No
Quick View	No	No	No	Yes
Resource Meter	No	No	No	No
Screen Savers	Yes[1]	No	No	No
System Monitor	No	No	No	Yes
Windows 95 Tour	Yes	No	No	Yes
WinPopup[2]	No	No	No	No
WordPad	Yes	Yes	No	No
Communications				
Dial-Up Networking	No	Yes	No	No
Direct Cable Connection	No	Yes	No	No
HyperTerminal	Yes	Yes	No	No
Phone Dialer	Yes	Yes	No	No

	Available on			
Component	Typical	Portable	Compact	CD-ROM Only
Disk Tools				
Backup	No	No	No	No
Disk Compression Tools[3]	No	No	No	No
Disk Defragmenter	Yes	Yes	Yes	No
ScanDisk	Yes	Yes	Yes	No
Microsoft Exchange				
Microsoft Fax	No	No	No	No
Microsoft Mail	No	No	No	No
Microsoft Network	No	No	No	No
Multilingual Support	No	No	No	Yes
Multimedia				
Audio Compression[4]	No	No	No	No
CD Player[5]	No	No	No	No
Media Player	Yes	Yes	No	No
Sound Schemes	No	No	No	Yes
Sound and Video Clips	No	No	No	Yes
Sound Recorder[4]	No	No	No	No
Video Compression	Yes	Yes	No	No
Volume Control[4]	No	No	No	No

[1]Flying Windows is the only screen saver installed. Others are available on both CD-ROM and on floppy disk.

[2]WinPopup is only installed if networking is detected.

[3]Disk Compression is only installed if DoubleSpace or DriveSpace is detected.

[4]Audio Compression, Sound Recorder, and Volume Control are only installed if a sound card is detected.

[5]CD Player is only installed if a CD-ROM is detected.

OSR 2 Components

OSR 2 The following additional components are included in the OSR 2 release of Windows 95:

Component Category	Component	Typical Install
Accessories	Desktop Management	No
	Imaging	Yes
Communications	Microsoft NetMeeting	No
Multimedia	Multimedia Sound Schemes	No
Windows Messaging[1]	Internet Mail Services	No[2]
	Microsoft Mail Services	Yes
	Window Messaging	Yes

[1]Windows Messaging is just a new name for the Microsoft Exchange.

[2]Internet Mail Service is not part of the Typical install, but it is automatically brought in when the Internet options are installed after completing the Windows 95 installation.

Index

To **speak to the support experts** who handle more than one million technical issues every month, call **Stream's** Microsoft® Windows 95® answer line. Trained specialists will answer your Microsoft Windows questions including setup, built-in networking, printing, multimedia, Microsoft Exchange Mail client, and Wizards.

Have all your questions been answered?

1-800-298-8215

$34.95 per problem (Charge to a major credit card.)

1-900-555-2009

$34.95 per problem (Charge to your phone bill.)

Visit our web site at www.stream.com.

The technical support specialists.